AF895094

Two-Step Approaches to Natural Language Formalisms

Studies in Generative Grammar 64

Editors

Henk van Riemsdijk
Harry van der Hulst
Jan Koster

Mouton de Gruyter
Berlin · New York

Two-Step Approaches to Natural Language Formalisms

by

Frank Morawietz

Mouton de Gruyter
Berlin · New York 2003

Mouton de Gruyter (formerly Mouton, The Hague)
is a Division of Walter de Gruyter GmbH & Co. KG, Berlin.

The series Studies in Generative Grammar was formerly published by
Foris Publications Holland.

∞ Printed on acid-free paper which falls within the guidelines
of the ANSI to ensure permanence and durability.

ISBN 3-11-017821-4

Bibliographic information published by Die Deutsche Bibliothek

Die Deutsche Bibliothek lists this publication in the Deutsche
Nationalbibliografie; detailed bibliographic data is available in the
Internet at <http://dnb.ddb.de>.

© Copyright 2003 by Walter de Gruyter GmbH & Co. KG, D-10785 Berlin.
All rights reserved, including those of translation into foreign languages. No part of this book may be reproduced in any form or by any means, electronic or mechanical, including photocopy, recording, or any information storage and retrieval system, without permission in writing from the publisher.

Printed in Germany.
Cover design: Christopher Schneider, Berlin.

Abstract

In this monograph, mathematical techniques from logic, automata theory and universal algebra are employed to define a provably equivalent denotational and operational approach toward the formalization of natural languages.

We start by exploring a classical technique connecting the three fields by specifying constraints on analyses of natural languages in monadic second-order (MSO) logic on trees following a proposal made by Rogers (1998). The weak interpretation of MSO logic on trees is intertranslatable with finite-state tree automata. Recall that finite-state tree automata characterize the class of recognizable languages – which are, up to a projection, weakly equivalent to the context-free languages. Therefore this classical technique is sufficient to cope (in principle) with context-free languages. Nevertheless, we will show that both for practical reasons and for reasons of the still too limited generative capacity an extension of the formalism is necessary.

The proposal outlined in this monograph proceeds with a two-step approach which still has provably equivalent denotational and operational descriptions. In this two-step approach we model linguistic formalisms – as for example tree adjoining grammars (TAGs) or minimalist grammars (MGs) – which can generate non-context-free languages with two regular or two logical steps. In the first step we model the linguistic formalisms with particular forms of tree grammars – either context-free tree grammars or multiple context-free grammars – which also have a higher generative capacity than context-free grammars. To make them amenable to characterizations with MSO logic, we insert a certain amount of implicit control information explictly into the generated structures. This is done by a process which has been called lifting in the literature (Mönnich 1999).

Unfortunately, the generated structures do not correspond to the ones linguists commonly assume for their analyses exactly because of the additional information. We need the second step to transform these lifted structures back into the intended ones. This can be done equivalently with tree-walking automata and macro tree transducers on the operational side and with MSO definable transductions on the denotational side such that we retain the desired duality.

In the course of the monograph I will show how the contemporary natural language formalisms of Government & Binding, Minimalism and Tree Adjoining Grammar can be captured within the two-step proposal.

Acknowledgments

> The study of mathematics is apt to commence in disappointment. The important applications of the science, the theoretical interest of its ideas, and the logical rigor of its methods, all generate the expectation of a speedy introduction to the processes of interest. We are told that by its aid the stars are counted and the billions of molecules in a drop of water are counted. Yet, like the ghost of Hamlet's father, this great science eludes the efforts of our mental weapons to grasp it – ''Tis here, 'tis there, 'tis gone' – and what we do see does not suggest the same excuse for illusiveness as sufficed for the ghost, that is too noble for our gross methods. 'A show of violence', if ever excusable, may surely be 'offered' to the trivial results which occupy the pages of some elementary mathematical treatises.
>
> The reason for this failure of the science to live up to its reputation is that its fundamental ideas are not explained to the student disentangled from the technical procedure which has been invented to facilitate their exact presentation in particular instances.
>
> (Whitehead 1911, p. 40)

Since the work presented in the following chapters utilizes a lot of material which stands in a mathematical tradition, the claims by Whitehead are also true for this book. Even the reader with a firm background in "formal" linguistics is faced with a large number of definitions from universal algebra, logic and automata theory.

Fortunately, I had a couple of inspiring and extremely competent guides for my forays into the realm of mathematical linguistics. First and foremost is Uwe Mönnich who not only understood my problems but also was patient enough to answer all of my (sometimes thick-headed) questions. On the practical side, I profited most from Tom Cornell. Not only did he raise my interest in MSO logic as a description language for P&P theories, he also was my constant partner for all things related to implementations. I am also grateful to Erhard Hinrichs, Klaus Schulz and Fritz Hamm for accepting the part of referee. Their comments and questions turned out to helpful indeed. Also, a lot of useful comments which improved the exposition of some parts of the monograph considerably were made by an anonymous referee. All their comments and insights led to a better work. Needless to say, all the errors that remain are my own.

Special thanks also go to Craig Thiersch who took over some of my teaching duties to allow me more time to finish the book.

Thanks go also to all the people I was privileged to work with, or simply to talk to; most notably my (other) co-authors Hans-Peter Kolb, Stephan Kepser and Jens Michaelis. Thanks also go to Laura Kallmeyer, Kai-Uwe Kühnberger and lots of others at the *Seminar für Sprachwissenschaft* and the *Graduiertenkolleg Integriertes Linguistik-Studium* at the University of Tübingen who provided help, advice and a stimulating, if sometimes distracting environment. Final thanks go to Carmella Payne who spend a lot of time correcting my English.

Since a large part of the work underlying this monograph was done while I worked in the project A8 of the *Sonderforschungsbereich 340*, thanks also go to the *Deutsche Forschungsgemeinschaft* for providing the necessary funding.

And last, but not least, I have to thank my wife and family who suffered with me through long years without any visible progress. Without their support, I wouldn't have been free to spend so much time on my work.

Parts of this book have been published in various papers: The part dealing with the classical result is an extended and modified version of topics presented in Morawietz and Cornell (1997a,b,c, 1999) and Morawietz (1999). The part with the presentation of the actual two-step approach is an extension of the work reported on in Kolb, Mönnich, and Morawietz (1999a,b, 2000), Kolb, Michaelis, Mönnich, and Morawietz (2003), Michaelis, Mönnich, and Morawietz (2000a,b) and Morawietz and Mönnich (2001).

Tübingen, Juli 2003
Frank Morawietz

Contents

III Two Steps Are Better Than One

List of Figures

List of Tables

Part I

Introduction

Chapter 1

Overview

This monograph is concerned with formal, mathematical approaches to linguistics. In particular, we will use classical techniques from logic, universal algebra and automata theory to define a formalism for natural language syntax

- which has a clearly defined limited generative capacity, but is still expressive enough to account for the empirical data,
- which has a provably equivalent operational and denotational interpretation and, furthermore,
- which forms the basis for some of the major approaches to linguistics proposed in the literature.

Since the book combines techniques from many areas of linguistics, (theoretical) computational linguistics, (theoretical) computer science and mathematics, it may require some intellectual effort even for readers with a firm background in formal linguistics. Therefore I will try throughout the course of this work to motivate unfamiliar notions and concepts and provide illustrating examples wherever possible.

Formal approaches to linguistics are necessary for many reasons. We will refrain from recapitulating the entire discussion here. Instead, we will focus on some crucial statements which motivate this work. Consider the following paragraph stated in Chomsky (1957):

> Precisely constructed models for linguistic structure can play an important role, both negative and positive, in the process of discovery itself. By pushing a precise but inadequate formulation to an unacceptable conclusion, we can often expose the exact source of the inadequacy and, consequently, gain a deeper understanding of the linguistic data. More positively, a formalized theory may automatically provide solutions for many problems other than those

> for which it was explicitly designed. Obscure and intuition-bound notions can neither lead to absurd conclusions nor provide new and correct ones, and hence they fail to be useful in two important respects. I think that some of those linguists who have questioned the value of precise and technical development of linguistic theory have failed to recognize the productive potential in the method of rigorously stating a proposed theory and applying it strictly to linguistic material with no attempt to avoid unacceptable conclusions by *ad hoc* adjustments or loose formulation.

We can summarize the reasons given by Chomsky analogously with the keywords given in Frank (1990) which put a slightly different emphasis on the points:

Theory Testing: Formalizing a theory leads to the discovery of errors and holes in a theory.

Perspicuity of Grammatical Representations: Modular formalization of linguistic analyses in an appropriate grammar formalism provides a way of writing a grammar cleanly without the need to deal with processing-specific or formalism-inherent details. Moreover, the formalism itself might encode linguistic universals such that it is impossible to write a grammar with certain undesired properties.

Psychological Modeling of Languages: The formalization might provide a psychologically plausible mechanism for the use of language.

Since theory testing seems to be widely accepted as a reason for formal approaches, we will not go into any detail here. But since the second point addresses the main motivation behind this monograph, it deserves some further clarification: If one can build a Turing machine to demonstrate that one can parse a particular syntactic construction, say, subject–verb agreement, (almost) nothing has been shown. If we can show that the same construction can be handled by context-free (CF) grammars, we have not only shown that it can be *decided* for every input whether the subject and the verb agree on some features, but also that we can parse such constructions in at most cubic time. While in this case the observation may seem trivial, we will hopefully point out more salient contributions in the course of this work. Most notably, we will be concerned with formalisms with an adequate *generative power* and with an adequate *descriptive complexity*.

While the *computational* complexity of a problem is usually defined in terms of the resources required for its computational solution on some machine model, *descriptive* complexity looks at the complexity of describing the problem (seen as a collection of relational structures) in a logic, measuring logical resources such as the type and number of variables, quantifiers, operators, etc. It is a non-trivial fact that there is a close correspondence between these two, with many natural logics corresponding exactly to independently defined complexity classes (cf. Fagin 1974; Immerman 1987).

The last point stated above, psychological modelability, will not play a role in this presentation. I do not believe that the formalism(s) presented in this book reflect psychological reality. Some of their properties, on the other hand, might indeed be relevant, but since this discussion leads too far off the main focus of the book I will leave this open for others to address.

The preceding paragraphs have already outlined the main questions addressed in this monograph: Can we find a formalism for natural languages which is empirically adequate but of limited generative capacity such that the formalism itself says something on natural languages? To specify more closely the kind of formalism we are looking for, we review some of the desiderata which have been posed for natural language formalisms.

1.1 Desiderata for a linguistic formalism

Since the main focus of this book is on the development and presentation of formalisms for the specification of natural language grammars, we will start by clarifying which properties are desired in this type of formalism.

As laid out at length in Pollard and Sag (1994), as in any science, modeling reality requires the formalization of the relation between the observable, empirical facts and the derivable theorems of the formal theory. Therefore we have to specify what the objects of our formalisms are and how they are related to the ontological categories we strive to model. Moreover, it seems mandatory that we want the formalism itself to be a theory in the technical sense, i.e., the well-formed or admissible structures are *characterized* or at least *described* by the theory.

Maybe the linguistic theory with the greatest impact in the last decades is what emerges from the work by Noam Chomsky (Chomsky 1965, 1982, 1985) as the *Government & Binding* (GB) approach in the *Principles-and-Parameter* (P&P) framework. The approach has three layers of (syntactic) analysis of linguistic utterances: deep- or D-structure, surface- or S-structure and logical form. The output or phonetic form (PF) is generated from the S-structure with phonological rules. Linguistic well-formedness conditions can then apply on all levels of representation. An utterance whose derivation yields a structural representation which is acceptable on all levels is deemed grammatical.

In all the approaches in this tradition of the work by Noam Chomsky, *trees* are used as the objects of the structural analyses of utterances. Therefore, in the case of this monograph, the objects of the theory which we will model will be nodes in labeled trees or the trees themselves. Historically, this might have been an artifact of the fact that for context-free grammars the *derivation* trees and the *derived* trees are identical. But since trees have proven to be very useful indeed, they continue to be used as the main explanatory method even in formalisms where the equivalence between derivation trees and derived trees does not hold any more.

It seems obvious that in order to facilitate the task of the grammar writer, it would be best to aim for the formal language defined by the formalisms, i.e., the constraint language, to be as natural as possible. With the term "natural", we mean here that the language is close enough to the basic explanatory mechanisms proposed by the particular formalism so that a direct translation of empirical analyses into the formal language is possible. To further help the grammar writer, it is also desirable for the formalism to be modular, i.e., to consist of (simple) *independent* parts which, through their interaction, achieve the necessary complexity to deal with natural languages. Modularity has the benefit that the parts of a theory can be developed and tested independent from each other. But at the same time the formalism must also meet the criterion to be efficiently processable, ideally, incrementally.

As presented in the section above, one of the central points of this book will be the specification of formalisms with a clearly defined descriptive complexity such that the question of *decidability* which is usually posited as a further desideratum, is trivially fulfilled. While we want a formalism with a strictly limited generative capacity, we need a formalism, on the other hand, which is expressive enough to handle the necessary empirical constructions needed for natural languages, especially those which go beyond the power of context-free grammars. Historically, the Chomsky Hierarchy (see Table 1.1 on the facing page) was the first approach towards capturing the descriptive complexity of natural languages. As we will see below, this classification turned out to be too simple to model the observable facts.

Table 1.1: The Chomsky Hierarchy

Chomsky Type	Language class	Rule type
0	recursively enumerable	no restrictions
1	context-sensitive	$\gamma_1 A \gamma_2 \longrightarrow \gamma_1 \alpha \gamma_2$
2	context-free	$A \longrightarrow \alpha$
3	regular	$A \longrightarrow aA \mid Aa$

The following notational conventions apply: Lowercase letters are terminals, uppercase ones nonterminals. $\alpha, \gamma_1, \gamma_2$ are strings of terminals or nonterminals.

Another set of desiderata comes form the research on Tree Adjoining Grammars (TAG, Joshi et al. 1975; Joshi 1985, 1987; Joshi and Schabes 1997) and therefore rather from the generative side of linguistic formalisms. Here the search is for a formal family of languages that contains all natural languages but also has "nice" computational properties. Since the Chomsky Hierarchy, according to Joshi, does not provide such a family, he proposed an additional class between the context-free and the context-sensitive languages which he called the *mildly context-sensitive languages*. These languages have to obey the following three conditions. Firstly, each language has to be *semi-linear* and therefore has to have the *constant growth* property. Secondly, each language has to be parseable in polynomial time. And thirdly, each language can only allow a limited number of cross-serial dependencies. In the case of TAGs, the boundary seems to be drawn at four crossing dependencies.

Semi-linear in this context means that the set of occurrence vectors of the alphabet symbols of the words of the language is semi-linear, i.e., it can be decomposed into a finite union of linear sets. The connection between semi-linearity and formal languages was first proven by Parikh who showed that every context-free language is semi-linear (Parikh 1966).

Constant growth here means that there exists a constant c and a finite set of constants C such that for any word w of length greater than c there exists a prefix w' of w such that the length of w equals the length of w' plus some element from C.

Typical examples of mildly context-sensitive languages are the copy language (e.g., ww for $w \in \Sigma^*$), the languages modeling crossing dependencies (e.g., $a^n b^m c^n d^m$) or the languages modeling multiple agreements (e.g., $a^n b^n c^n$).

While the search for a formalism with all these properties might seem like the search for the philosopher's stone, the criteria all deserve our attention and will be considered during the deliberations laid out in the course of this book.

1.2 Logic, algebra and formal language theory

The languages we use in everyday communication are called natural languages. What we will use and discuss in this book, though, are formal languages – exactly defined and formally specified artificial languages which serve particular purposes. Examples of the use of formal languages can be found in a variety of areas such as arithmetic, set theory, logic, algebra, programming languages or in the languages of the Chomsky Hierarchy. Even in theoretical linguistics they are employed for numerous tasks on all levels of linguistic "processing" such as phonology, morphology, syntax, semantics etc. The idea behind the use of formal languages is that by modeling a natural language with a formal language, one can learn about the underlying principles and properties of natural languages. In this book I will focus on the use of formal languages for the specification of the syntax of natural languages – in particular within the paradigm of theories as proposed by Noam Chomsky, the Principles & Parameters (P&P) approach, although some of the tools and methods that I present and employ might well be suited to other tasks as well.

It is important to carefully distinguish the usages of the words *syntax* (structure of a sentence) and *semantics* (meaning of a sentence) in linguistics from the ones in relation to formal languages. In formal language theory the distinction between syntax and semantics is one between form, i.e., expressions, axioms, rules of inference, etc., and content, i.e., the relation of the system to its models.

Another important question concerns the chosen methodology. In this monograph the most prominent "tools" will be logic and algebra.

In science we attempt to model reality (to a certain degree) with formal methods. It then seems natural to choose logic as a way to formalize the deductive or inferencing process which allows us to draw conclusions from some basic assumptions; particularly, since logic allows us to reason about reasoning. While this might seem circular, a clear distinction between object- and meta-language enables us to use logic for both purposes.

In approaches dealing with natural languages we are faced with an infinite amount of data needing to be systematicized. So what is more "logical" than trying to reduce our empirical observations to a small number of observable facts (axioms) and then specifying the inference rules which allows the reasoning about the facts we want to explain.

On the other hand we are interested not only in licensing utterances, but also in the structures which provide an analysis of these utterances. At this point we have to define these structures and relate them to our logical language. Both algebra – to formalize the underlying models – and model theory – to formalize the relation between these models and the chosen logical language – become necessary.

Additionally, logic offers a very concise way of modeling natural languages. Usually a few simple constraints are sufficient to ensure the correct formalization of complex phenomena. And, since logic does not talk about how the necessary models are generated, it is not dependent on a particular mode of processing, e.g., parsing or generation.

To my knowledge, Johnson and Postal (1980) were the first to propose a logical description language for a linguistic formalism (Arc-Pair Grammar, which used predicate logic). In connection with the P&P approaches, the first papers seems to have been by Marcus et al. (1983) who proposed their *D-Theory* (description theory) to deal with specific aspects of parsing. Marcus' proposals have been taken up in other papers (Barton and Berwick 1985; Berwick and Weinberg 1985; Weinberg 1988; Stabler 1992), but these approaches have, until Rogers (1998), not received the same rigorous mathematical treatment as the approaches formalizing feature structures with logics (Kasper and Rounds 1986; Kasper 1987a,b; Moshier and Rounds 1987; Moshier 1988, 1993; Johnson 1988, 1990, 1991; King 1989; Carpenter 1992).

A different, historically older view, advertises the fact that natural languages are generative, i.e., they can be produced by humans with finite resources. Again, we take a finite number of basic items, a lexicon, and a number of rules and can generate bigger items/utterances from the basic ones. The advantages of this view are more oriented towards processing: a specification of a grammar in this form can easily be implemented and there are a huge number of well-known techniques making the resulting program efficient. This generative view is maybe best exemplified with Generalized Phrase Structure Grammar (GPSG, Gazdar et al. 1985) where the "standard" approach of processing consists of the compilation of a given GPSG into a context-free grammar used for parsing. Historically, the early works by Chomsky on *Transformational Grammar* (Chomsky 1956, 1959) had a strong connection to formal languages and therefore to the generative paradigm.

Active research in the 1980s for other formalisms led to the proof of the weak equivalence of a number of mildly context-sensitive formalisms used in connection with natural languages. Specifically, tree-adjoining grammars (TAG), combinatory categorial grammars (CCG, Steedman 1988), linear indexed grammars (LIG, Gazdar 1988), and head grammars (HG, Pollard 1984) have been shown to be weakly equivalent. Recently, another class of mildly context-sensitive grammar formalisms has been proven to be weakly equivalent. Among others, the following families of (string) languages are identical:

$MCFL$	languages generated by multiple context-free grammars,
$MCTAL$	languages generated by set local multi-component tree adjoining grammars,
$LCFRL$	languages generated by linear context-free rewriting systems,
$LUSCL$	languages generated by local unordered scattered context grammars,
$STR(HR)$	languages generated by string generating hyperedge replacement grammars,
$OUT(DTWT)$	output languages of deterministic tree-walking tree-to-string transducers,
$yDT_{fc}(REGT)$	yields of images of regular tree languages under deterministic finite-copying top-down tree transductions

(more on these equivalences can be found, e.g., in Engelfriet 1997; Rambow and Satta 1999; van Vugt 1996; Weir 1992). We summarize the formalisms which will be considered in the course of this book and their (weak) "generative power" in Table 1.2 on the next page. We added some well known formalisms to further illustrate the area we are working in, e.g., Lambek Calculus (LC, Lambek 1958) and Indexed Grammars (IG, Aho 1968).

Commonly, the logical approaches to theoretical linguistics are referred to as the *constraint-based* or *representational* approaches, whereas the latter ones are referred to as the *generative* or *operational* ones.

In mathematical logic, as we stated above, a formal language is defined to be a deduction system – which is subject to proof theory – and the definition of a class structures which interpret the symbols of the deductive language and which are subject to model theory. The resulting logic is correct if the deductive calculus manipulates the formal symbols in such a way that their meaning is provably preserved.

Table 1.2: Grammar Formalisms in a Refined Chomsky Hierarchy

Chomsky Type	Grammar Formalism
context-free	LC, CFG
	$\subsetneq$
mildly context-sensitive	TAG, CCG, LIG, HG, MCFTG
	$\subsetneq$
	LCFRS, MCFG, HRG, DTWT, MCTAG, LUSCG
	$\subsetneq$
indexed	CFTG, IG

There is a comparable situation in computer science. If we consider our formal language to be a programming language, then the *operational semantics* tells us *how* something is computed whereas the *denotational semantics* tells us *what* is computed. The procedural view of the operational semantics is akin to proof theory. The denotational semantics can be compared to the model theory of mathematical logic. And, again, it is desired that both are provably equivalent. The difference appears to be on the level of abstraction: it is very well possible that an algorithm implemented in two programming languages has an identical denotational semantics since they compute the same function, but the way they achieve the computation is completely different operationally.

As stated above, the same dichotomy exists in linguistics, sometimes even within the same paradigm as is exemplified within the Chomskian tradition with the P&P-based approaches (Chomsky 1965, 1982, 1985) and the Minimalist Program (Chomsky 1995) or in the shift in Head-Driven Phrase Structure Grammar (HPSG) from a more unification oriented view (Pollard and Sag 1987) to a licensing theory (Pollard and Sag 1994).

In more detail, linguists use transformational or unification-based derivations as well as chain-based representations or descriptions of (typed) feature structures to code the sound-meaning pairs of a grammar. But in linguistics the two views are not treated as two sides of the same coin which complement one another. Rather the contrary is the case: Linguists discuss which of the alternatives is better. And, even worse, in Brody (1995) it is claimed that a linguistic theory which contains both chains and movement is lacking explanatory adequacy since one of the two mechanisms is redundant.

Table 1.3: Two Ways of Formalizing Grammar

Logic:	Proof Theory	vs.	Model Theory
Computation:	Operational Semantics	vs.	Denotational Semantics
Linguistics:	Derivations	vs.	Licensing Conditions

In direct contrast to this line of thought, we think that a linguistic theory needs both a denotational and an operational semantics which are provably equivalent in analogy to the views in computer science and mathematical logic. Both views contribute important insights and seem essential to bridge the gap between the high-level languages commonly employed by grammar writers and the practical needs of the implementor.

We are aware that the situation in linguistics is not as clear cut as in computer science and logic. Formalizations of transformational theories, in particular, treat movement as a relation between trees, i.e., the relation is formalized in the object language and trees are the objects of the theory (e.g., Stabler 1992). Compared to that, representational theories most often have a single model and chains are sequences of nodes in that single tree (e.g., Rogers 1998). Are these chains the denotational equivalent of the movement steps? But the attempt of formulating both theories may actually help in isolating the real differences – if there are any – between the two views. The crucial fact here is that it is necessary to show that the relation between sound and meaning is preserved no matter how they are characterized or generated. In case we can indeed show that movement-based and chain-based approaches can be handled within one formalism, we would have shown that the difference between the usage of entire trees or collections of nodes is not a deep or substantive difference, but an artifact of the formalization.

So, we think that by providing a formal system with both a representational and an operational interpretation, it becomes possible to focus on the relevant differences between linguistic theories, i.e., differences of an empirical kind. And, furthermore, we are attempting to provide this formal system in such a general way that it is independent of the particular linguistic theory involved. While we draw our main motivation from the realm of the Chomskian tradition, we remain open to other theories as well. A summary of the connection between denotation and operation in the various fields is given in Table 1.3.

Since there are almost no approaches putting the same emphasis on a provably equivalent denotational and operational system for linguistic formalisms, there is almost no literature to review. But in the following paragraphs we try to give a brief overview of the history of the methodology employed in this monograph.

The advances – not the least through important contributions by Chomsky (e.g., Chomsky 1956, 1959) – of formal language theory in the 1950s and 1960s, which had provided much initial evidence for the feasibility of the generative approach, seemed to suggest a stronger role of the formal framework in Generative Grammar research. It had established, for the classes of the Chomsky Hierarchy of formal languages, an intimate connection between the form of a grammar (the types of rules employed), the computational resources needed to process it, and the type of (string) language specified by it, see Table 1.1 on page 7. In its application to natural languages, this line of thought aims at establishing a formal system which is defined automata-theoretically and/or via rule types and which by its inherent restriction of expressive power provides guidance through the empirical mine-fields of linguistic theory formation.

The first attempt at an algebraic treatment of language classes goes back to the late 1950s. Maybe most influential were the works of Büchi (1960). Right from the start, descriptive complexity played a prominent role. The beginning of the enterprise is marked by a paper by Elgot (1961). In this paper he proved the equivalence between monadic second-order logic (MSO) with one successor function (S1S) with finite-state automata and therefore with the regular (string) languages. This paper provoked a whole series of papers in the 1960s and 1970s (Mezei and Wright 1967; Thatcher and Wright 1968; Rabin 1969; Thatcher 1970; Doner 1970) transferring the results on strings to trees. The finite-state tree automata introduced by both Thatcher & Wright and Doner needed for the decidability proof of MSO logic with multiple successor functions (SωS) opened a new field for both automata theory and formal languages (see Gécseg and Steinby 1984) and finite model theory and descriptive complexity theory (see Ebbinghaus and Flum 1995). Of particular importance for this work is the expansion to many-sorted algebras (Maibaum 1974; Engelfriet and Schmidt 1977, 1978). The new technique allowed an algebraic characterization of the indexed languages with the help of context-free tree grammars (CFTGs) by Fischer (1968) and Rounds (1970a,b) and an algebraic refinement of the Chomsky Hierarchy (Mönnich 1993).

Because of the growing distance between linguistics and the theory of formal languages there has almost been no impact of this in linguistic theorizing with respect to the approaches in the P&P paradigm. When in the early 70s Peters and Ritchie formulated their famous (though not necessarily well-understood) result that there is an Aspects-style transformational grammar for any recursively enumerable language, i.e., that the formal framework of transformational grammar in itself not only does not restrict the class of natural languages in any way, but does not even ensure computability of the grammars couched in these terms (Peters and Ritchie 1971, 1973), almost all research in that direction ceased. The enthusiasm for questions of computational complexity was seriously abated, and the stage was set for a major shift in emphasis of linguistic theorizing towards *substantive* issues: Not to get the formal framework "exactly right" became the primary goal now, but the discovery of "exactly the right" structural properties of natural language – in what ever way formulated. Except for paying lip-service, most of the little formal work done on the basis of P&P theory has not addressed questions of finding a weak but adequate theory. Either formalization was restricted to some *fixed* version of the theory – usually in some "machine-readable" language under the heading of GB-parsing (Macías 1990; Kolb and Thiersch 1991; Fong 1992; Johnson and Stabler 1993; Veenstra 1998) – without consideration for alternatives or future developments, or a strong meta-theory like full predicate logic – maybe even of higher order – was used to accommodate the wide variety of means of P&P theory formation (Stabler 1992).

Despite the indisputable merits of this work in elucidating many aspects of P&P theory neither strategy is likely to yield a formal framework for Generative Grammar in the sense outlined above: The former, while relatively close to the ultimate purpose of the P&P model, is premature: change seems to be about the only constant in linguistic theorizing and consequently there has not been a consistent, let alone complete, set of principles at any stage of GB-development. The latter, on the other hand, seems to go nicely with actual linguistic practice since it provides all the flexibility needed to express new generalizations. However, in a Swiss-Army-Knife-type framework the particular structural properties of natural language grammars will just be accidents without any explanatory force. Neither can such formalizations, due to their unrestrictive character, provide any significant guidance for linguistic theorizing, nor are there general decision procedures for such strong logics, hence these attempts are in danger of formalizing for formalization's sake.

Only the dissertation by Jim Rogers (1994) addressed the growing competence in formal language theory. His MSO-based approach to linguistic theories (most notably P&P-based approaches and towards tree adjoining grammar (TAG)) uses the results by Doner, Thatcher & Wright and Rabin on decidability and descriptive complexity. He was able to show in a rigorous formalization of a large grammar of English (implementing the ideas from Rizzi 1990) that most parts of a modern P&P grammar can be captured by context-free means.

His non-decidability results are interesting as well. The long debate among linguists whether free indexation is an appropriate method for linguistic theorizing can be answered in the negative since free indexation is not decidable.[1] Unfortunately it turns out that the logic is too weak to capture languages such as Dutch or Swiss German precisely because of this descriptive complexity result.

In this monograph, I will start with Rogers's work and use methods from universal algebra, logic and automata theory to extend the formalism of MSO logic in such a way that we retain the nice properties but gain enough generative capacity to address the linguistic facts.

So, let us restate our objective: The goal of this work is to develop a meta-theory for the expression of theories of natural language syntax on the basis of a weak logic, which makes direct use of the primitive notions of grammatical theories. Thus complexity theory and formal language theory regain their former importance, although they appear slightly different from the early days.

1.3 Outline

Let us now briefly outline the structure of the monograph. This first part deals with the introductions and the most basic technical preliminaries.

The second part introduces what has been coined *model-theoretic syntax*, most notably approaches dealing with P&P formalisms from a logic oriented point of view with a strong emphasis on model-theory and decidability and definability results. We pick the most prominent member of its kind, namely Rogers's work and elucidate the underlying mathematical results while preparing the field for the techniques we will use in the third part of the book. We will call the work which directly builds upon Rogers thesis the *classical approach* since it uses the results from formal language theory in an undiluted form. After the introductory overview, we present the necessary formal tools for the classical approach, MSO logic and finite-state devices, before turning to the relation between the two, namely a short recapitulation of the important parts of the decidability proof which has been enhanced with two sections of definability issues, both of which we need later in the course of this work. The first of those is concerned with inductive definability, the second one with the definability of MSO transductions. Before concluding this part with a review of the strengths and weaknesses of the classical approach, we also outline a couple of applications and experiences which we have had with the MSO to tree automata compilation process.

The third part deals with our proposal for the extension of the classical approach with a second step. In particular, we recall the argumentation why we need more generative capacity by presenting arguments for the non-context-freeness of natural languages and by reviewing formalisms which can handle them. In the next chapter we present the fist step of our proposal, namely the coding of the linguistic formalisms with special kinds of tree grammars. Since those can generate structures with non-context-free yields, and we want to keep MSO logic as the description language, we have to lift these structures by explicitly inserting control information. Thereby we make them characterizable with regular means, in particular regular tree grammars or finite-state tree automata, and therefore with MSO logic as well. As presented in another chapter, the extra symbols have to be "removed" to recover the intended information both by logical and operational means.

The last part contains a summary of the presented results as well as an outlook about work which is yet to be done. And finally, we collect some relevant but distracting details in an appendix. What may be especially helpful to the reader is the table of acronyms on page 193 and the list of mathematical symbols.

Chapter 2

Technical preliminaries

> Mathematics is often considered a difficult and mysterious science, because of the numerous symbols which it employs. Of course, nothing is more incomprehensible than a symbolism which we do not understand. Also a symbolism, which we only partially understand and are unaccustomed to use, is difficult to follow. In exactly the same way the technical terms of any profession or trade are incomprehensible to those who have never been trained to use them. But this is not because they are difficult in themselves. On the contrary they have invariably been introduced to make things easy.
>
> (Whitehead 1911, p. 40)

In this spirit, we will lay out a number of basic definitions and notations (mostly) from universal algebra which will be used throughout this analysis of natural language formalisms. We hope that they are chosen in such a way that they are helpful to the reader and not an obstacle in understanding. Nevertheless, we will assume that almost all of the terms are fairly well known to most of the readers, therefore we do not try to explain or motivate them in any depth.

The definitions in this section are fairly general and used throughout the monograph. Therefore they have been separated from the particular chapters and are presented in their own section. Since most of the definitions are basic ones from the realm of universal algebra, readers familiar with universal algebra might skip this part of the book and come back only as needed.

2.1 Alphabets, words and languages

Whenever we will talk about strings or trees, we will use *alphabets* to denote the symbols which can appear as the elements of the string or as the labels of the trees. Since one can associate other information, e.g., their sort, rank or arity information, with these symbols, we give the full definition of a many-sorted alphabet although sometimes simpler versions are enough.

A string or word over an alphabet is a finite sequence of symbols from the alphabet.

Definition 2.1 (words and alphabets). Let A be a finite set of symbols (an alphabet). Then

$$A^* = \bigcup_{n \in \mathbb{N}} A^n$$

is the set of all words (or strings) over the set A. Each element $w \in A^n$ is called a word of length n. The empty word is denoted by ε. So, words are simply special cases of ordered tuples which we choose to write in a particular fashion.

In algebraic terms, A^* is the free monoid generated from A with respect to concatenation and identity ε.

Most of the time we will omit an explicit concatenation symbol $(\cdot)$ by simple juxtaposition of words, i.e., $w_1 w_2 = w_1 \cdot w_2$.

The length of a word w is denoted with $|w|$. By definition $|\varepsilon| = 0$.

A word v is a sub-word of w if there exist $v_1, v_2 \in A^*$ such that $w = v_1 \cdot v \cdot v_2$. If $v_1 = \varepsilon$ v is called a *prefix* (of w) and if $v_2 = \varepsilon$ v is called a *suffix* (of w).

Definition 2.2 (many-sorted alphabet). For a given set of sorts $\mathcal{S}$, a *many-sorted alphabet* Σ *(over* $\mathcal{S}$*)* is an indexed family $\langle \Sigma_{w,s} \mid w \in \mathcal{S}^*, s \in \mathcal{S} \rangle$ of disjoint sets. A symbol $\sigma \in \Sigma_{w,s}$ is an *operator of type* $\langle w, s \rangle$, *arity* w, *sort* s and *rank* $|w|$. The rank of σ is denoted by $rank(\sigma)$. The elements of $\Sigma_{\varepsilon,s}$ are also called constants (of sort s).

In case $\mathcal{S}$ is a singleton $\{s\}$, i.e., in case Σ is a *single-sorted or ranked alphabet (over sort s)*, we usually write Σ_n to denote the (unique) set of operators of rank $n \in \mathbb{N}$ since for $\mathcal{S} = \{s\}$ each $\langle w, s \rangle \in \mathcal{S}^* \times \mathcal{S}$ is of the form $\langle s^n, s \rangle$ for some $n \in \mathbb{N}$. Therefore we can simplify the notation by focusing on the arity of the alphabet symbol.

To leave the sorting information underspecified, we will simply use the term alphabet to denote both the many-sorted and the single-sorted case. Sometimes alphabets are also called *signatures*.

A (string) language is just a collection of words over an alphabet.

Definition 2.3 (language). Let A be an alphabet. Then each subset $\mathcal{L} \subseteq A^*$ is called a language over A. We call the set of all languages over A $\mathcal{L}(A)$.

We can use operations on these sets to create new sets, i.e., we can build languages out of other languages.

Definition 2.4 (operations on languages). Let $\mathcal{L}_1$ and $\mathcal{L}_2$ be two languages over A. Then we can define the regular operations of intersection, union, concatenation, complement and Kleene closure of $\mathcal{L}_1$ and $\mathcal{L}_2$ as follows:

$$
\begin{aligned}
\mathcal{L}_1 \cap \mathcal{L}_2 &= \{w \mid w \in \mathcal{L}_1 \text{ and } w \in \mathcal{L}_2\} \\
\mathcal{L}_1 \cup \mathcal{L}_2 &= \{w \mid w \in \mathcal{L}_1 \text{ or } w \in \mathcal{L}_2\} \\
\mathcal{L}_1 \cdot \mathcal{L}_2 &= \{w_1 w_2 \mid w_1 \in \mathcal{L}_1 \text{ and } w_2 \in \mathcal{L}_2\} \\
\overline{\mathcal{L}_1} &= A^* - \mathcal{L}_1 \\
\mathcal{L}_1^* &= \{w \mid w = w_1 w_2 \cdots w_n \text{ for } n \geq 0 \text{ and } w_i \in L_1\}
\end{aligned}
$$

A language is called *regular* if it can be obtained from the empty language $\emptyset$ and the "basic" languages $\mathcal{L}_a = \{a\}$ for all $a \in A$ by applying the regular operations a finite number of times.

2.2 Trees

So far, all the definitions dealt with strings. Now we turn to trees which are the main topic of this monograph. Trees are used in various applications not only in linguistics, but also in computer science or mathematics. The study of trees is a rich field since fairly often the step from strings to trees is not only natural, but also provides new insights and opens new perspectives. Maybe the most easily accessible example is the fact that in the case of strings automata are reversible, i.e., usually they can work from left-to-right or right-to-left without any consequences, whereas in the case of trees it does matter whether one starts from the root or from the leaves (cf. Section 4.2 on page 49).

Due to the diverse areas of applications of trees, we have a choice of how to define them: as restricted, labeled graphs, as ground terms or as a set of node addresses with a labeling function. We will start with the second way of defining trees, but will also define them with a labeling function below. Since the definitions are all equivalent, there is no harm in choosing the most convenient definition for the task at hand. For the automata theory, we prefer the term-based view, whereas for the logical applications we prefer the view using node addresses. We do not need the power of the definition built upon graphs.

Definition 2.5 (tree (via alphabets)). Let Σ be a many-sorted alphabet and $\mathcal{S}$ a set of sorts. The *set of trees* $T(\Sigma)$ *(over a many-sorted alphabet* Σ*)* is built up using the operators in the usual way:

(i) If $\sigma \in \Sigma_{\varepsilon,s}$ for some $s \in \mathcal{S}$ then σ is a (trivial) tree of sort s.

(ii) If, for some $s \in \mathcal{S}$ and $w = s_1 \cdots s_n$ with $s_i \in \mathcal{S}$, $\sigma \in \Sigma_{w,s}$ and $t_1, \ldots, t_n \in T(\Sigma)$ with t_i of sort s_i then $\sigma(t_1, \ldots, t_n)$ is a tree of sort s.

Sometimes we will refer to $T(\Sigma)$ with T_Σ.

The usage of a single-sorted alphabet simplifies the above construction in the sense that we can ignore the information about the sorts and simply focus on the arity. Intuitively, the leaves of the trees are formed by the constants of the alphabet whereas the other elements form the interior nodes and have as many daughters as is required by their rank.

The next definition is needed in the second part of the book when we will use trees with variables as leaves in tree grammars.

Definition 2.6 (trees with variables). Let Σ be a many-sorted alphabet, $\mathcal{S}$ a set of sorts and $\mathrm{X} = \langle X_s \mid s \in \mathcal{S} \rangle$ a family of disjoint sets of variables. Each set $X_s = \{x_1, x_2, \ldots\}$ contains only variables of sort s. By X_n, $n \in \mathbb{N}$, we denote the subset $\{x_1, \ldots, x_n\}$. Variables are considered to be constants, i.e., operators of rank 0. Then the family $T(\Sigma, \mathrm{X})$ is defined as $T(\Sigma(\mathrm{X}))$, where $\Sigma(\mathrm{X})$ is a new many-sorted alphabet built as follows:

(i) $\Sigma(\mathrm{X})_{\varepsilon,s} = \Sigma_{\varepsilon,s} \cup X_s$

(ii) $\Sigma(\mathrm{X})_{w,s} = \Sigma_{w,s}$ for $w \neq \varepsilon$.

Analogously to the string case, we define a tree language to be a collection of trees.

Definition 2.7 (tree language). Let Σ be a many-sorted or ranked alphabet. A tree language $\mathcal{L}$ is a subset of $T(\Sigma)$.

As mentioned above, there is an alternative way of specifying trees via tree domains.

Definition 2.8 (tree domain). A tree domain $\mathcal{T}$ is a subset of strings over a linearly ordered set which is closed under prefix and left sister.

$\mathcal{T} \subseteq \mathbb{N}^*$ is a **tree domain** if for all $u, v \in \mathbb{N}^*$ and $i, j \in \mathbb{N}$ the following holds:

(i) $uv \in \mathcal{T} \Rightarrow u \in \mathcal{T}$ (prefix closure) and

(ii) $ui \in \mathcal{T}$ and $j < i \Rightarrow uj \in \mathcal{T}$ (left-sister closure).

If we limit $\mathcal{T}$ to be a *finite* subset, we are dealing with finite trees.

For the following example (see Figure 2.1), we use the set $\{0, 1\}$ in place of $\mathbb{N}$, yielding the binary branching tree domain $\mathcal{T}_2$.

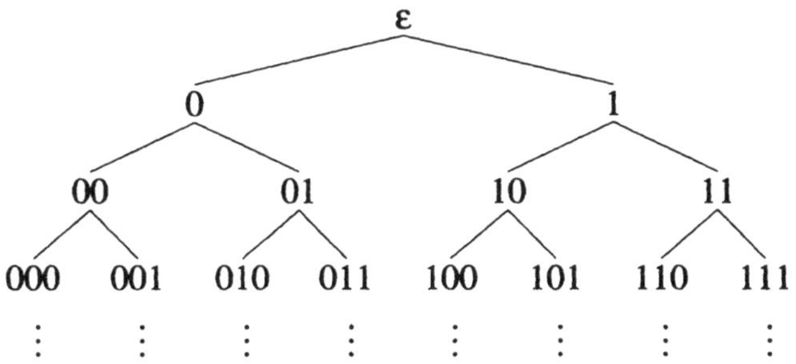

Figure 2.1: An example of a tree domain

The elements of a tree domain are called nodes. For each $n \in \mathcal{T}_2$, n is a daughter of $m \in \mathcal{T}_2$ if there exists an $i \in \{0, 1\}$ such that $n = m \cdot i$. A node is called a leaf if it has no children. The distinguished node ε forms its root. Paths are simply prefixes of the string of numbers denoting a node.

Definition 2.9 (tree (via tree domains)). Let A be a set and $\mathcal{T}$ a tree domain. A tree over A is a (partial) function $t : \mathcal{T} \longrightarrow A$.

The domain of the tree t is denoted $\mathcal{T}(t)$. For $n \in \mathcal{T}(t)$, $t(n)$ is called the label of n.

The two definitions of trees are obviously related. In fact, a tree under this second definition is only well-formed if A is a many sorted (or ranked) alphabet and all nodes have the right number of daughters according to the rank of the elements from A.

2.3 Algebras

In later stages of the book we will make use of a technique called lifting (cf. Mönnich 1999) which is based on the notion of *derived algebras*. Intuitively, terms from one sort of algebra will be translated into terms in another sort of algebra. To this end, we have to formally introduce the notion of an algebra. Furthermore, we have to give a definition of the way in which the operator symbols induce operations on an algebra, i.e., we need a precise definition how term forming symbols can be regarded as operations.

Definition 2.10 (Σ-algebra). Let $\mathcal{S}$ be a set of sorts and Σ a many-sorted alphabet. A Σ-*algebra* $\mathcal{A}$ consists of an $\mathcal{S}$-indexed family $\langle A^s \mid s \in \mathcal{S} \rangle$ of disjoint sets, the carriers of $\mathcal{A}$, and for each operator $\sigma \in \Sigma_{w,s}$, $\sigma_{\mathcal{A}} : A^w \rightarrow A^s$ is a function, where $A^w = A^{s_1} \times \cdots \times A^{s_n}$ and $w = s_1 \cdots s_n$ with $s_i \in \mathcal{S}$.

The set $T(\Sigma)$ can be made into a Σ-algebra $\mathcal{T}$ by specifying the operations as follows. For every $\sigma \in \Sigma_{w,s}$, where $s \in \mathcal{S}$ and $w = s_1 \cdots s_n$ with $s_i \in \mathcal{S}$, and every $t_1, \ldots, t_n \in T(\Sigma)$ with t_i of sort s_i we identify $\sigma_{\mathcal{T}}(t_1, \ldots, t_n)$ with $\sigma(t_1, \ldots, t_n)$.

We also need structure preserving mappings between these algebras. As usual, they are called homomorphisms. So, different algebras, defined over the same operator domain, are related to each other if a mapping between their carriers exists that is compatible with the basic structural operations.

Definition 2.11 (Σ-homomorphism). Let $\mathcal{A}$ and $\mathcal{B}$ be Σ-algebras and $\mathcal{S}$ a set of sorts. A Σ-homomorphism $h : \mathcal{A} \longrightarrow \mathcal{B}$ is an indexed family of functions $h_s : A^s \longrightarrow B^s$, $s \in \mathcal{S}$ such that for every operator of type $\langle w, s \rangle = \langle w_1 \cdots w_n, s \rangle$

$$h_s(\sigma_{\mathcal{A}}(a_1, \ldots, a_n)) = \sigma_{\mathcal{B}}(h_{w_1}(a_1), \ldots, h_{w_n}(a_n))$$

for every n-tuple $(a_1, \ldots, a_n) \in A^w$.

A particular homomorphism is constituted by the function which computes the yield of a tree.

Definition 2.12 (*yield*). Let Σ be a many-sorted (or ranked) alphabet. The yield of a tree is defined such that each operator $\sigma \in \Sigma$ with $rank(\sigma) = n$ is interpreted as n-ary concatenation.

(i) $yield(\sigma) = \sigma$ for $\sigma \in \Sigma_{\varepsilon,s}$ (or Σ_0)

(ii) $yield(\sigma(t_1,\ldots,t_n)) = yield(t_1)\cdots yield(t_n)$ for $\sigma \in \Sigma_{w,s}$ with $rank(\sigma) = n$ (or Σ_n) and $t_i \in T(\Sigma)_{w_i}$ (or $T(\Sigma)$)

We can also accommodate the trees which contain variables: The set of trees $T(\Sigma,X)$ can be made into a Σ-algebra by defining the operations in the following way. For every f in $\Sigma_{w,s}$, for every $(t_1,\ldots,t_n)$ in $T(\Sigma,X)^w$: $f_{\mathcal{T}(\Sigma,X)}(t_1,\ldots,t_n) = f(t_1,\ldots,t_n)$.

Every variable-free tree $t \in T(\Sigma)$ has a value in every Σ-algebra $\mathcal{A}$. It is the value at t of the unique homomorphism $h : \mathcal{T}(\Sigma) \to \mathcal{A}$.

The existence of a unique homomorphism from the Σ-algebra of trees into an arbitrary Σ-algebra $\mathcal{A}$ provides also the basis for the view that regards the elements of $T(\Sigma(X_w))$ as *derived operations*. Each tree $t \in T(\Sigma(X_w),s)$ with $w = w_1\cdots w_n$ induces an n-ary function $t_{\mathcal{A}} : A^w \to A^s$.

The meaning of the function $t_{\mathcal{A}}$ is defined in the following way. For every tuple $(a_1,\ldots,a_n) \in A^w$: $t_{\mathcal{A}}(a_1,\ldots,a_n) = \hat{a}(t)$, where $\hat{a} : \mathcal{T}(\Sigma,X_w) \to \mathcal{A}$ is the unique homomorphism with $\hat{a}(x_i) = a_i$.

In the particular case where $\mathcal{A}$ is the Σ-algebra $\mathcal{T}(\Sigma,X_m)$ of trees over Σ that contain at most variables from $X_m = \{x_1,\ldots,x_m\}$ at their leaves the unique homomorphism extending the assignment of a tree $t_i \in T(\Sigma,X_m)$ to the variable x_i in X_n acts as a substitution $t_{\mathcal{T}(\Sigma,X_m)}(\langle t_1,\ldots,t_n\rangle) = t[\langle t_1,\ldots,t_n\rangle]$ where the right hand side indicates the result of substituting t_i for x_i in t.

The notion of a *Lawvere*-algebra (Lawvere 1963) will play an important role in the second part of this book. Those algebras are generalizations of algebras coming from category theory. Lawvere algebras can always be seen as a special kind of category where the set of objects is the set of strings on a given alphabet. The morphisms of the category are the carriers of the algebra.

Definition 2.13. Given a set of sorts $\mathcal{S}$, an *algebraic (Lawvere) theory*, as an algebra, is an $\mathcal{S}^* \times \mathcal{S}^*$-sorted algebra $\mathcal{A}$ whose carriers $\langle A^{\langle u,v\rangle} \mid u,v \in \mathcal{S}^*\rangle$ consist of the morphisms of the theory and whose operations are of the following types, where $n \in \mathbb{N}$, $u = u_1\cdots u_n$ with $u_i \in \mathcal{S}^*$ for $1 \leq i \leq n$ and $v,w \in \mathcal{S}^*$,

projection:	$\pi_i^u \in A^{\langle u,u_i\rangle}$
composition:	$c_{(u,v,w)} \in A^{\langle u,v\rangle} \times A^{\langle v,w\rangle} \to A^{\langle u,w\rangle}$
target tupling:	$(\quad)_{(v,u)} \in A^{\langle v,u_1\rangle} \times \cdots \times A^{\langle v,u_n\rangle} \to A^{\langle v,u\rangle}$

As should be clear from the chosen names, the operations of projection, composition and tupling have the the following intended interpretations: Consider a tuple t. Then the projection $\pi^t_{t_i}$ returns the ith element of t. Given functions C, f and g_i of appropriate types, i.e., $\langle w,s\rangle, \langle v,s\rangle, \langle w,v_i\rangle$, composition satisfies the rule $C(t) = f(g_1(t),\ldots,g_n(t))$ with $n = |v|$ and t a tuple of sort w. Similarly, tupling satisfies $T(t) = (g_1(t),\ldots,g_n(t))$.

From category theory we have that the projections and the operations of target tupling are required to satisfy the identities for products. The composition operations must satisfy associativity, i.e.,

$$c_{(v,u,u_i)}\big((\alpha_1,\ldots,\alpha_n)_{(v,u)},\pi^u_i\big) = \alpha_i \text{ for } \alpha_i \in A^{\langle v,u_i\rangle}, 1 \leq i \leq n$$

$$\big(c_{(v,u,u_1)}(\beta,\pi^u_1),\ldots,c_{(v,u,u_n)}(\beta,\pi^u_n)\big)_{(v,u)} = \beta \quad \text{for } \beta \in A^{\langle v,u\rangle}$$

$$c_{(u,v,z)}\big(\alpha, c_{(v,w,z)}(\beta,\gamma)\big) = c_{(u,w,z)}\big(c_{(u,v,w)}(\alpha,\beta),\gamma\big)$$
$$\text{for } \alpha \in A^{\langle u,v\rangle}, \beta \in A^{\langle v,w\rangle}, \gamma \in A^{\langle w,z\rangle}$$

$$c_{(u,u,v)}\big((\pi^u_1,\ldots,\pi^u_n)_{(u,u)},\alpha\big) = \alpha \text{ for } \alpha \in A^{\langle u,v\rangle}$$

where $u = u_1 \cdots u_n$ with $u_i \in \mathcal{S}^*$ for $1 \leq i \leq n$ and $v,w,z \in \mathcal{S}^*$.

Definition 2.6 on page 20 simplifies in case of a single sorted signature. Let Σ be a single-sorted signature and $X = \{x_1,x_2,x_3,\ldots\}$ a countable set of variables. For $k \in \mathbb{N}$ define $X_k \subseteq X$ as $\{x_1,\ldots,x_k\}$. Then, the set of *k-ary trees $T(\Sigma,X_k)$ (over Σ)* is the set of trees $T(\Sigma')$ over the single-sorted signature $\Sigma' = \langle \Sigma'_n \,|\, n \in \mathbb{N}\rangle$, where $\Sigma'_0 = \Sigma_0 \cup X_k$ and $\Sigma'_n = \Sigma_n$ for $n > 0$. Note that $T(\Sigma,X_k) \subseteq T(\Sigma,X_l)$ for $k \leq l$. Let $T(\Sigma,X) = \bigcup_{k\in\mathbb{N}} T(\Sigma,X_k)$.

The power set $\wp(T(\Sigma,X))$ of $T(\Sigma,X)$ constitutes the central example of interest for formal language theory. The carriers $\langle \wp(T(k,m)) \,|\, k,m \in \mathbb{N}\rangle$ of the corresponding $\mathcal{S}^* \times \mathcal{S}^*$-Lawvere algebra are constituted by the power sets of the sets $T(k,m)$, where each $T(k,m)$ is the set of all m-tuples of k-ary trees, i.e., $T(k,m) = \{(t_1,\ldots,t_m) \,|\, t_i \in T(\Sigma,X_k)\}$. Since $\mathcal{S}$ is a singleton, $\mathcal{S}^*$ can be identified with $\mathbb{N}$, because up to length each $w \in \mathcal{S}^*$ is uniquely specified (cf. Definition 2.2 on page 18). For $i,k \in \mathbb{N}$ with $1 \leq i \leq k$ the projection constant π^k_i is defined as $\{x_i\}$. Composition is defined as substitution of the projection constants and target tupling is simply tupling.

Much later in this monograph, we will note that an arbitrary number of nonterminals on the right hand sides (RHSs) of rules of an multiple context-free grammar entails the use of tuples of tuples in the definition of the corresponding mapping. That is to say, each nonterminal on the RHS generates a tuple of terminal strings rather than a single string (cf. Definition 10.8 on page 140). Therefore we defined the Lawvere algebra in such a way that each component u_i of any u is from $\mathcal{S}^*$. Since in the illustrating examples we will use only rules with one nonterminal on the RHS, each u_i we employ there is of length one (i.e., from $\mathcal{S}$) such that we can safely ignore the "outer" tupling.

More on algebraic Lawvere theories in general can be found in, e.g., Wagner (1994). More on the connection to linguistics is elaborated in Mönnich (1998, 1999).

Part II

The Classical Approach

Using MSO Logic as a Description Language for Natural Language Syntax

Chapter 3

Model-theoretic syntax and monadic second-order logic

In recent years there has been a growing interest in the combination of licensing and generative approaches to linguistic formalisms. As we argued previously, in the ideal case, both are provably equivalent. The identical question arises in logic as well as in computational deliberations and in the design of grammatical theories. All three areas must be brought together to bridge the gap between theoretical and computational linguistics.

It was somewhat surprising that Jim Rogers showed in his dissertation (Rogers 1998) that this desideratum could actually be fulfilled even for approaches in the P&P paradigm by using a classical logical approach, namely monadic-second order (MSO) logic on trees. Not only is this logic decidable, but – if limited to quantification over finite sets – the decidability proof allows a direct translation into finite-state (tree) automata.[2] By presenting large parts of Rizzi's book *Relativized Minimality* (Rizzi 1990) in MSO logic, he was able to show that these parts of contemporary theorizing could be rigorously formalized so that a descriptive complexity result could be obtained.

This licensing and logic-based approach to P&P theories (Cornell 1992, 1994; Rogers 1997, 1996, 1998) together with the ones using modal logics by Marcus Kracht (Kracht 1993, 1995; Michaelis and Kracht 1997; Kracht 1999) and Patrick Blackburn (Blackburn et al. 1993; Blackburn and Meyer-Viol 1994) have then been coined *model-theoretic syntax*. For a recent overview of the field, see Cornell (1996). We will only briefly recapitulate the aspects which pertain to our monograph.

Not surprisingly, after our initial discussion, model-theoretic techniques are the underlying principle of a large number of grammar formalisms for natural language, not only for approaches in the P&P tradition, but also for Lexical Functional Grammar (LFG, Kaplan and Bresnan 1983; Blackburn and Gardent 1995), Head-Driven Phrase Structure Grammar (HPSG, Pollard and Sag 1987, 1994; King 1989, 1994b; Carpenter 1992), Dependency Grammar (Hays 1964; Gaifman 1965; Kunze 1977; McCawley 1986; Duchier and Thater 1999; Duchier 1999), Functional Unification Grammar (FUG, Kay 1983, 1984), and Tree Adjoining Grammar (TAG, Joshi et al. 1975; Joshi 1985, 1987; Rambow et al. 1995; Vijay-Shanker et al. 1995).

More concretely, constraint-based formalisms characterize objects with logical description languages declaratively, i.e., without the specification of how to generate admissible structures. Both the logical approaches to GB and HPSG use well-formedness conditions on particular structures, i.e., trees and (typed) feature structures, respectively. In the case of GB this presupposes that we use a monostratal grammar formalism. Movement has to be encoded as well-formedness conditions of chains of traces and fillers. To be able to use these formalisms in applications, computational linguistics has to provide a connection between model theory and theorem proving on the one hand, and natural language processing on the other. We bridge the gap between the two in this first part of the book by exploiting the connection between constraints in MSO logic on trees and tree automata. Since the solutions to constraints expressed in MSO logic are represented by tree automata which recognize the assignment trees satisfying the formulas, we can directly use the automata as the operational interpretation of our formalism; the aim of this part being the exploitation of Rogers's formalization in relation to tree automata.

In this book, we focus in this second part on the use of MSO logic for formalizations of Principle and Parameter (P&P) approaches in the Government and Binding tradition (Chomsky 1982). But since the advent of Chomsky's *Minimalist Program* (Chomsky 1995), there has been a shift back from using licensing conditions to generating theories. With that in mind, in the third part we are concerned with two open problems from the direct use of MSO logic as a specification language for linguistic theories. Structures characterizable by MSO logic yield only context-free (string) languages – natural languages, on the other hand, are argued to be at least mildly context-sensitive. Secondly, the advent of the minimalist program forces one to reconsider the derivational approaches. It was essential to find a way to address both of these problems while retaining the (desirable) properties of the original formalism.

3.1 Overview of the classical approach

In this part of the monograph we will explore the logic-automaton connection, i.e., we will introduce monadic second-order (MSO) logic on trees. In particular, $\mathcal{L}^2_{K,P}$, the tree description language proposed by Rogers will serve as the main source of examples. Afterwards we will introduce several types of finite state machines which will be needed in the course of the work. To a certain extent, we will introduce abstract machines which are only needed in the third part of the book. In this sense this part also serves as an extended presentation of the necessary preliminaries for the later work. However, it seemed more convenient and better accessible for the reader to introduce all finite-state devices in one chapter. This presentation is followed by the core of this second part: the outline of the proof of the decidability of MSO logic by the compilation to tree automata. We will show that it is enough to present tree automata for the basic relations from the signature since the rest of the proof simply rests on an induction which relies on closure properties of tree automata. Before we relate the findings of the previous chapters to notions of model-theoretic syntax, we will introduce some more facts about the definability of relations and transductions within MSO logic. In the next chapter we will examine the practical use which can be gotten from the classical techniques for natural language processing by discussing some applications. The final chapter of this second part reviews the strengths and weaknesses inherent in this "classical" compilation technique.

3.2 Monadic second-order logic

The techniques we are introducing here come originally from an old result in logic, namely that the weak MSO theory of two successor functions (WS2S) is decidable (Thatcher and Wright 1968; Doner 1970). A "weak" second-order theory is one in which the set variables are allowed to range only over finite sets. There is a more powerful result available: it has been shown by Rabin (1969) that the strong second-order theory (variables range over infinite sets) of even countably many successor functions (SωS) is decidable. However, in our linguistic applications we need only to quantify over finite sets, so the weaker theory is enough, and the techniques correspondingly simpler. In fact, since we are interested in using the technique of the decidability proof for natural language processing and the proof works by showing a correspondence between formulas in the language of WS2S and tree automata and there is no efficient minimization algorithm for the corresponding class of Rabin automata on infinite sets, using strong SωS is not an option.

All of these results are generalizations to trees of a result on strings originally due to Büchi (1960). Thus, the applications we mention here could be adapted to strings with finite-state automata replacing tree automata. There are also MSO languages on graphs (Courcelle 1990, 1997), but since there are no automata with the desired closure properties for graphs we will ignore those approaches.

3.2.1 Monadic second-order logic on trees

In this section we will present the formal definitions for MSO logic on trees, i.e., multiple successor structures and introduce the necessary notation. In most cases we use only two successor functions. Since one can always compile multiply branching structures down to binary branching ones, we do not loose expressive power.

Note that it is an ongoing debate whether binary trees are sufficient for P&P theories. This debate is beyond the scope of the topics presented here. The reason for using only binary branching structures in this monograph is merely to keep the technical presentation simpler.

We begin with the specification of the syntax of an MSO language on trees. Intuitively, an MSO logical language is like standard first-order predicate logic extended with variables ranging over sets and quantifiers ranging over these MSO variables. More specifically, it has a syntax of both first and (monadic) second-order quantification, all the usual logical connectives, a (countably infinite) set of first-order variables ranging over nodes and a (countably infinite) set of monadic second-order variables ranging over (finite) sets.

Definition 3.1 (MSO Language). The MSO-Language $\mathcal{L}$ (of WS2S) consists of

- a set of *monadic* second-order variables: $X, Y, \ldots, X_i, Y_i, \ldots$;
- a set of individual variables: $x, y, \ldots, x_i, y_i, \ldots$;
- boolean connectives: $\neg, \wedge, \vee, \ldots$;
- quantifiers over individuals and sets: $\exists, \forall$;
- binary predicates for the successor functions ($i \in \{1,2\}$): s_i;

– prefix, equality and membership: $\leq$, $\approx$, $\in$.

Free variables, terms, well-formed formulas and sentences are defined as for first-order predicate logic.

Definition 3.2 (Terms, Well-Formed Formulas, Free Variables and Sentences).

– The variables are the only *terms* of the MSO language.[3]

– the set of the *well-formed formulas* (WFF) is defined as the smallest set fulfilling the following conditions:

  - if x and y are individual variables and s_i is a successor relation, then the application of s_i to the arguments is also a well-formed formula, i.e, $s_i(x,y) \in WFF$,
  - if x and y are individual variables and X is a monadic second-order variable, then $x \approx y$, $x \leq y$ and $x \in X$ (alternatively $X(x)$) are in WFF,
  - if φ and ψ are in WFF, then $\neg\varphi$, $\varphi \wedge \psi$ and $\varphi \vee \psi$ are also in WFF,
  - if x is an individual variable and X is a monadic second-order variable and φ is in WFF, then $(\exists x)[\varphi]$, $(\exists X)[\varphi]$ and $(\forall x)[\varphi]$, $(\forall X)[\varphi]$ are in WFF.

– the set of *free variables* of an MSO formula ϕ is defined as follows:[4]

$$
\begin{aligned}
Free(x_i) = &\quad \{x_i\} \\
Free(s_i(x,y)) = &\quad \{x,y\} \\
Free(x \circ y) = &\quad \{x,y\} && \text{for } \circ \in \{\approx, \leq\} \\
Free(x \in X) = &\quad \{x,X\} \\
Free(\neg\phi) = &\quad Free(\phi) \\
Free(\phi \circ \psi) = &\quad Free(\phi) \cup Free(\psi) && \text{for } \circ \in \{\wedge, \vee, \rightarrow, \ldots\} \\
Free((\forall x)[\phi]) = &\quad Free(\phi) - \{x\} \\
Free((\exists x)[\phi]) = &\quad Free(\phi) - \{x\} \\
Free((\forall X)[\phi]) = &\quad Free(\phi) - \{X\} \\
Free((\exists X)[\phi]) = &\quad Free(\phi) - \{X\}
\end{aligned}
$$

– *Sentences* are well-formed formulas without free variables, i.e., $Free(\phi) = \emptyset$ for ϕ an MSO formula.

We will sometimes write $\phi(x_1,\ldots,x_n,X_1,\ldots,X_m)$ for the formula ϕ with free individual variables $x_1,\ldots,x_n$ and free set variables $X_1,\ldots,X_m$.

Informally, we create a tree description logic by fixing the domain of the interpretation to "trees" and adding binary relations to the syntax which will be interpreted as the successor functions. So, for the structure of WS2S, we are going to assume a (binary) tree domain with the extension of (at least) the two successor relations. These correspond intuitively to the relations of left and right daughter and are used to navigate through the tree. As we will show, the structure can be extended with interpretations of other definable relations we may want to use. We will call this basic structure of WS2S N_2.

Recalling the necessary definition of the binary tree domain $\mathcal{T}_2$ from the section with the preliminaries, we have the prerequisites to define N_2.

Definition 3.3. The *structure of* WS2S (N_2) is a tuple $\langle \mathcal{T}_2, \varepsilon, s_0, s_1 \rangle$ such that $\mathcal{T}_2$ is a binary tree domain with root ε and s_0, s_1 the left and right successor relations respectively.

Note that this is an infinite, though only binary branching tree. The extension to arbitrary, but fixed branching trees simply consists in choosing more successor functions and the corresponding tree domain. Note that we have an infinite model whereas we allow quantification only over finite sets. Since we are only interested in finite trees for linguistic analyses, we have two choices to achieve the desired limitation. We either can use a separate MSO variable in all our formalizations which denotes the finite tree that we are interested in and make all quantification relative to that variable. Or we can switch to finite model theory, viz., finite tree domains. In the following sections we will tacitly assume the necessary distinguished MSO variable for the tree that we want to define since using the infinite model corresponds to the usage in the classical results. But in Section 5.3.3 on page 72, we will also state the necessary definitions for finite model theory. At this point, both approaches work equally well. We will overload the term WS2S to mean the structure of two successor functions as well as its MSO language.

Formally, each MSO formula represents a constraint on the valuation of its free variables which is determined by the assignment of the variables to (sets of) nodes.

Definition 3.4 (variable assignment and satisfiability). Let $\mathcal{T}$ be a tree domain and VAR a set of (MSO) variables. A *variable assignment* is a total function $\alpha : \mathsf{VAR} \rightarrow \wp(\mathcal{T})$.

Satisfaction is relative to these assignments. We will write satisfaction as $N_2 \models \phi[\alpha]$ for ϕ an MSO formula, α a variable assignment. As for first-order logic, *satisfiability* of a formula means that there exists a variable assignment which makes the formula true (in the given model).

Since these assignments are such that they map variables to nodes in a tree, i.e., the assignments together with the domain of interpretation form a (labeled) tree, we will also speak of assignment trees.

Intuitively, MSO predicates, i.e., monadic second-order variables, pick out sets of nodes. We can think of the predicates as features labeling the nodes. A tree, then, is just a rooted, dominance connected subset T of the domain of N_2. A labeled tree is a $k+1$-tuple $\langle T, F_1, \ldots, F_k \rangle$ of the tree T and k features.[5] Therefore, MSO formulas with the underlying interpretation on N_2 are constraints on trees. And a grammar in this setting becomes just the specification of a $k+1$-ary relation characterizing the well-formed trees. An example can be found in Section 3.2.3 on page 39.

As we will see later, the proofs of the decidability results are inductive on the structure of MSO formulas. So, we can choose our particular tree description language rather freely, knowing (a) that the resulting logic will be decidable and (b) that the translation to automata will go through as long as the atomic formulas of the language represent relations which can be translated (by hand if necessary) to tree automata recognizing the "right" assignments to their free variables. We will see how this is done in the next section. However, note that further proof is required that these languages have the full power of WS2S.

Because of the flexibility concerning the signature of the MSO languages, the use of the decidability result is not fixed to a particular area of natural language formalisms. For example, Ayari et al. (1998) have investigated the usefulness of these techniques in dealing with record-like feature trees which unfold feature structures; there the attributes of an attribute-value term are translated to distinct successor functions. On the other hand, we will base our work on Rogers (1998) who has developed a language rich in long-distance relations (dominance and precedence) which is more appropriate for work in GB theory. Compact automata can be easily constructed to represent dominance and precedence relations.

3.2.2 An example language: $\mathcal{L}^2_{K,P}$

In this monograph, we draw our examples from tree description logics used in the P&P paradigm. In particular $\mathcal{L}^2_{K,P}$, the logic proposed in Rogers (1998), will serve as our main source. Note that $\mathcal{L}^2_{K,P}$ has been demonstrated to offer concise and well founded formalizations of concepts involved in P&P approaches. In fact, Rogers encodes in his monograph most of the proposals made in *Relativized Minimality* by Rizzi (1990) naturally and perspicuously. Although Rogers has shown that $\mathcal{L}^2_{K,P}$ is intertranslatable with SnS and therefore not limited to either binary or finite trees, we use it only in the weak sense over finite binary trees since in linguistics as well as in natural language processing it seems a reasonable assumption that we are dealing with finite trees only. The limitation to the binary case, on the other hand, is just for convenience (see the remark above).

The strength and naturalness of Roger s's formalization stems from two facts. First of all, he is able to define a set of primitive relations which formalize linguistically relevant tree configurations such as dominance, immediate dominance and precedence. This links the formal definitions given above with the notions linguists use in their analysis of natural languages. And secondly, the monadic second-order variables allow to designate sets of nodes in the tree. Therefore they serve the purpose of features or labels as well as general sets of nodes and, since we can also quantify over these sets, the resulting language is surprisingly flexible.

Therefore, the language of $\mathcal{L}^2_{K,P}$ is designed to express relationships between nodes in trees representing linguistic structures. There are local relations on nodes such as the immediate dominance relation as well as nonlocal ones such as the reflexive transitive closure of immediate dominance, which is simply called dominance. Various other theory independent relations for reasoning about relations between nodes can be defined in WS2S and added freely, e.g., proper precedence to express ordering information. We parameterize the language with both individual and predicate constants.

Example 3.5. Let $\mathcal{L}^2_{K,P}$ be defined by a set K of countably many individual constants; a set P of countably many predicate constants; a countably infinite set $\mathbf{X} = \mathbf{X}_0 \cup \mathbf{X}_1$ of first-order and monadic second-order variables; $\wedge, \vee, \neg$ – logical connectives; $\forall, \exists$ – quantifiers; $(,),[,]$ – brackets; $\triangleleft, \triangleleft^*, \triangleleft^+$ – immediate, reflexive, and proper dominance; $\prec$ – proper precedence; and $\in, \approx$ – set membership and equality.

In the remainder of the book we will mostly use $\mathcal{L}^2_{\emptyset,\emptyset}$. The change does not limit the power of the language since both the predicate and individual constants correspond to free (global) variables. In fact, if one uses a tool to compile the automata from the formulas, one *must* use free variables since the compilation process cannot handle constants. We deviate slightly from Rogers's definition of the language and use $X(x)$ and $x \in X$ interchangeably.

We will freely use appropriate symbols for standard combinations of the boolean operators (for example $\Rightarrow$, $\not\Leftarrow$, $\Leftrightarrow$, ...), uppercase letters to denote set variables and lowercase ones to denote individual ones. As an example for relations definable in this language, take the subset relation in (3.1), the constraint for a set to contain exactly one member in (3.2) and, more linguistically motivated, the formula denoting the relation of directed asymmetric c-command in the sense of Kayne (1994), see (3.3).

The following notational conventions apply: Comments are preceeded by a % sign, defined predicates will appear in sans-serif font whereas MSO variables will simply be italicized. Recall that we presuppose a further MSO variable for the designated tree to ensure finiteness of the defined tree. For better readability, we will leave this variable implicit.

(3.1) $$X \subseteq Y \overset{def}{\Longleftrightarrow} (\forall x)[x \in X \Rightarrow x \in Y]$$

(3.2) $$\begin{aligned} \mathsf{Sing}(X) \overset{def}{\Longleftrightarrow} & \text{ \% for all subsets } Y \text{ of } X, Y = X \text{ or } Y = \emptyset \\ & (\forall Y)[Y \subseteq X \Rightarrow (\forall Z)[(X \subseteq Y \lor Y \subseteq Z)]] \land \\ & \text{\% and } X \text{ is not the empty set} \\ & (\exists Y)[X \not\subseteq Y] \end{aligned}$$

(3.3) $$\begin{aligned} \mathsf{AC\text{-}Com}(x,y) \overset{def}{\Longleftrightarrow} & \text{ \% } x \text{ c-commands } y \\ & (\forall z)[z \lhd^+ x \Rightarrow z \lhd^+ y] \land \neg(x \lhd^* y) \land \\ & \text{\% but } y \text{ does not c-command } x \\ & \neg((\forall z)[z \lhd^+ y \Rightarrow z \lhd^+ x] \land \neg(y \lhd^* x)) \land \\ & \text{\% and } x \text{ precedes } y \\ & x \prec y \end{aligned}$$

The relation in (3.3) is not monadic, but reducible via syntactic substitution to an MSO signature. We can define and use these explicitly definable relations freely, but we cannot quantify over them. A relation r is explicitly MSO definable iff there exists an MSO formula ϕ such that $\mathsf{r}(X_1, \ldots, X_n) \Longleftrightarrow$

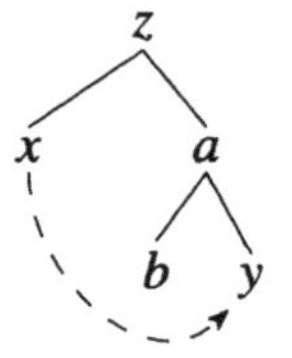

Figure 3.1: An example for asymmetric directed c-command

$\phi(X_1,\ldots,X_n)$. For a more exhaustive discussion of definability issues, see Section 5.5 on page 75.

The formula in (3.1) is simple enough to be self-explanatory, whereas the one in (3.2) demonstrates how to use second-order quantification. Therefore we will explain it briefly. A set is a singleton iff all its subsets are either equal to it or the empty set and it itself is nonempty. This formalization uses the fact that the empty set is a subset of all sets. So, if we find a set which is not a superset of X, one knows that X is non-empty. The definition in (3.3) is more linguistically motivated and specifies asymmetric, directed c-command. As can be seen directly in the formula, two nodes asymmetrically c-command each other from "left-to-right" iff x c-commands y, y does not c-command x and x precedes y. As usual, a node x c-commands another node y if all of x's ancestors also dominate y, but x itself is not on a common path with y. We depict an example tree in Figure 3.1. The dashed arrow represents the c-command relation. Note that x also c-commands a and b, but does not asymmetrically c-command a.

In linguistic applications, we generally use versions of c-command which are restricted to be local, in the sense that no element of a certain type is allowed to intervene. The general form of such a locality condition LC might then be formalized as follows.

$$\begin{aligned}\mathsf{LC}(x,y) \overset{def}{\Longleftrightarrow}\ & \mathsf{AC\text{-}Com}(x,y) \wedge \\ & \%\ \text{there does not exist } z \text{ with property } P\text{:} \\ & (\neg\exists z)[z \in P \wedge \\ & \%\ \text{such that it intervenes between } x \text{ and } y\text{:} \\ & (\exists w)[w \triangleleft x \wedge w \triangleleft^+ z \wedge z \triangleleft^+ y]]\end{aligned}$$

Here property P is meant to be the property identifying a relevant intervener for the relation meant to hold between x and y. Note that this property could include that some other node be the left successor of z with certain properties, that is, this general scheme fits cases where the intervening item is not itself directly on the path between x and y. The reader may note that the definition of LC is a building-block for definitions of government. So, with this language we can easily express even complex linguistic relations.

A structure for $\mathcal{L}^2_{K,P}$ consists of an appropriate set of nodes, i.e., a tree domain, with relations interpreting the elements from the signature. We limit the structure to dominance, parent and precedence since proper dominance can be defined in these terms. This structure is a more specific alternative for the one given in Def. 3.3 on page 34 for N_2.

Example 3.6. A model for $\mathcal{L}^2_{K,P}$ is a tuple $\langle \mathcal{T}, I, \mathcal{P}, \mathcal{D}, \mathcal{L}, \mathcal{R}_p \rangle_{p \in P}$ with:

$\mathcal{T}$	a nonempty tree domain
I	a function from K to $\mathcal{T}$
$\mathcal{P}$, $\mathcal{D}$, $\mathcal{L}$	binary relations on $\mathcal{T}$ which interpret $\triangleleft$, $\triangleleft^*$ and $\prec$
$\mathcal{R}_p$	are relations of appropriate arity on $\mathcal{T}$ interpreting $p \in P$.

A model for $\mathcal{L}^2$ is then just a tuple $\langle \mathcal{T}, \mathcal{P}, \mathcal{D}, \mathcal{L} \rangle$.

We will presuppose the use of this type of models whenever we speak of $\mathcal{L}^2_{K,P}$ and the more general one of N_2 otherwise. Again, appropriate steps have to be taken to ensure the finiteness of the resulting trees either via a designated MSO variable or by the limitation to finite tree domains.

3.2.3 A small example grammar

In this section we will present a set of formulas as an example grammar which allow, among many other things, trees with a GBish distribution of features marking nodes which belong to a projection line and the maximal elements of these lines. Let it be noted here that this example grammar is not meant to represent a serious approach to P&P grammars. It is simply supposed to give some intuition what one can do with the logical formulas, or better, with these constraints, to achieve a certain distribution of features in trees.

First of all we have to ensure that all the nodes which appear in the trees T in question are indeed licensed by the grammar, i.e., either by a rule or by a lexical element.

$$\mathsf{Licensed}(T) \stackrel{def}{\Longleftrightarrow} (\forall x \in T)[\mathsf{Lex}(x) \vee \mathsf{Rule}(x)]$$

A lexicon in this setting simply becomes a disjunction. Each disjunct encodes the possible distribution of features on a lexical node. For simplicity, we treat the words or lexical items as features, i.e., MSO variables. The following lexicon has just six words and four features indicating the respective categories.

$$\begin{array}{rlcl} \mathsf{Lex}(x) \stackrel{def}{\Longleftrightarrow} & (C(x) & \wedge & \mathrm{weil}(x)) \\ \vee & (V(x) & \wedge & \mathrm{schlug}(x)) \\ \vee & (N(x) & \wedge & (\mathrm{Schuft}(x) \vee \mathrm{Hund}(x))) \\ \vee & (D(x) & \wedge & (\mathrm{der}(x) \vee \mathrm{den}(x))) \end{array}$$

The predicate $\mathsf{Rule}(x)$ also licenses single nodes by requiring the existence of appropriate daughters as well as by ensuring the correct labeling. This example grammar has only three rules, one building CPs, one for a transitive verb and one for NPs. The rules are simply of the form that they posit the necessary daughters with their respective labeling. Note that the precedence constraint excludes equality of the daughters.

$$\begin{aligned} \mathsf{Rule}(x) \stackrel{def}{\Longleftrightarrow} (\exists y,z)[(C(x) &\Rightarrow x \lhd y \wedge x \lhd z \wedge C(y) \wedge V(z) \wedge y \prec z) \\ \vee (V(x) &\Rightarrow x \lhd y \wedge x \lhd z \wedge D(y) \wedge V(z) \wedge y \prec z) \\ \vee (D(x) &\Rightarrow x \lhd y \wedge x \lhd z \wedge D(y) \wedge N(z) \wedge y \prec z)] \end{aligned}$$

For simplicity we have already assumed the trees to be at most binary branching. Now we also want to make sure that there are no unlicensed unary branches, i.e., each node in the tree has to have either exactly two daughters (and therefore it can not be lexical) or it has to be lexical, i.e., it can not have any daughters.

$$\begin{aligned} \mathsf{Bin\_Branch}(T) \stackrel{def}{\Longleftrightarrow} & \ \%\ x \text{ has at least two daughters} \\ & (\forall x \in T)\big[(\exists y,z \in T)[x \lhd y \wedge x \lhd z \wedge \neg(y \approx z) \wedge \\ & \%\ x \text{ has at most two daughters} \\ & (\forall w \in T)[x \lhd w \Rightarrow (w \approx y \vee w \approx z)] \wedge \\ & \%\ \text{and is not lexical} \\ & \neg\mathsf{Lex}(x)] \\ & \%\ \text{unless it is a leaf} \\ & \vee \neg(\exists y \in T)[x \lhd y]\,\big] \end{aligned}$$

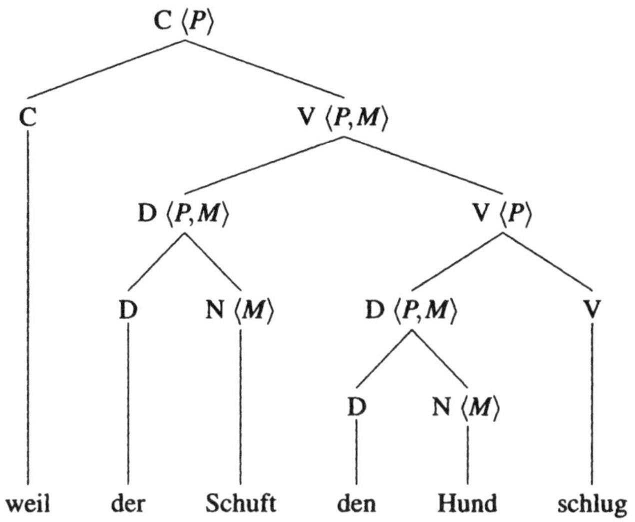

Figure 3.2: Distribution of *Max* and *Proj*

Cat(x,y) is just an auxiliary predicate which is true if two nodes have the same category feature.

$$\mathsf{Cat}(x,y) \stackrel{def}{\Longleftrightarrow} (C(x) \Leftrightarrow C(y)) \lor (V(x) \Leftrightarrow V(y)) \lor (N(x) \Leftrightarrow N(y)) \lor (D(x) \Leftrightarrow D(y))$$

Finally, after having defined the shape of the tree and the basic distribution of the category features, we can turn to the distribution of the features marking projection lines and their respective maximal element. The nodes lying on a projection line are marked with the feature *Proj* and the maximal element with *Max*. If two nodes stand in the immediate dominance relation and they have the same category feature, then the mother is labeled with *Proj*.

$$\mathsf{Proj\_Princ}(T) \stackrel{def}{\Longleftrightarrow} (\forall x \in T)[(\exists y \in T)[x \lhd y \land \mathsf{Cat}(x,y)] \Leftrightarrow Proj(x)]$$

If two nodes which stand in the immediate dominance relation do not carry the same category label, then the lower one is labeled with *Max* since its projection line ends here.

$$\mathsf{Max\_Princ}(T) \stackrel{def}{\Longleftrightarrow} (\forall x \in T)[(\exists y \in T)[y \lhd x \land \neg\mathsf{Cat}(x,y)] \Leftrightarrow Max(x)]$$

Then the well-formed tree T has to obey all the principles, i.e.,

$$\begin{aligned}\text{well-formed}(T) \stackrel{def}{\Longleftrightarrow} & \ \text{Licensed}(T) \wedge \text{Bin\_Branch}(T) \wedge \\ & \ \text{Proj\_Princ}(T) \wedge \text{Max\_Princ}(T)\end{aligned}$$

The following is an example tree allowed by the grammar given above. It is presented graphically in Figure 3.2 on the page before. We use M for Max and P for $Proj$ and split the nodes licensed by the lexicon into a terminal labeled with the actual word and a preterminal labeled with the category for convenience.

Chapter 4

Finite-state devices

Finite-state devices constitute an efficient, powerful and flexible tool in diverse areas such as program compilation, hardware modeling or database management. Their use in computational linguistics is an area of active research as is indicated by a recent survey (Roche and Schabes 1997) on finite-state language processing (FSNLP). The mathematical and algorithmic results presented in that volume unfortunately do not cover most of the types of finite-state machines that we will use throughout the book. Neither the tree automata we will introduce in this chapter, nor the tree-walking automata and the macro tree transducer used in the second part of this monograph seem to be used in these application oriented approaches to natural language processing. This is partly due to the fact that this area of research utilizing finite-state devices has completely different goals compared to the ones we have in this monograph. Whereas they want to build actual machines for particular tasks such as parsing, we want to characterize language classes as collections of entities which can be recognized by a particular type of automaton. Nevertheless, we can certainly transfer some of their claims to our setting. Therefore we will very briefly outline some of the standard techniques and results.

Generally, there are two main benefits cited for finite-state devices. They are efficient, e.g., a finite-state automaton can process a given sentence in time linear in the length of the sentence. And furthermore, they are flexible, e.g., finite-state machines are closed under a variety of operations.

One limitation of finite-state devices consists in their limited expressive power. Finite-state automata, for example, are only able to capture regular languages. By using tree automata we retain the flexibility, but gain one step in the Chomsky hierarchy from regular to context-free languages.

Some familiarity with finite state devices is assumed in this chapter. For readers who want to refresh their memory, I'll recommend Yu (1997).

4.1 Finite-state language processing

In this section I will briefly recapitulate some of the work from Roche and Schabes (1997) to prepare the groundwork for the switch to tree automata which appear as a natural generalization of the work presented in Roche and Schabes. But I will neither discuss particular applications in any detail nor do more than mention variations of the standard definitions.

Finite-state automata (FSAs) and finite-state transducer (FSTs) are the main concepts used in this section. Note that both work on strings. This will already be the main difference to the classes of automata we will introduce in the following section.

4.1.1 Finite-state automata

Let us review the definition of *deterministic* FSAs, the generalization to non-deterministic automata is straightforward.

Definition 4.1 (Finite-State Automaton). A *(deterministic) finite-state automaton* $\mathfrak{A}$ is a 5-tuple $\langle Q, \Sigma, \delta, q_0, F \rangle$ with Q the (finite) set of states, Σ a finite set of symbols (an alphabet), $q_0 \in Q$ the initial state, $F \subseteq Q$ the final states and $\delta : Q \times (\Sigma \cup \{\varepsilon\}) \to Q$ the transition function.

Nondeterministic FSAs are also 5-tuples $\langle Q, \Sigma, \delta, I, F \rangle$, but they may have more than one rule for a given (alphabet, state)-pair. Therefore transitions of nondeterministic automata have sets of states as the result of a transition, i.e., $\delta : Q \times (\Sigma \cup \{\varepsilon\}) \to \wp(Q)$, and they have a set of start states I.

Since FSAs can always be determinized (see below), we will silently assume that we are always dealing with deterministic FSAs unless stated otherwise.

FSAs are usually represented graphically such that states are indicated by nodes and transitions by arcs. Furthermore, the initial state is marked with an ingoing arrowhead and final states by two concentric circles. A simple example is shown in Figure 4.1 on the facing page. This graphical representation corresponds to the following definition of the FSA $\mathfrak{A} = \langle \{q_0, q_1\}, \{a, b\}, \delta, q_o, \{q_0\} \rangle$ with δ as given below:

q	q_0	q_0	q_1	q_1
σ	a	b	a	b
$\delta(q,\sigma)$	q_0	q_1	q_1	q_0

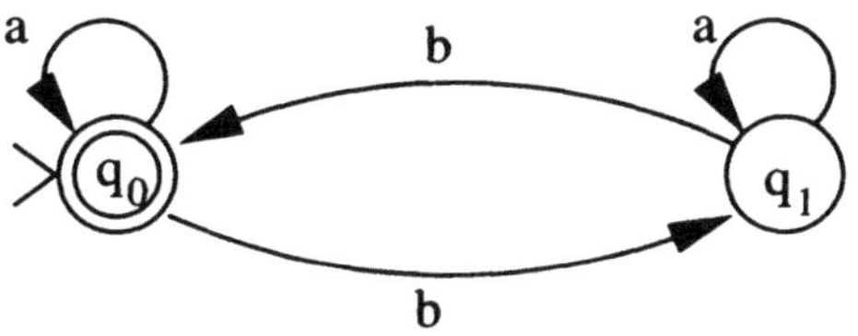

Figure 4.1: A simple FSA

Each FSA represents a set of strings over the alphabet Σ where for each string there are transitions from the initial to a final state of the automaton while consuming the string, the language recognized by the FSA. More precisely, a single transition of an FSA is defined from state $q \in Q$ on reading symbol $\sigma \in \Sigma$ to be $\delta(q,\sigma)$. We can generalize these transitions from single symbols to strings in the following way.

Definition 4.2. Let $\mathfrak{A} = \langle Q, \Sigma, \delta, q_0, F \rangle$ be an FSA. The extended transition function $\hat{\delta}$ from $Q \times \Sigma^*$ to Q is defined as follows:

(i) for all $q \in Q$, $\hat{\delta}(q,\varepsilon) = q$

(ii) for all $w \in \Sigma^*$ and $a \in \Sigma$, $\hat{\delta}(q,wa) = \delta(q_1,a)$ where $\hat{\delta}(q,w) = q_1$.

Definition 4.3. Let $\mathfrak{A} = \langle Q, \Sigma, \delta, q_0, F \rangle$ be an FSA. The language $\mathcal{L}(\mathfrak{A})$ of a deterministic FSA $\mathfrak{A}$ is defined to be:[6]

$$\mathcal{L}(\mathfrak{A}) = \{w \in \Sigma^* \mid \hat{\delta}(q_0,w) \in F\}$$

Languages recognized by FSAs are called *regular*.

The example automaton given in Figure 4.1 above recognizes the language $\mathcal{L}(\mathfrak{A}) \subset \{a,b\}^*$ where each string $w \in \mathcal{L}(\mathfrak{A})$ has an even number of *b*s.

The central results about FSAs were proven in papers by Kleene (1956) and Rabin and Scott (1959). The results relate the class of languages recognized by FSAs to closure properties. The idea is to construct automata from other automata with "natural" operations and showing that the result is still regular. In particular, FSAs are closed under union ($\mathcal{L}(\mathfrak{A}_1 \cup \mathfrak{A}_2) = \mathcal{L}(\mathfrak{A}_1) \cup \mathcal{L}(\mathfrak{A}_2)$), concatenation ($\mathcal{L}(\mathfrak{A}_1 \cdot \mathfrak{A}_2) = \mathcal{L}(\mathfrak{A}_1) \cdot \mathcal{L}(\mathfrak{A}_2)$), complementation ($\mathcal{L}(\overline{\mathfrak{A}}) = \Sigma^* - \mathcal{L}(\mathfrak{A})$), intersection ($\mathcal{L}(\mathfrak{A}_1 \cap \mathfrak{A}_2) = \mathcal{L}(\mathfrak{A}_1) \cap \mathcal{L}(\mathfrak{A}_2)$) and Kleene star ($\mathcal{L}(\mathfrak{A}^*) = \mathcal{L}(\mathfrak{A})^*$). I will not repeat the proofs here, the interested reader is referred to any textbook on formal language theory, e.g. Lewis and Papadimitriou (1998). These results directly relate FSAs with regular expressions. In fact, they characterize the same languages.

Note that the naive constructions usually are augmented with two useful techniques. First of all, one considers only the states which are *reachable* from the initial state(s) by some transitions. This can directly be used in constructing the new automata by starting from the initial states and using only those which can be generated from there on. The other construction is the one which removes *useless* states. A state is useless, if no final state can be reached from it. One can simply compute the useless states by doing a reverse reachability construction starting with the final states. Both of these fairly simple improvements can be folded into the basic constructions – as for example the intersection construction – and help to speed up building the automata by keeping them small.

Furthermore, FSAs are also closed under determinization (via a subset construction of the states) which means that we can pick the more convenient version of FSA and be certain that the other closure properties still hold. Again, particulars of this construction can be found in any textbook, e.g. Lewis and Papadimitriou (1998).

The closure properties are powerful and not all other formalisms in natural language processing have them, e.g., as is well-known, context-free grammars are not closed under intersection nor under complementation. FSAs, on the other hand, can be used to build other automata incrementally from sets of constraints according to these natural operations.

FSAs can also be minimized and therefore have a normal form which ensures optimal space and time efficiency. Minimization works by removing any useless states (and the transitions using them), followed by forming equivalence classes of states which behave identically. The details are outlined in any standard textbook on automata theory.

We conclude this brief introduction of FSAs by giving a number of important decidable properties regarding their languages:

(4.1)

Membership:	$w \in \mathcal{L}(\mathfrak{A})$
Emptiness:	$\mathcal{L}(\mathfrak{A}) = \emptyset$
Totality:	$\mathcal{L}(\mathfrak{A}) = \Sigma^*$
Subset:	$\mathcal{L}(\mathfrak{A}_1) \subseteq \mathcal{L}(\mathfrak{A}_2)$
Equality:	$\mathcal{L}(\mathfrak{A}_1) = \mathcal{L}(\mathfrak{A}_2)$

The results all rely on the crucial fact that the emptiness of the language recognized by an automaton is decidable together with the closure operations outlined above. The emptiness can be decided by a simple fixpoint construction on the set of states which can be reached with arbitrary alphabet symbols from the initial states. If a final state can be found in this way, the language is non-empty. The process terminates since there are only a finite number of states to consider. Note that minimization gives us another way of deciding this question: the canonical empty automaton has just one state which is initial but non-final. Again, this turns FSAs into a flexible framework which can be used to incrementally build applications.

The applications of FSAs in natural language processing include, among others, morphology, phonology, lexica, dictionaries, pattern matching, speech processing, optical character recognition and grammar approximation (Roche and Schabes 1997). Occasionally, the applications require the extension or modification of the basic definitions, e.g., to weighted finite automata. I will not go into the details here, the interested reader is referred to the relevant literature, e.g., Pereira and Riley (1997).

4.1.2 Finite-state transducer

I will be even briefer about finite-state transducers. Since we will need tree transducer in the second part of the book it seems helpful to recall at least the basic definitions and properties of FSTs.

But first, we have to define what a transduction is. Let A and B be two (arbitrary) sets of, e.g., words or trees. A binary relation $T \subseteq A \times B$ can be considered to be a (partial) mapping between elements of A and B. These mappings associate some elements from A with one or many elements from B. These relations are more commonly called *transductions*, $T : A \longrightarrow B$.

Intuitively, the main difference between automata and transducers is the fact that transducer produce an output while consuming the input. Therefore they have two (not necessarily disjoint) alphabets; one for the input and one for the output string. So, whereas all an FSA can tell us is whether it has reached the end of a string in a final state, i.e., whether the string is well-formed, a transducer can at the same time generate an output string. In fact, a transducer defines such a relation between two languages.

Definition 4.4 (Finite-State Transducer). A *finite-state transducer* $\mathfrak{T}$ is a 6-tuple $\langle Q, \Sigma, \Omega, \delta, q_0, F \rangle$ with Q the (finite) set of states, Σ, Ω finite sets of

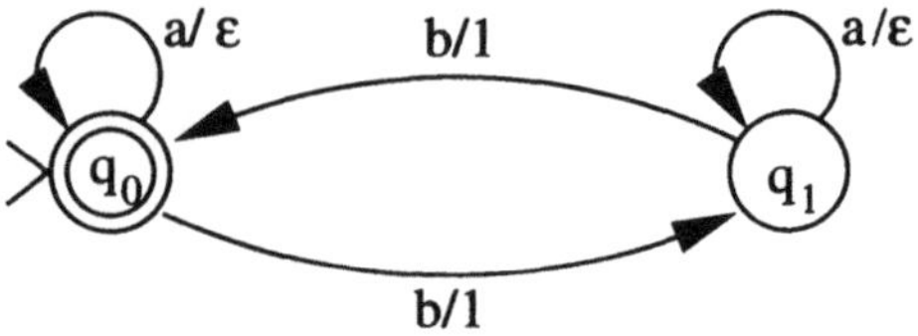

Figure 4.2: A simple FST

symbols (input and output alphabet), $q_0 \in Q$ the initial state, $F \subseteq Q$ the final states and $\delta : Q \times (\Sigma \cup \{\varepsilon\}) \rightarrow Q \times (\Omega \cup \{\varepsilon\})$ the transition function.

$\mathfrak{T}$ is deterministic if for all $q \in Q$ and $\sigma \in \Sigma$ $|\delta(q,\sigma) \cup \delta(q,\varepsilon)| = 1$, otherwise it is called non-deterministic.

We can associate an underlying FSA with each FST by just defining the FSA to work on an alphabet of pairs from $\Sigma \times \Omega$.

An example is again graphically displayed in Figure 4.2. The only difference to the FSA in Figure 4.1 on page 45 is that the arcs are now labeled with pairs of symbols where the first one is the input and the second one the output symbol.

Transitions are defined as for automata. If we are in state q_i and read symbol σ_j of the input word $w = \sigma_1 \cdots \sigma_n$ and have generated the output $\omega_1 \cdots \omega_{l-1}$ and a transition exists in $\mathfrak{T}$ $\delta(q_i, \sigma_j, q_k, \omega_l)$, we continue the computation in state q_k and append ω_l to the output $u = \omega_1 \cdots \omega_l$.

Definition 4.5. Let $\mathfrak{T} = \langle Q, \Sigma, \Omega, \delta, q_0, F \rangle$ be an FST and $w = w_1 \cdots w_n \in \Sigma^*$. Then $\mathfrak{T}(w)$ is the set of all output words $v = v_1 \cdots v_n \in \Omega^*$ of $\mathfrak{T}$ for w if there exists a sequence of transitions from q_0 to some $q_i \in F$

$$(q_1, v_1) \in \delta(q_0, w_1), (q_2, v_2) \in \delta(q_1, w_2), \ldots, (q_n, v_n) \in \delta(q_{n-1}, w_n)$$

and $q_n \in F$.

In this sense the transition realized by $\mathfrak{T}$ is $\{(w, v) \mid v \in \mathfrak{T}(w)\}$.

Our example transducer from Figure 4.2 transduces the words with even occurrences of *b*s into strings of 1s such that it counts the *b*s, e.g., *aabbaba* is transduced to 111.

As with FSAs, the power and flexibility of FSTs come from the diverse closure results, although it should be noted that FSTs as defined here (they allow ε-transitions) are not closed under intersection. The reader is referred to Roche and Schabes (1997) for details.

4.2 Tree automata

Recall that we are not solely interested in strings but in their structural description which can be modeled with trees. Therefore we will introduce an appropriate class of automata working on trees. And furthermore, the switch to tree automata also results in a gain of expressive power since the yields of recognizable trees are the context-free languages (Gécseg and Steinby 1984).

Since we are only using MSO logic on *finite* trees, the introduction of tree automata is sufficient. We do not have to follow Rabin (1969) in the specification of automata on infinite trees.

Intuitively, FSAs work on a rather special sort of tree already. Consider turning a string by 90 degrees and re-interpreting the old precedence information as dominance. Then FSAs work on unary branching trees, i.e., on a special *monadic* alphabet. Now we generalize this to arbitrarily branching trees by switching to a ranked alphabet for the input symbols and generalizing the transition function from (state, alphabet symbol)-pairs to multiple states on the left hand side of a transition. This is quite natural from the perspective which views automata recognizing terms over a ranked alphabet as a special form of algebra. More specifically, terms are seen as finite labeled trees as defined in the preliminaries (cf. Section 2 on page 17). Strings over a finite alphabet are simply terms over a unary ranked alphabet and the generalization to arbitrarily branching terms is straightforward. For example, the string *aba* becomes the tree $a(b(a(\varepsilon)))$ via a bijection defined such that each word $w \in \Omega^*$ is taken to $t_w \in T_\Sigma(\{\varepsilon\})$, with $\Sigma = \Sigma_1 = \Omega$ a ranked alphabet, in the following way:

(i) $t_\varepsilon = \varepsilon$, ε a new symbol, and

(ii) $t_w = u(t_v)$ for $w = uv$, $v \in \Sigma^*$, $u \in \Sigma$.

Now we can generalize the terms and automata correspondingly. We already introduced terms over a ranked alphabet in the preliminaries (see, again, Section 2 on page 17). Therefore we can immediately turn to the tree automata which recognize them. As can be seen, we prefer in this case an algebraic definition of trees.

To be able to define deterministic tree automata, we follow Gécseg and Steinby (1997) in assuming that leaves have two daughters which are both in the initial state. Algebraically, this corresponds to the addition of a terminating "null"-symbol λ labeling special nodes below the intended leaves. These

$$\mathfrak{A} = \langle \{a_0, a_1\}, \{A, B\}, \delta, a_0, \{a_0\} \rangle$$

$$\begin{array}{ll} \delta(a_0, a_0, A) = a_0 & \delta(a_0, a_1, A) = a_1 \\ \delta(a_1, a_0, A) = a_1 & \delta(a_1, a_1, A) = a_1 \\ \delta(a_0, a_0, B) = a_1 & \delta(a_0, a_1, B) = a_1 \\ \delta(a_1, a_0, B) = a_1 & \delta(a_1, a_1, B) = a_1 \end{array}$$

Figure 4.3: A simple FSTA

are connected with a null-ary transition function into the intended initial state. Most of the time we will omit both these nodes and the transitions for better readability.

Intuitively, a finite-state bottom-up tree automaton (FSTA) creeps up the tree from the frontier to the root using the labels as alphabet symbols for the transitions and assigning a state to each subtree. If the root is reached in a final state, the tree has been recognized.

Definition 4.6 (Tree Automaton). A *(deterministic) finite-state bottom-up tree automaton* (FSTA) $\mathfrak{A}$ is a 5-tuple $\langle A, \Sigma, \delta, a_0, F \rangle$ with A the (finite) set of states, Σ a ranked alphabet, $a_0 \in A$ the initial state, $F \subseteq A$ the final states and $\delta : \bigcup_n (A^n \times \Sigma_n) \to A$ the transition function.

Again, we can extend the transition function inductively from labels to entire trees by defining

(i) $\hat{\delta}(\lambda) = a_0$ and

(ii) $\hat{\delta}(\sigma(t_1, \ldots, t_n)) = \delta(\hat{\delta}(t_1), \ldots, \hat{\delta}(t_n), \sigma)$, for $t_i \in T_\Sigma, 1 \leq i \leq n, \sigma \in \Sigma_n$.

An automaton $\mathfrak{A}$ accepts a tree $t \in T_\Sigma$ iff $\hat{\delta}(t) \in F$. The language recognized by $\mathfrak{A}$ is denoted by $T(\mathfrak{A}) = \{t \mid \hat{\delta}(t) \in F\}$. Sets of trees which are the language of some tree automaton are called *recognizable*.

As an example, the automaton in Figure 4.3 recognizes trees from an alphabet with $\Sigma_2 = \{A, B\}$ where all the nodes are labeled with A. Unfortunately, there is no suitable graphical representation for FSTAs. Therefore it is necessary to give the full specification as outlined in the formal definition.

This admittedly very simple tree automaton recognizes all binary trees whose interior nodes are labeled with A by staying in the initial and, at the same time, final state a_0. As soon as we encounter a node labeled B, we go into a sink state (a_1). We will eliminate the transitions to the sink state in the

$$\mathfrak{A} = \langle \{a_0, a_1\}, \{A, B\}, \delta, a_0, \{a_1\} \rangle$$

$$\begin{array}{ll} \delta(a_0, a_0, A) = a_0 & \delta(a_0, a_1, A) = a_1 \\ \delta(a_1, a_0, A) = a_1 & \delta(a_1, a_1, A) = a_1 \\ \multicolumn{2}{c}{\delta(a_0, a_0, B) = a_1} \end{array}$$

Figure 4.4: A tree automaton recognizing an non-context-free tree set

remainder of the paper since they do not contribute knowledge on acceptable structures.

As can be seen from the definition of the *yield*-homomorphism in Definition 2.12 on page 22, the tree language recognized by a tree automaton can be turned into a string language by interpreting all the nonterminals as concatenation operators of the appropriate arity, i.e., the string language $\mathcal{L}(\mathfrak{A})$ associated with a tree automaton $\mathfrak{A}$ is defined to be $\mathcal{L}(\mathfrak{A}) = \{w \mid w = yield(t) \text{ for } t \in T(\mathfrak{A})\}$.

As mentioned previously, Gécseg and Steinby (1984) show that for any tree automaton $\mathfrak{A}$, $\mathcal{L}(\mathfrak{A})$ is a context-free language and that for any context-free language $\mathcal{L}$ there is a tree automaton $\mathfrak{A}$ such that $\mathcal{L} = \mathcal{L}(\mathfrak{A})$. But note that tree automata are only equivalent to context-free grammars up to a projection! Consider for example the tree automaton given in Figure 4.4. It recognizes trees which have exactly one node labeled with b. There is no context-free grammar which will have this set of trees as derivation trees since if in a rule an A can be rewritten into a B once, it can happen for any A. But if we take as nonterminals pairs of states and alphabet symbols, then we can write an appropriate grammar. If we then project the states away, the resulting trees are the ones recognized by the tree automaton.

Let us re-state briefly the results about boolean operations which can be directly transfered from the previous discussions of standard FSAs, before we explain the new ones. As for FSAs, bottom-up tree automata are closed under complementation, intersection, union, Kleene star, projection and cylindrification of alphabets, determinization[7] and minimization. Most of the constructions are adaptions from the corresponding ones on finite-state automata. Most notably, the binary constructions are all variants of building the cross-product of the two automata involved and then computing the "right" set of final states.

We will use the constructions during the compilation from formulas to automata to parallel connectives and quantifiers in MSO formulas. Again, the questions presented in (4.1) on page 46 remain decidable since we are still dealing with finite sets of states such that reachability is decidable and the automata retain the necessary closure properties.

There are two operations which have not been introduced so far, but which are necessary for the decidability proof of MSO logic on trees, namely projection and cylindrification of alphabets. Intuitively, when we quantify a variable in MSO logic and have a corresponding tree automaton, then we have to remove the element corresponding to that variable from the alphabet. Here we need the projection operation. Conjoining two automata (formulas) requires that they work on the same alphabet, i.e., the boolean constructions assume that $T(\mathfrak{A}_1)$ and $T(\mathfrak{A}_2)$ are both subsets of T_Σ, for some fixed Σ – we need cylindrification.

Therefore, for the handling of the projection and the conjunction of the alphabets we need a general construction which takes us from a set of trees in one alphabet Σ to another, call it Ω. Assume that we are given a mapping $P : \Sigma \to \Omega$; we extend it to a mapping $\overline{P}$ from $T_\Sigma \to T_\Omega$ in the natural way. That is:

$$\overline{P}(\sigma) = P(\sigma) \text{ for } \sigma \in \Sigma_0$$
$$\overline{P}(\sigma(t_1,\ldots,t_n)) = P(\sigma)(\overline{P}(t_1),\ldots,\overline{P}(t_n)) \text{ for } \sigma \in \Sigma_n$$

Now suppose that $T(\mathfrak{A}) \subseteq T_\Sigma$, with $\mathfrak{A} = \langle A,\Sigma,\delta,a_0,F\rangle$. We construct a nondeterministic automaton $\mathfrak{B}$ working on the new "projected" alphabet as presented in (4.2). But first we have to introduce some notation. Let G be a set of functions. Then $G(x_1,\ldots,x_n)$ is meant to denote $\{z \mid (\exists g \in G)[g(x_1,\ldots,x_n) = z]\}$.

(4.2)
$$\mathfrak{B} = \langle A,\Omega,\delta_P,a_0,F\rangle$$
$$\delta_P(a_1,\ldots,a_n,\omega) = \delta(a_1,\ldots,a_n,P^{-1}(\omega)) \qquad \text{for } \omega \in \Omega$$

Then one can show that (see Morawietz and Cornell 1997b)

$$\overline{P}(T(\mathfrak{A})) = T(\mathfrak{B}).$$

Considering the remark on notation above, $\delta(a_1,\ldots,a_n,P^{-1}(\omega))$ denotes the set of a such that, for some σ with $P(\sigma) = \omega$, the following equation holds: $\delta(a_1,\ldots,a_n,\sigma) = a$. The result is a non-deterministic automaton. Since bottom-up tree automata are closed under determinization, we can always determinize the resulting automata afterwards and gain the desired new automaton.

We can also define cylindrification, i.e., an inverse to the projection function. Suppose, again, that we have a projection $P : \Sigma \to \Omega$ and a tree automaton $\mathfrak{A} = \langle A, \Omega, \delta, a_0, F \rangle$. By definition, $T(\mathfrak{A})$ is recognizable. Then we can define a new automaton $\mathfrak{B}$ recognizing $T(\mathfrak{B}) = \overline{P}^{-1}(T(\mathfrak{A}))$ as follows:

$$\begin{aligned} \mathfrak{B} &= \langle A, \Sigma, \delta_P, a_0, F \rangle \\ \delta_P(a_1, \ldots, a_n, \sigma) &= \delta(a_1, \ldots, a_n, P(\sigma)) \qquad \text{for } \sigma \in \Sigma \end{aligned}$$

More details on both the specification and implementation of FSTAs and their constructions can be found in Morawietz and Cornell (1997b) and Klarlund (1998). Standard references for tree automata on finite sets are Gécseg and Steinby (1984, 1997), for FSTAs on infinite ones, see Thomas (1990).

4.3 Tree-walking automata

Furthermore, we will need a variant of finite-state automata: *tree-walking automata with tests* (FSTWA). Intuitively, those automata – which are a variation of the tree-walking automata introduced in Aho and Ullman (1971) – make transitions from nodes in a tree to other nodes along its branches. Each single transition can either test a label of a node, move up in the tree or down to a specific daughter.

Definition 4.7 (Tree–Walking Automaton). A *finite-state tree-walking automaton with tests*, (FSTWA) over a ranked alphabet Σ is a finite automaton $\mathfrak{A} = \langle Q, \Delta, \delta, I, F \rangle$ with states Q, directives Δ, transitions $\delta : Q \times \Delta \to Q$ and the initial and final states $I \subseteq Q$ and $F \subseteq Q$ which traverses a tree $t \in T_\Sigma$ along connected edges using three kinds of directives:

$\uparrow_i$ – "move up to the mother of the current node (if the current node has a mother and is its i-th daughter)"

$\downarrow_i$ – "move to the i-th daughter of the current node (if it exists)", and

$\varphi(x)$ – "verify that φ holds at the current node".

For any tree $t \in T_\Sigma$, such an automaton $\mathfrak{A}$ computes a node relation

$$R_t(\mathfrak{A}) = \{(x,y) \mid (x,q_i) \Rightarrow^* (y,q_f) \text{ for some } q_i \in I \text{ and } q_f \in F\}$$

where for all states $q_i, q_j \in Q$ and nodes x, y in t, $(x, q_i) \Longrightarrow (y, q_j)$ if and only if $\exists d \in \Delta : (q_i, d, q_j) \in \delta$ and y is reachable from x in t via d. Note that x is reachable from itself if the directive was a (successful) test.

It is important not to confuse this relation with the *walking language* recognized by the automaton, i.e., the string of directives needed to come from the initial to the final node in a path.

If all the tests $\varphi(x)$ of $\mathfrak{A}$ are definable in MSO logic, $\mathfrak{A}$ specifies a *regular tree-node relation*. Bloem and Engelfriet (1997a), who may be consulted for details, prove that any regular tree-node relation is itself MSO definable and provide a general translation of $\mathfrak{A}$ into an MSO formula which we will present in Section 5.5 on page 75. We, however, will not exploit the full power of the definition: a *basic* tree-walking automaton restricting φ to simple tests of node labels (which are trivially MSO definable via the membership relation) is sufficient for our purposes.

4.4 Tree transducer

We need yet another type of finite-state machine later in the paper: Macro Tree Transducer (MTTs). Since those are not so well known, we will introduce them via the more accessible standard top-down tree transducers. These are not so different from the bottom-up tree automata or the standard FSTs introduced above. Instead of working from the leaves towards the root, the top-down tree transducer start from the root and work their way downwards to the leaves. And, of course, they produce an output tree along the way. In the following paragraphs we will use the notation as introduced in Engelfriet and Vogler (1985). Our presentation is also inspired by Engelfriet and Maneth (2000). A full introduction to tree transductions can be found in Gécseg and Steinby (1997).

4.4.1 Top-down tree transducer

Intuitively, top-down tree transducers transform trees over a ranked alphabet Σ into ones over a ranked alphabet Ω. They traverse a tree from the root to the leaves (the input tree) and output on each transition step a new tree whose nodes can contain labels from both alphabets, states and variables. More formally, the right hand sides of such a production are trees from $T(\Omega \cup \Sigma(X) \cup Q)$. For this definition we assume that Q is a ranked alphabet containing only unary symbols.

Figure 4.5: One step of a TDTT derivation

Definition 4.8 (Top-Down Tree Transducer). Let X be a set of variables. A top-down tree transducer (TDTT) is a a tuple $T = \langle Q, \Sigma, \Omega, q_0, P \rangle$ with states Q, ranked alphabets Σ and Ω (input and output), initial state q_0 and a finite set of productions P of the form

$$q(\sigma(x_1, \ldots, x_n)) \longrightarrow t$$

where $n \geq 0$, $x_i \in X$, $\sigma \in \Sigma_n$ and $t \in T(\Omega \cup \Sigma(X) \cup Q)$.

The transition relation ($\stackrel{T}{\Longrightarrow}$) is defined similarly to the string case (see Definition 4.5 on page 48). We traverse a tree and construct a new tree while doing so (see Engelfriet and Vogler (1985) for a full definition). The transduction realized by a top-down tree transducer T is then defined to be $\{(t_1, t_2) \in T(\Sigma) \times T(\Omega) \mid q_0(t_1) \stackrel{T}{\Longrightarrow}^* t_2\}$.

Consider as a very simple example the transducer T which maps binary trees whose interior nodes are labeled with a's into ternary trees whose interior nodes are labeled with b's. The leaves are labeled with p and are transduced into q's. Furthermore, new leaves labeled c are introduced at every branching point. Σ consists of one binary symbol a and one constant p, Ω of one ternary symbol b and two constants q and c. The transducer has only one state q_0 and the two productions below:

$$q_0(a(x_1, x_2)) \longrightarrow b(q_0(x_1), c, q_0(x_2))$$
$$q_0(p) \longrightarrow q$$

Figure 4.5 shows one application of the nontrivial rule. The left hand side displays the rule in tree notation whereas the right hand side displays an actual transition.

If we have already transduced a subtree β of the input and are in state q_0 and currently working on a node labeled with a with immediate subtrees t_1

and t_2, then we can rewrite it into a tree labeled with b whose leftmost and rightmost daughter are in state q_0 applied to t_1 and t_2 respectively and the middle daughter is labeled with the terminal symbol c.

4.4.2 Macro tree transducer

By generalizing the set of states to a ranked alphabet, we can extend the notion of a top-down tree transducer to a macro tree transducer. This allows to pass parameters – which contain a limited amount of context from the part of the input tree we have already seen – into the right hand sides. We formalize these new right hand sides as follows:

Definition 4.9. Let Σ and Ω be ranked alphabets and $n, m \geq 0$. The set of right hand sides $RHS(\Sigma, \Omega, n, m)$ over Σ and Ω with n variables and m parameters is the smallest set $rhs \subseteq T(\Sigma \cup \Omega, X_n \cup Y_m)$ such that

1. $Y_m \subseteq rhs$
2. For $\omega \in \Omega_k$ with $k \geq 0$ and $\varphi_1, \ldots, \varphi_k \in rhs$, $\omega(\varphi_1, \ldots, \varphi_k) \in rhs$
3. For $q \in Q_{k+1}$ with $k \geq 0$, $x_i \in X_n$ and $\varphi_1, \ldots, \varphi_k \in rhs$, $q(x_i, \varphi_1, \ldots, \varphi_k) \in rhs$

The productions of macro tree transducers contain one "old" parameter (an alphabet symbol with the appropriate number of variables, the x_i's) and additionally a number of context parameters (the y_j's). In Engelfriet and Vogler (1985), the x_i's are called *input variables* and the y_j's *formal parameters*.

Definition 4.10 (Macro Tree Transducer). Let X and Y be two sets of variables. A macro tree transducer (MTT) is a five-tuple $M = \langle Q, \Sigma, \Omega, q_0, P \rangle$ with Q a ranked alphabet of states, ranked alphabets Σ and Ω (input and output), initial state q_0 of rank 1, and a finite set of productions P of the form

$$q(\sigma(x_1, \ldots, x_n), y_1, \ldots, y_m) \longrightarrow t$$

where $n, m \geq 0$, $x_i \in X$, $y_j \in Y$, $q \in Q_{m+1}$, $\sigma \in \Sigma_n$ and $t \in RHS(\Sigma, \Omega, n, m)$.

The productions $p \in P$ of M are used as subtree rewriting rules, i.e., one can construct new terms out of the old ones by replacing the x_i's with elements from T_Σ and the y_j's by *sentential forms*.[8] The transition relation of M is denoted by $\stackrel{M}{\Longrightarrow}$. The transduction realized by M is the function $\{(t_1, t_2) \in T(\Sigma) \times T(\Omega) \mid (q_0, t_1) \stackrel{M}{\Longrightarrow}^* t_2\}$.

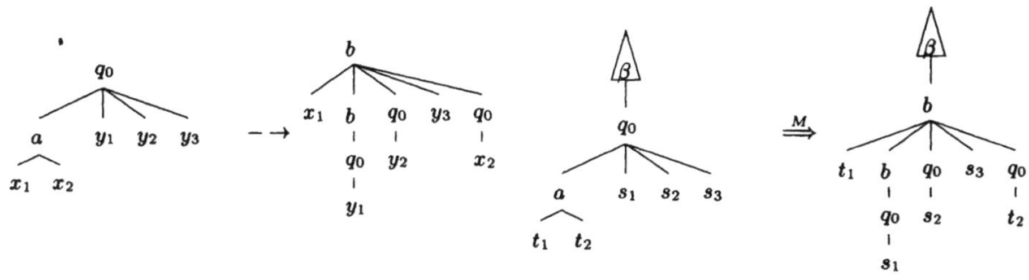

Figure 4.6: One step of an MTT derivation

An MTT is *deterministic* if for each pair $q \in Q_{m+1}$ and $\sigma \in \Sigma_n$ there is at most one rule in P with $q(\sigma(x_1,\dots,x_n),y_1,\dots,y_m)$ on the left hand side.

An MTT is called *simple* if it is simple in the input (i.e., for every $q \in Q_{m+1}$ and $\sigma \in \Sigma_n$, each $x \in X_k$ occurs exactly once in $RHS(\Sigma,\Omega,n,m)$) and simple in the parameters (i.e., for every $q \in Q_{m+1}$ and $\sigma \in \Sigma_k$, each $y \in Y_m$ occurs exactly once in $RHS(\Sigma,\Omega,n,m)$). The MTT discussed in the remainder of the paper will be simple. Note that if we disregard the input, MTTs turn into CFTGs.

A little care has to be taken in the definition of the transition relation with respect to the occuring parameters y_i. Derivations are dependent on the order of tree substitutions. Inside-out means that trees from $T(\Omega)$ have to be substituted for the parameters whereas in outside-in derivations any subtree must not be rewritten if it is in some context parameter. Neither of these classes contains the other.[9] Since we are only dealing with *simple* MTTs in our approach, all modes are equivalent and can safely be ignored.

TDTTs result from MTTs by dropping the context parameters. If we drop the input variables from TDTTs, they turn into regular tree grammars.

Consider for example the following rule of an MTT M.

$$q_0(a(x_1,x_2),y_1,y_2,y_3) \longrightarrow b(x_1,b(q_0(y_1)),q_0(y_2),y_3,q_0(x_2))$$

In analogy to the presentation in Figure 4.5 on page 55, we illustrate the the rule above in Figure 4.6 without being too concerned about the formal details of specifying a full transducer.

The only difference (apart from a totally different transduction) is that we now have parameters which appear as trees s_1 through s_3. Those trees can also be freely used on the right hand sides of the MTT productions.

Chapter 5

Decidability and definability

The theorem given below is the cornerstone of this first part of our approach. It was discovered independently by Doner (1970) and Thatcher and Wright (1968).

Theorem 5.1 (Doner; Thatcher & Wright). *The weak monadic second-order theory of 2 successor functions (*WS2S*) is decidable.*

In this section I will help the reader to develop an intuition for the decidability proof in at least one direction. Since the proof of the theorem above is constructive, the goal is to present how automata represent constraints, i.e., formulas in MSO logic. The consequence of the theorem for us is the immediate application of compiling a representational theory into an operational device.

Let it be noted again that an even stronger result exists: *SnS*, the *strong* MSO theory of two successor functions, is decidable as well (Rabin 1969). But since finite trees are sufficient for our purposes, we can safely use the weak theory. This has the additional advantage that we can use standard finite-state or tree automata which work on finite strings or trees, instead of the more complicated Rabin automata which work on infinite objects. This makes the entire approach more applicable to the techniques developed and used in finite-state language processing as presented in Section 4.1.

5.1 Representing MSO formulas with tree automata

In this section we take a closer look at the connection between MSO formulas and tree automata. It should be pointed out immediately that the translation from formulas to automata, while effective, is of non-elementary complexity. In the worst case, the number of states can be given as a function of the number of free variables in the input formula with a stack of exponents as tall as the number of the formula's quantifier alternations. However, there is a growing body of work in the computer science literature on computer hardware and system verification (e.g., Kelb et al. 1997; Klarlund 1998; Basin and Klarlund 1998) and software development (e.g., Sandholm and Schwartzbach 1998; Damgaard et al. 1999; Elgaard et al. 2000; Møller and Schwartzbach 2001) suggesting that in practical cases the extreme explosiveness of this technique can be effectively controlled, and our own experiments suggest that this should be the case in most linguistic applications as well. Experiences with a software tool are documented in Morawietz and Cornell (1999).

The attraction of the proposed approach is obvious: the connection allows the linguist the specification of ideas about natural language in a concise manner in logic and at the same time provides a representation of the constraints which can be efficiently used for processing.

The decidability proof works by showing a correspondence between formulas in the language of WS2S and tree automata, developed in such a way that the formula is satisfiable iff the set of trees accepted by the corresponding automaton is nonempty.

More specifically, Doner (1970) and Thatcher and Wright (1968) show that each formula in MSO logic can be represented by a tree automaton which recognizes the relevant assignment trees. One step in the proof is to encode the variable assignments as the inverse of the labeling function, another the inductive construction of automata. Then WS2S is decidable since the emptiness problem for tree automata is decidable.

Please recall that an assignment function maps first order variables to nodes and second-order variables to sets of nodes in N_2. The labeling function on the trees the automaton accepts does the converse: it maps nodes to the set of free variables to which that node is assigned. Concretely, we can think of nodes as being labeled with bit-strings such that bit i is on at node n if and only if n is to be assigned to variable X_i.

More formally, let again N_2 be the structure of WS2S and $\phi(\vec{X})$ a formula with free variables $\vec{X}$. We can safely ignore individual variables since they can be encoded as properly constrained set variables with the formula for $\mathsf{Sing}(X)$ given in (3.2) on page 37. For each relation $r(\vec{X})$ from the signature of the MSO logic, we have to define a tree automaton $\mathfrak{A}^r$ recognizing the proper assignment trees. Recall that we need a special variable to ensure the finiteness of our trees.

Then we can inductively build a tree automaton $\mathfrak{A}^{\phi}$ for each MSO formula $\phi(\vec{X})$, such that

$$N_2 \models \phi[\tau] \Longleftrightarrow t \in T(\mathfrak{A}^{\phi})$$

where τ assigns sets of nodes to the free variables $\vec{X}$ and t is the corresponding assignment tree. The automaton compactly represents the (potentially infinite) number of valuations, i.e., the solutions to constraints.

5.2 Coding of relations

Before we turn to the inductive construction of the automata, we have to make the notion of "representing" an MSO formula by a tree automaton more concrete. For simplicity we again limit the discussion to the binary case.

The key to the correspondence between automata and formulas is the use of a certain family of alphabets with a particular interpretation – a *coding scheme* – according to which a tree can represent a tuple of sets of nodes in N_2. In this section we set out the essentials of that coding scheme. This scheme is somewhat easier to present if we think of trees as tree domains together with a labeling function than if we think of them as terms.

For an n-ary relation we choose an alphabet

$$\Sigma^n = \{\underline{0}, \underline{1}\}^n,$$

that is, the set of n-ary strings of bits. Then, given a binary tree $t : \{0,1\}^* \to \{\underline{0}, \underline{1}\}^n$, if a node $w \in \{0,1\}^*$ has a label $t(w) = \langle k_1, \ldots, k_n \rangle$, then wherever $k_i = \underline{1}$, we interpret w as a member of set X_i, the ith set variable. In this way we can interpret a Σ^n tree as encoding an assignment function for variables in the (monadic second-order) language of WS2S. The tree t is interpreted as a function assigning to each X_i the set of nodes in which the ith bit is "on".

Recall that technically we can only encode tuples of sets this way, so we can only encode assignments to sequences of set variables. However, it is relatively easy to deal with individual variables as well. At very least, we can translate to a language in which all individual variables have been replaced one-for-one with set variables which are constrained to denote singleton sets. We can do this because singletonhood is definable in a language without individual variables (cf. (3.2)).[10]

Note that the set of trees which represent a certain tuple of sets will necessarily be infinite. To see this note that the n-tuple $\underline{0}^n$ labels a node which plays no direct role in the sets being picked out. Now suppose we have a tree

t which represents the desired tuple. Furthermore suppose that some of its leaves are labeled with λ, a zero-place function symbol which plays no role in the representation of the tuple. Clearly we can take any of these λ-labeled nodes and replace it with $\underline{0}^n(\lambda, \lambda)$[11] without either adding, removing or displacing any node marked for membership in one of the sets. Furthermore we can repeat this process as often as we like. Any tree we derive in this manner will represent the same tuple of sets as the tree with which we started. The same procedure can go in the other direction as well: any subtree of the form $\underline{0}^n(\lambda, \lambda)$ can be replaced with λ, and we can do this as often as we like without affecting the tuple of sets which the tree represents.

There are two ways of doing this. If we want to be able to say "the tree" that officially encodes a tuple, then we must take steps to isolate one member of this infinite set for special treatment. Both Doner (1970) and Thatcher and Wright (1968) ultimately follow this course. On the other hand, as Doner (1970) shows, given any set of trees which represent a given tuple, both its minimal member and its "closure" under extension with and removal of filler-trees $\underline{0}^n(\lambda, \lambda)$ form recognizable sets. In spite of historical precedent, it seems to us that the encoding via the closure is simpler to implement than the encoding via minimal representatives, and that is how we will precede. From now on we will distinguish the following two notions:

- a set of trees *represents* the relation made up of the tuples the trees encode;

- a set of trees *encodes* a relation just in case it contains *all* of the trees that encode each tuple of the relation.

Note that encoding is a strictly stronger notion than representation; a set which encodes a relation necessarily represents it, but a set which (merely) represents a relation does not necessarily encode it. We will be at some pains to ensure that the automata we construct for a given formula recognize that formula's encoding. A more extensive discussion why this distinction is necessary is presented in Morawietz and Cornell (1997b). Since it is directly related to the implementation of a tool to translate MSO formulas into tree automata, we do not go into any details.

So now we can say what it means for a relation R on $\wp_{fin}(\mathcal{T}_2)$ to be *recognizable*, $\mathcal{T}_2$ being the domain of N_2. An n-ary set-valued relation R is a subset of $(\wp_{fin}(T_2))^n$. Each member r of $R \subseteq (\wp_{fin}(T_2))^n$ is thus an n-tuple of (finite) sets of nodes, and can be encoded by a (finite) Σ^n-labeled tree. The

$$\mathfrak{A} = \langle A, \Sigma^2, \alpha, a_0, F \rangle,$$
$$A = \{a_0, a_1, a_2, a_3, a_4, a_5\},$$
$$\Sigma^2 = \{\langle x,y\rangle, \langle x,\neg y\rangle, \langle \neg x, y\rangle, \langle \neg x, \neg y\rangle\}$$
$$F = \{a_4\},$$

$$\begin{array}{ll}
\alpha(a_0,a_0,\langle \neg x,\neg y\rangle) = a_0 & \alpha(a_0,a_0,\langle\ x,\neg y\rangle) = a_3 \\
\alpha(a_0,a_0,\langle \neg x,\ y\rangle) = a_1 & \alpha(a_0,a_1,\langle \neg x,\neg y\rangle) = a_2 \\
\alpha(a_0,a_2,\langle \neg x,\neg y\rangle) = a_2 & \alpha(a_0,a_4,\langle \neg x,\neg y\rangle) = a_4 \\
\alpha(a_1,a_0,\langle \neg x,\neg y\rangle) = a_2 & \alpha(a_2,a_0,\langle \neg x,\neg y\rangle) = a_2 \\
\alpha(a_3,a_2,\langle \neg x,\neg y\rangle) = a_4 & \alpha(a_4,a_0,\langle \neg x,\neg y\rangle) = a_4
\end{array}$$

all other transitions are to a_5

Figure 5.1: The automaton for AC-Com(x,y)

relation R is, then, encodable by a set of trees, namely the full set of trees which encode its members. So we have the following.

Definition 5.2. An n-ary relation R is *recognizable* if and only if it can be encoded by a recognizable set of Σ^n-trees.

Consider as a first example the tree automaton corresponding to Kayne's asymmetric c-command relation from (3.3) on page 37, see Figure 5.1. For readability, we denote the alphabet of node labels in such a way that the tuples indicating for each free variable whether a node is assigned to it or not consist of the variable names (standing for $\underline{1}$) or their negations (standing for $\underline{0}$), respectively. In this case we have only free variables x and y, so the alphabet consists in this concrete case of the tuples $\langle x,y\rangle$, $\langle \neg x,y\rangle$, $\langle x,\neg y\rangle$ and $\langle \neg x,\neg y\rangle$.

On closer examination of the transitions, we note that we just percolate the initial state as long as we find nodes which are neither x nor y.[12] From the initial state on both the left and the right subtree we can either go to the state denoting "found x" (a_3) if we read symbol $\langle x,\neg y\rangle$ or to the state denoting "found y" (a_1) if we read symbol $\langle \neg x,y\rangle$. After finding a dominating node while being in a_1 – which switches the state to a_2 – we can percolate a_2 as long as the other branch does not immediately dominate x. If we come into the situation that we have a_3 on the left subtree and a_2 on the right one, we go to the final state a_4 which again can be percolated as long as empty symbols are read. Clearly, the automaton recognizes all trees which have the desired c-command relation between the two nodes. But in addition to the arbitrary number of intermediate nodes, we can also have an arbitrary number

$$\mathfrak{A} = \langle \{a_0, a_1, a_2, a_3\}, \{\langle \neg X \rangle, \langle X \rangle\}, \alpha, a_0, \{a_0, a_1, a_2\} \rangle$$

$$\begin{array}{ll}
\alpha(a_0, a_0, \langle \neg X \rangle) = a_0 & \alpha(a_0, a_0, \langle \ X \rangle) = a_1 \\
\alpha(a_0, a_1, \langle \neg X \rangle) = a_2 & \alpha(a_0, a_1, \langle \ X \rangle) = a_1 \\
\alpha(a_1, a_0, \langle \neg X \rangle) = a_2 & \alpha(a_1, a_0, \langle \ X \rangle) = a_1 \\
\alpha(a_0, a_2, \langle \neg X \rangle) = a_2 & \alpha(a_2, a_0, \langle \neg X \rangle) = a_2
\end{array}$$

all other transitions are to a_3

Figure 5.2: The automaton for Path(X)

of $\langle \neg x, \neg y \rangle$ labeled nodes dominating the constellation or being dominated by it such that we recognize the closure of the (AC-Com) relation in the sense of Doner. The relation can now serve as a new primitive in further MSO formulas.

A further example which uses second-order variables is given with the definition of the predicate Path. A path is a connected set of nodes where all nodes are related by dominance.

(5.1) Connected(P) $\overset{def}{\Longleftrightarrow}$

% If an element falls between any two other elements

% wrt domination it has to be in P.

$(\forall x, y, z)[(x \in P \wedge y \in P \wedge x \triangleleft^* z \wedge z \triangleleft^* y) \Rightarrow z \in P]$

(5.2) Path(P) $\overset{def}{\Longleftrightarrow}$

% P is connected and linearly ordered.

Connected(P) $\wedge (\forall x, y \in P)[x \triangleleft^* y \vee y \triangleleft^* x]$

The tree automaton recognizing the relation looks as given in Figure 5.2. The automaton works on a very simple alphabet: either a node is a member of the set X or it isn't. Let us briefly review the workings of the automaton. The initial state is a_0. We remain in the initial state until we encounter a node labeled for membership in X, at which point we transit to state a_1. As long as we are in a_1 on exactly one daughter and the mother node is also assigned to X, we remain in a_1. Note that if we find ourselves in a_1 on *both* daughters, then we enter a_3, the sink state. If we are in a_1 on one daughter and the mother is not in X, then we enter state a_2, indicating that we have completed our search for the path X. Any further X-nodes force us into state a_3: this tree cannot represent an assignment function satisfying the constraints on Path-hood. All of states a_0, a_1 and a_2 are final states: X may be the empty set

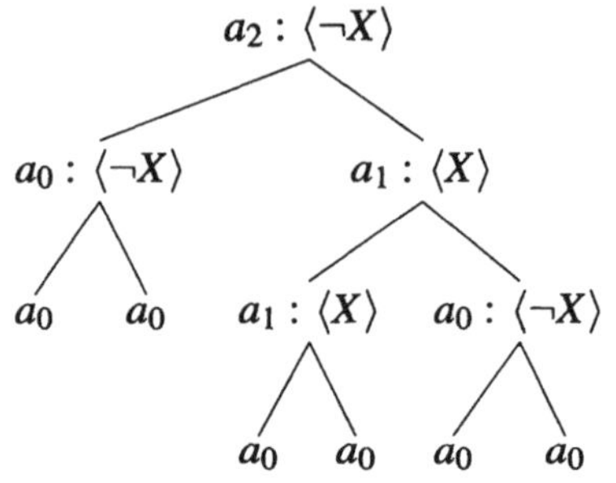

Figure 5.3: An example run of the Path(X) automaton

(a_0), it may include the root (a_1) or not (a_2). See the example tree given in Figure 5.3. The tree in the figure is annotated with the states and the labels the automaton finds upon traversing it.

There are many other ways one can define the property of a set of nodes as constituting a path. However, any other equivalent definition would still yield an automaton isomorphic to the one given for the formula Path in Figure 5.2 on the page before. That is, minimized automata are normal forms.

5.3 Constructing automata from MSO formulas

How do we construct the necessary automata from the MSO formulas?

Due to the inductive nature of the proof, all we have to do is present automata exhibiting the relations from our signature, say for $\mathcal{L}^2_{K,P}$. And then we can use the closure of tree automata under the operations of complementation, union, intersection and projection to "mimic" the corresponding connectives from the logic.

We start by simply presenting the automata for equality, dominance, precedence and set membership to prove the base case.

5.3.1 The decidability proof (various base steps)

The base of the induction involves proving that the relations definable by atomic formulas of the relevant language are recognizable. In the case of $\mathcal{L}^2_{K,P}$, we must prove five cases.

Theorem 5.3. *The relations defined by the following formulas are all recognizable.*

1. $x \triangleleft^* y$, 2. $x \triangleleft y$, *3.* $x \prec y$, *4.* $x \approx y$, *5.* $x \in X$.

We prove theorem 5.3 by brute force, exhibiting five automata which recognize the encodings of the five relations defined in the theorem.

Keep in mind, however, that our encoding scheme is defined as if all our variables were set variables. We will see below that in all of these proofs the assignments to individual variables appearing in these formulas are constrained to be unique. Put another way, it is as if we translated our formulas to a language containing only set variables, but where certain of these sets were in addition constrained to be singletons. (That is, we appear to adopt a typographical convention which requires all lower-case variables to denote singleton sets. Note that we still write $x_i \in X_j$, not $x_i \subseteq X_j$.)

Unless defined differently, the following automata work on the ranked alphabet $\Sigma = \{\langle x,y\rangle, \langle x,\neg y\rangle, \langle \neg x,y\rangle, \langle \neg x,\neg y\rangle\}$.

Case 1: Dominance. We define here a tree automaton $\mathfrak{A}$ such that $T(\mathfrak{A})$ encodes the relation $x \triangleleft^* y$.

$$\begin{aligned}
\mathfrak{A} &= \langle \{a_0,a_1,a_2,a_3\},\Sigma,\alpha,a_0,\{a_2\}\rangle \\
\alpha(a_0,a_0,\langle \neg x,\ y\rangle) &= a_1, \\
\alpha(a_1,a_0,\langle\ x,\neg y\rangle) &= a_2, \\
\alpha(a_0,a_1,\langle\ x,\neg y\rangle) &= a_2, \\
\alpha(a_i,a_0,\langle \neg x,\neg y\rangle) &= a_i, \qquad a_i \in \{a_0,a_1,a_2\}, \\
\alpha(a_0,a_i,\langle \neg x,\neg y\rangle) &= a_i, \qquad a_i \in \{a_0,a_1,a_2\}, \\
&\text{all other transitions are to } a_3.
\end{aligned}$$

Note that for any tree recognized by $\mathfrak{A}$, only a single node can be labeled $\langle x,\neg y\rangle$ and only a single node can be labeled $\langle \neg x,y\rangle$. That is, variables x and y are assigned to unique nodes by any variable assignment encoded by a tree in $T(\mathfrak{A})$. This is assured by the fact that all subtrees peripheral to a path containing denotata for x and y must be assigned a_0 by $\mathfrak{A}$. But no subtree containing either $\langle \neg x,y\rangle$ or $\langle x,\neg y\rangle$ (or for that matter $\langle x,y\rangle$) can be assigned a_0. So nodes for x and y must be found on a single path to the root, and, clearly, they can only be found once on any given path. Informally, the automaton $\mathfrak{A}$ is in state a_0 while it is searching for an occurrence of a node labeled $\langle \neg x, y \rangle$. Once it has found such a node it changes to a_1, which means that it is currently searching for a node labeled $\langle x, \neg y \rangle$. In case it has found a node of that type it switches to the final state a_2.

As long as $\mathfrak{A}$ sees only nodes labeled $\langle \neg x, \neg y \rangle$, it remains in whatever state it is currently in, so the node denoted by x can be arbitrarily far above the node denoted by y, and both can be embedded arbitrarily deeply in the tree, and arbitrarily far above the frontier. This last point assures that $\mathfrak{A}$ recognizes a true encoding.

Case 2: Immediate Dominance. The immediate dominance automaton is a simple variant of the dominance automaton of the last paragraph. We need only disallow $\langle \neg x, \neg y \rangle$ from intervening between the node labeled $\langle \neg x, y \rangle$ and the node labeled $\langle x, \neg y \rangle$. That is, we can remain in state a_1 only momentarily.

$$
\begin{aligned}
\mathfrak{A} = \langle \{a_0, a_1, a_2, a_3\}, \Sigma, \alpha, a_0, \{a_2\} \rangle \\
\alpha(a_0, a_0, \langle \neg x, \ \ y \rangle) = a_1, \\
\alpha(a_1, a_0, \langle \ \ x, \neg y \rangle) = a_2, \\
\alpha(a_0, a_1, \langle \ \ x, \neg y \rangle) = a_2, \\
\alpha(a_i, a_0, \langle \neg x, \neg y \rangle) = a_i, \qquad a_i \in \{a_0, a_2\} \\
\alpha(a_0, a_i, \langle \neg x, \neg y \rangle) = a_i, \qquad a_i \in \{a_0, a_2\} \\
\text{all other transitions are to } a_3.
\end{aligned}
$$

Case 3: Precedence. Essentially, $x \prec y$ just in case there is a pair of sisters the leftmost one of which (reflexively) dominates x and the rightmost one of which (reflexively) dominates y. The automaton encodes this fairly directly.

$$
\begin{aligned}
\mathfrak{A} = \langle \{a_0, a_1, a_2, a_3, a_4\}, \Sigma, \alpha, a_0, \{a_3\} \rangle \\
\alpha(a_0, a_0, \langle \ \ x, \neg y \rangle) = a_1, \\
\alpha(a_0, a_0, \langle \neg x, \ \ y \rangle) = a_2, \\
\alpha(a_1, a_2, \langle \neg x, \neg y \rangle) = a_3, \\
\alpha(a_i, a_0, \langle \neg x, \neg y \rangle) = a_i, \qquad a_i \in \{a_0, a_1, a_2, a_3\}, \\
\alpha(a_0, a_i, \langle \neg x, \neg y \rangle) = a_i, \qquad a_i \in \{a_0, a_1, a_2, a_3\}, \\
\text{all other transitions are to } a_4.
\end{aligned}
$$

Once again, the set of nodes labeled $\langle x, \neg y\rangle$ is a singleton, and likewise for $\langle \neg x, y\rangle$. Also, $\mathfrak{A}$ does recognize the official encoding of the precedence relation, though this fact is a little trickier to establish. A simple argument suffices, however, to show that whenever $\hat{\delta}(t_1) = a_0$ and $\hat{\delta}(t_2) = a_0$, then $\hat{\delta}(\langle \neg x, \neg y\rangle(t_1, t_2)) = a_0$. So, in essence, all representations of the tuple of empty sets are treated equivalently.

Case 4: Equality. The automaton for $x \approx y$ is designed to scan an input tree for a single node labeled $\langle x, y\rangle$.

$$
\begin{gathered}
\mathfrak{A} = \langle \{a_0, a_1, a_2\}, \Sigma, \alpha, a_0, \{a_1\}\rangle \\
\alpha(a_0, a_0, \langle x, y\rangle) = a_1, \\
\alpha(a_i, a_0, \langle \neg x, \neg y\rangle) = a_i, \qquad a_i \in \{a_0, a_1\}, \\
\alpha(a_0, a_i, \langle \neg x, \neg y\rangle) = a_i, \qquad a_i \in \{a_0, a_1\}, \\
\text{all other transitions are to } a_2.
\end{gathered}
$$

Again, only a single node labeled $\langle x, y\rangle$ is tolerated. All other nodes must be labeled $\langle \neg x, \neg y\rangle$.

Case 5: Set membership (a.k.a. 'singleton subset'). The automaton for $x \in X$ (properly, $X_1 \subseteq X_2 \wedge Sing(X_1)$) is essentially similar to the automaton for equality, except that now only x is constrained to appear uniquely. Nodes labeled $\langle \neg x, X\rangle$ may appear freely; in fact they are indistinguishable from $\langle \neg x, \neg X\rangle$, reflecting that the relation defined here is completely indifferent to the size of X, as long as it is at least 1. The careful reader will have noted that we are working on a different alphabet now:

$$
\begin{gathered}
\mathfrak{A} = \langle \{a_0, a_1, a_2\}, \Sigma, \alpha, a_0, \{a_1\}\rangle, \\
\Sigma = \{\langle x, X\rangle, \langle x, \neg X\rangle, \langle \neg x, X\rangle, \langle \neg x, \neg X\rangle\} \\
\alpha(a_0, a_0, \langle x, X\rangle) = a_1, \\
\alpha(a_i, a_0, \langle \neg x, k\rangle) = a_i, \qquad k \in \{\neg X, X\}, a_i \in \{a_0, a_1\}, \\
\alpha(a_0, a_i, \langle \neg x, k\rangle) = a_i, \qquad k \in \{\neg X, X\}, a_i \in \{a_0, a_1\}, \\
\text{all other transitions are to } a_2.
\end{gathered}
$$

This completes the "brute force" proof of the base case for decidability of our language.

5.3.2 The decidability proof (inductive step)

The "modular" nature of the decidability proof is emphasized by the fact that the inductive step is independent of the particular variety of MSO language we choose. This step is common to proofs of the decidability of both the language of WS2S and $\mathcal{L}^2_{K,P}$, and indeed it assures the decidability of any monadic second order language with "automaton-definable" atomic formulas. So we can choose an arbitrary monadic second-order language $\mathcal{L}$, assuming only that all relations definable by $\mathcal{L}$'s atomic formulas alone are recognizable.

First, all sentences of $\mathcal{L}$ are either of the form $(\exists X)[\phi]$ or of the form $\neg(\exists X)[\phi]$. We know that

$$\mathrm{N}_2 \models (\exists X)[\phi] \text{ iff there is an } A \subseteq \mathcal{T}_2 \text{ and } \mathrm{N}_2 \models \phi(A)$$

for $\mathcal{T}_2$ the domain of N_2. Such an A exists just in case the (unary) relation defined by ϕ is non-empty. (Each member of that unary relation is a potential candidate for X.) By the same token, $\mathrm{N}_2 \models \neg(\exists X)[\phi]$ just in case the relation defined by ϕ *is* empty. So the decidability of $\mathcal{L}$ reduces to the decidability of emptiness for the $\mathcal{L}$-definable relations.

The argument runs as follows. If we can show that all $\mathcal{L}$-definable relations are *recognizable*, then, knowing that the emptiness of recognizable sets is decidable, we have immediately that the emptiness of $\mathcal{L}$-definable relations is decidable, and so membership of $\mathcal{L}$-sentences in the $\mathcal{L}$-theory of N_2 is decidable as well.

We prove this by induction. In the previous section we showed that the atomic well-formed formulas of $\mathcal{L}^2_{K,P}$ define recognizable relations, by the brute force approach of actually exhibiting the automata which witness this fact. To prove the inductive step, we must prove the following claim (which is essentially Lemma 19 in Thatcher and Wright (1968), and the second half of Theorem 3.7 in Doner (1970)):

Theorem 5.4. *If formulas ϕ and ψ define recognizable relations, then so do*

1. $\phi \wedge \psi$, *2.* $\neg\phi$, *3.* $(\exists X)[\phi]$.

Assuming that $\mathfrak{aut}$ stands for an automaton constructor, the proof is a matter of exhibiting the constructions by which we arrive at $\mathfrak{aut}(\phi \wedge \psi)$, $\mathfrak{aut}(\neg\phi)$ and $\mathfrak{aut}((\exists X)[\phi])$, given $\mathfrak{aut}(\phi)$ and $\mathfrak{aut}(\psi)$.

Case 1: Conjunction. Unsurprisingly, the construction which proves the conjunction case is based on the construction for the intersection of two recognizable sets. However, simple intersection is not quite enough, since ϕ and ψ may differ on their variables. Suppose that ϕ has free variables X_1 and X_2, while ψ has free variables X_2 and X_3. That is, ϕ defines relation $R(X_1,X_2)$ while ψ defines relation $S(X_2,X_3)$. Our first problem is to get the relations to "line up". The solution is as follows. Clearly, R is the projection of some relation $R'(X_1,X_2,X_3)$, under a projection P_3 which maps $\langle k_1,k_2,k_3\rangle \mapsto \langle k_1,k_2\rangle$. Similarly, S is the projection of a relation $S'(X_1,X_2,X_3)$ under a projection P_1 which maps $\langle k_1,k_2,k_3\rangle \mapsto \langle k_2,k_3\rangle$. Since the recognizable sets are closed under inverse projection ("cylindrification"), and by assumption both R and S are recognizable, it must be the case that R' and S' are recognizable as well.

So the first step is to identify the relevant projections and invert them, giving us automata $\mathfrak{A}'$ and $\mathfrak{B}'$ working on a new, common alphabet Σ' and recognizing R' and S', respectively. Now $R' \cap S'$ is a 3-ary relation which is just the set of trees recognized by the cross-product automaton

$$\langle A \times B, \Sigma', \alpha' \times \beta', a_0 \times b_0, A_F \times B_F\rangle$$

(Recall that the inverse projection construction preserves the initial and final states of its inputs; for example, $\mathfrak{A}' = \langle A, \Sigma', \alpha', a_0, A_F\rangle$, where only the transition function and the alphabet differ from $\mathfrak{A}$.) The same construction can be extended to handle formulas that overlap on any number of variables.

Case 2: Negation. This case is relatively straightforward, as long as we can make the following assumption. If we are attempting to construct $\mathfrak{aut}(\neg\phi)$, we must be able to assume that $\mathfrak{aut}(\phi)$ is deterministic. The conjunction construction and the complementation construction itself preserve this property of their inputs. Since all of the atomic automata are deterministic, we need only worry about this constraint in the case of existential quantification, to be considered below.

As long as our determinism constraint is satisfied, the construction for $\mathfrak{aut}(\neg\phi)$ is just complementation. If the input automaton is

$$\mathfrak{aut}(\phi) = \langle A, \Sigma, \alpha, a_0, A_F\rangle,$$

then its complement is

$$\mathfrak{aut}(\neg\phi) = \langle A, \Sigma, \alpha, a_0, A - A_F\rangle$$

and that is that.

Case 3: Quantification. The core of this construction is the projection construction from Section 4.2 on page 49. We wish to construct $\mathtt{aut}((\exists X_i)[\phi])$, given $\mathtt{aut}(\phi)$. Suppose ϕ defines a relation

$$R(X_1,\ldots,X_i,\ldots,X_n).$$

Then $\mathtt{aut}(\phi)$ is a tree automaton that recognizes trees each of which encodes a tuple $\overline{S}$ of subsets $\langle S_1,\ldots,S_n\rangle$. The formula $((\exists X_i)\phi)(\overline{S})$ is satisfiable by any sequence of sets $\overline{S}$ whose i-th member can be replaced by a set S_i' such that $\phi(\overline{S}[S_i'/X_i])$ is satisfiable. That formula is satisfiable if the set of tuples of sets which satisfy it is not empty. That set of tuples is the relation ϕ defines. So $(\exists X_i)\phi$ defines a relation which is a projection of the relation defined by ϕ, where the projection removes or suppresses the ith member of the elements of Σ^n to yield Σ^{n-1}.

The projection function corresponding to the quantifier prefix $(\exists X_i)$ is the following.

$$P_i : \Sigma^n \to \Sigma^{n-1} = \langle k_1,\ldots,k_i,\ldots,k_n\rangle \mapsto \langle k_1,\ldots,k_{i-1},k_{i+1},\ldots,k_n\rangle$$

Unfortunately, one can easily observe that the output of this construction need not recognize an encoding, even when its input does.

Suppose we have an automaton $\mathfrak{A}$ which recognizes the following tree, together with all of its extensions by $\underline{00}$.

$$\begin{array}{c}\underline{10}\\ |\\ \underline{01}\end{array}$$

Now take the projection function P defined as follows:

$$P : \Sigma^2 \to \Sigma^1 = \langle k_1,k_2\rangle \mapsto \langle k_1\rangle$$

Then applying $\overline{P}$ to the tree above yields

$$\begin{array}{c}\underline{1}\\ |\\ \underline{0}\end{array}$$

So the automaton we derive by applying the projection construction to $\mathfrak{A}$ will recognize this tree and all of its extensions by $\underline{0}$.

Now, our original automaton, $\mathfrak{A}$, recognized the official encoding of a certain relation (essentially the relation holding between nodes which are the root and nodes which are the first successor of the root). But this is no longer true of the projected automaton! In particular, it will not recognize the following tree which was obtained by replacing the subtree $\underline{0}$ with the empty tree, even though this tree encodes the same 1-tuple of sets as the tree above.

$$\underline{1}$$

Therefore we need to do a little clean-up work if we want our automata to maintain the official encoding. This is not just a matter of pointless bookkeeping! If $T(\mathfrak{A})$ encodes a given relation, then its complement encodes the complement of the relation. But now if we complemented the projected automaton (even after making it deterministic!), we would wind up with a set of trees containing the tree above, which therefore does not even *represent* the complement of the projection of $T(\mathfrak{A})$, since that tree encodes a tuple in $T(\mathfrak{A})$.

For this purpose we need a further operation on automata: the truncation operation. Intuitively, this operation "updates" the initial states to ensure that no spurious "empty" nodes are required by the automaton.

First, let us define the set V of trees as being those subtrees of trees in $\overline{P}(T(\mathfrak{A}))$ which are labeled only with $\underline{0}$. We need to compute the set of states A_V which are assigned by $\hat{\delta}$ to members of V. This is easy to do: we need only a slight variant of the procedure computing the reachable states mentioned for checking the emptiness of an automaton's recognized forest. There we allowed node-labels to range freely over the alphabet. All we need to do now is to fix our attention on transitions for nodes labeled with $\underline{0}$'s. We proceed as follows.

$$A_V^0 = \alpha(\Sigma_0)$$

$$A_V^{m+1} := A_V^m \cup \bigcup\{Q \mid (\exists a_1, a_2 \in A_V^m)[\alpha(a_1, a_2, \underline{0}^n) = Q]\}$$

$$\text{i.e., } A_V^m \cup \alpha(A_V^m \times A_V^m \times \underline{0}^n)$$

$$A_V := \bigcup_{m<\omega} A_V^m$$

Once again, the construction is guaranteed to reach a fixpoint in a number of steps bounded by the size of A. At that point, $A_V = A_V^m$. Note that the definition presupposed a nondeterministic automaton as input.

Now we construct from $\mathfrak{A}$ a nondeterministic automaton $\mathfrak{A}'$ by just changing the initial states: $\mathfrak{A}' = \langle A, \Sigma, \alpha, A_V, A_F \rangle$. Note that the resulting automaton $\mathfrak{A}'$ is only truly nondeterministic at the leaves of a tree.

This gives us a "roll-up" or *truncation* construction. For completeness we should provide also a *closure* construction which guarantees that the entire extension got by replacing empty trees with $\underline{0}^n$-labeled trees is recognized. Note however that in practice, while we need the truncation construction, we do not need the closure construction, since its behavior can be easily built into the primitive automata and is inherited under the various constructions.[13]

Coming back to our construction of the relevant automata for quantification, we have to apply truncation here. But we are not done yet! Both projection and truncation introduce nondeterminacy into the automaton, and we must therefore determinize the output in case we later apply the complementation operation.[14] So the sequence of steps we must go through are as follows.

1. Apply the projection construction.
2. Apply the truncation construction.
3. Apply the subset construction.

This gives us a deterministic automaton which recognizes the projection of the encoding of $T(\mathfrak{aut}(\phi))$.

5.3.3 Computational complexity

We now have all the ingredients to take a look at the sources for the non-elementary complexity of the translation from MSO formulas to automata.

In fact, the explosion is caused by the alternation between quantifier blocks, since quantification results in nondeterministic automata, but negation needs deterministic ones as input. That is to say, for each universal quantifier followed by an existential one (and vice versa) we need the subset construction which has an exponential worst case complexity: the number of states can grow according to a function with a stack of exponents whose height is determined by the number of $\forall$–$\exists$ quantifier alternations. As we will see later, this is not just a theoretical problem but results in a real "practical" problem, see Section 6.3 on page 95.

5.4 Finite model theory

Instead of considering a single infinite model (in our case N_2) with a dedicated MSO variable for the resulting (finite) tree, we can alternatively switch to finite model theory and consider a priori finite strings or finite trees as models for the MSO formulas.

As mentioned, while the *computational* complexity of a problem is usually defined in terms of the resources required for its computational solution on some machine model, *descriptive* complexity looks at the complexity of describing the problem (seen as a collection of relational structures) in a logic, measuring logical resources such as the type and number of variables, quantifiers, operators, etc.

The correspondence between a syntactically restricted class of logical formulas and a time-restricted class of computations has attracted considerable attention both in the logic and the computer science community and was the beginning of a series of important results that provide analogous logical descriptions of other complexity classes. This research program, i.e., the systematic study and development of logical resources that capture complexity classes is well documented in the monograph on finite model theory by Ebbinghaus and Flum (1995) to which we refer for further information.

The problems addressed in this monograph where, on the computational side, finite automata are taken into account rather than resource-bounded Turing machines, as is usually done, has been called *descriptive theory of recognizability* in the recent overview by Thomas (1997) and is handled in its own section in Ebbinghaus and Flum (1995), *Finite Automata and Logic: A Microcosm of Finite Model Theory.*

If we follow the tradition of finite model theory, our formalizations have to be changed accordingly. We begin with the definition of the finite models we will use, i.e., words and trees. The careful reader will later notice a similarity to the structures introduced in connection with the MSO definable transductions (see Section 5.6 on page 80).

Definition 5.5 (word models). Let Σ be an alphabet and let $\tau(\Sigma)$ be the vocabulary $\{s\} \cup \{P_\sigma \mid \sigma \in \Sigma\}$, where s is binary and the P_σ are monadic. A *word model* for $u \in \Sigma^*$ is a structure of the form

$$W = (A, s, P_\sigma)$$

where $|A| = length(u)$, s is an ordering of A and the P_σ correspond to positions in u carrying the label σ:

$$P_\sigma = \{a \in A \mid label(a) = \sigma\}.$$

Both definitions, i.e., the one for words and the one for trees given below, use a finite set of objects with some imposed order to represent strings and trees. The order basically defines the edges between the nodes. In the string case this is simple linear precedence, in the tree case a lexicographic order. In order to talk about the labels at certain positions in the structures, we have to include predicates denoting the relevant alphabet symbols.

Definition 5.6 (labeled tree models). Let Σ be a ranked alphabet and let $\tau(\Sigma)$ be the vocabulary $\{s_1,\dots,s_n\} \cup \{P_\sigma \mid \sigma \in \Sigma\}$, where the s_i are binary and the P_σ monadic. A *tree model* for $t \in T_\Sigma$ is a structure of the form

$$T = (A, s_i, <, P_\sigma)_{1 \le i \le n}$$

where A is in one-one correspondence with $dom(t)$, the tree domain of t, the s_i $(i = 1,\dots,n)$ are the successor functions over the tree domain, $<$ is the prefix order and the P_σ correspond to positions with label σ:

$$P_\sigma = \{a \in A \mid label(a) = \sigma\}.$$

Then we can state the two theorems relating these finite structures with MSO logic as follows:

Theorem 5.7 (Elgot). *$\mathcal{L}$ is a regular language over the alphabet Σ iff $\mathcal{L}$ is definable in monadic second order logic over the vocabulary $\tau(\Sigma)$. More succinctly (for φ an MSO sentence):*

$\mathcal{L}$ is a regular language iff there exists φ such that

$$\mathcal{L} = Mod(\varphi) = \{u \in \Sigma^* \mid u \models \varphi\}.$$

Theorem 5.8 (Doner, Thatcher–Wright). *Let Σ be a ranked alphabet. $\mathcal{L} \subseteq \Sigma^*$ is a context-free language iff $\mathcal{L}$ is the yield of a set of tree models definable in monadic second order logic over the vocabulary $\tau(\Sigma)$.*

Let φ be an MSO sentence. Then $\mathcal{L}$ is a context-free language iff there exists φ such that

$$\mathcal{L} = yield(Mod(\varphi)) = yield(\{t \in T_\Sigma \mid t \models \varphi\}).$$

By this simple expedient of switching from a single infinite to a set of finite models, the non-elementary complexity of checking satisfiability via the logic-automaton compilation can be tackled from a different angle.

We can also switch from looking at the question of deciding satisfiability (is there a model) to the question of deciding satisfaction (for a given model, can the formula be made true). Assuming a fixed MSO formula, i.e., a tree automaton, it can be decided in linear time whether a given finite tree is accepted by that automaton. But since we cannot generally assume that we are dealing with a fixed formula, this technical trick is not always open to us.

The switch to finite models also allows to address the problem of the decidability of extensions of MSO logic on trees with further relations. It is trivially decidable whether a given MSO formula holds for a given finite set of finite trees by the simple expedient of running the corresponding automaton on all trees. The non-decidability facts cited by Rogers in his thesis address satisfiability and rely on the use of the classical technique with the single infinite model.

It clearly is a philosophical question which approach is psychologically more appropriate. Since the ensuing discussion clearly would lead too far afield, we will leave this, admittedly very interesting and important, question open for further research.

The reformulation of the theorems does not play a prominent role in the succeeding chapters, but please note that we have to presuppose finite relational structures for the MSO transductions.

5.5 Definability of relations in MSO logic

After presenting the decidability of MSO logic we face the related question of what is *definable* within the logic. Particularly, which *relations* between nodes and sets of nodes are definable to be used freely.

Firstly, we can use all relations which are explicitly definable in WS2S. An example of an explicit definition is the one of asymmetric c-command given in (3.3), i.e., those relations which reduce via syntactic substitution.

Definition 5.9 (explicit MSO definability). A relation r is explicitly MSO definable iff there exists an MSO formula ϕ such that

$$\mathsf{r}(X_1,\ldots,X_n) \Longleftrightarrow \phi(X_1,\ldots,X_n).$$

As alluded to in Section 3.2.2 on page 36, we can define and use these explicitly definable relations, but we cannot quantify over them. This allows us to define more complex building blocks for more complex definitions, e.g., the direct use of predicates for c-command instead of having to specify the relevant node configurations over and over again. Basically, we can tailor the description language to our needs.

In further parts of this book, we will also need to define binary relations recursively. While that is not possible in general, there are special cases where the definability can be ensured.

Moschovakis (1974) provides the notions of first and second-order inductive definability to designate those relations which are recursively definable.[15] The following paragraphs relate the model-theoretic notions with the operational ones built upon fixpoints.

We are going to define the relations recursively via an operator which computes all the tuples of sets contained in it. Since we will be limiting ourselves to positive occurrences of the relation symbol, the operator is monotone and a least fixed point exists. An inductive definition is not satisfiable by a single relation but by a whole set of them. These are the fixed points of the operator. Intuitively, an inductive definition corresponds to a recursive definite clause definition in a logic programming language (see for example the definitions in Höhfeld and Smolka 1988) where the relation we define is to be added to the signature of our model. In general, the name of the predicate in the definite clause corresponds to a third-order variable. For example in a fact like the base case of $\mathsf{append}(X,Y,Z)$ (cf. Figure 5.4 on the facing page),[16] we can view append as a third-order variable with monadic second-order arguments. In the following all the X_i and X are meant to be (monadic) second-order variables. $\mathbf{X}$ is a third-order variable with monadic arguments. Naturally we do not allow quantification over the non-monadic and third-order variables. We assume the extension of the variable assignments to these second- and third-order variables such that they assign sets of nodes, i.e., relations on individuals or sets of sets of nodes, i.e., relations on sets. Recall that $\vec{X}$ denotes a tuple of distinct variables; $\vec{X}_n$ stands for a tuple of length n.

Definition 5.10. Let $R \subseteq \wp(\mathcal{T})^n$ and ϕ be a formula with $Free(\phi) = \{\vec{X}_n, \mathbf{X}\}$ such that $\mathbf{X}$ has arity n and occurs only positively. Then we define the operator $\Gamma_\phi : \wp(\wp(\mathcal{T})^n) \to \wp(\wp(\mathcal{T})^n)$ as

$$\Gamma_\phi(S) := \{\alpha(\vec{X}_n) \mid N_2 \models \phi[\alpha] \text{ and } \alpha(\mathbf{X}) = S\}.$$

$$
\begin{aligned}
\mathsf{append}(X,Y,Z) &\leftarrow \\
&\{\mathsf{Elist}(X) \wedge Y \approx Z\} \\
\mathsf{append}(X,Y,Z) &\leftarrow \\
&\{\mathsf{Head}(x,X) \wedge \mathsf{Head}(x,Z) \wedge \mathsf{Tail}(X,U) \wedge \mathsf{Tail}(Z,V)\}\ \& \\
&\mathsf{append}(U,Y,V)
\end{aligned}
$$

$$
\begin{aligned}
\mathsf{Max}(x,X) &\overset{def}{\Longleftrightarrow} x \in X \wedge (\forall y \in X)[y \not\approx x \Rightarrow x \lhd^+ y] \\
\mathsf{Elist}(X) &\overset{def}{\Longleftrightarrow} \neg(\exists x)[x \in X] \\
\mathsf{Nelist}(X) &\overset{def}{\Longleftrightarrow} (\exists x)[x \in X] \wedge \mathsf{Path}(X) \\
\mathsf{List}(X) &\overset{def}{\Longleftrightarrow} \mathsf{Elist}(X) \vee \mathsf{Nelist}(X) \\
\mathsf{Head}(x,X) &\overset{def}{\Longleftrightarrow} \mathsf{Nelist}(X) \wedge \mathsf{Max}(x,X) \\
\mathsf{Tail}(X,Y) &\overset{def}{\Longleftrightarrow} Y \subseteq X \wedge \mathsf{Nelist}(X) \wedge \mathsf{List}(Y) \\
&\quad \wedge (\forall x \in X)[\neg\mathsf{Head}(x,X) \Longleftrightarrow x \in Y]
\end{aligned}
$$

Figure 5.4: Definite clauses and auxiliary definitions for the append relation

The corresponding least fixpoint of $\Gamma_\phi^\omega(\emptyset) = \Gamma_\phi\left(\bigcup_{n<\omega}\Gamma_\phi^n(\emptyset)\right)$, i.e., the least Γ_ϕ^ω such that $\Gamma_\phi(\Gamma_\phi^\omega(\emptyset)) = \Gamma_\phi^\omega(\emptyset)$ will be called $F(\Gamma_\phi)$.

The relation R is called *(second-order) inductively definable* iff there exists such a formula $\phi(\vec{X}_n, \mathbf{X})$ such that $R = F(\Gamma_\phi)$.

Note that the relations we define here are sets of sets and computed as fixpoints. The main fact to note is that the inductive definitions must not contain a negated occurrence of the variable which is used to denote the relation. We can classify the inductively definable relations as follows.

Definition 5.11. Let ϕ be the formula defining the relation r of arity n, i.e., $\phi(\vec{X}_n, \mathbf{X})$ and $\alpha(\mathbf{X}) = r$.

(i) If the definition of the relation r uses only first-order induction, i.e., ϕ is of the form $\phi(\vec{X}_n, X)$ with each $X_i \in \vec{X}_n$ being only a singleton set and $\Gamma_\phi(r) = \{\alpha(\vec{X}_n) \mid N_2 \models \phi[\alpha] \text{ and } \alpha(X) = r\}$ with fixpoint $F(\Gamma_\phi) = r$. The fixpoint exists if X occurs only positively. The relation is *explicitly second-order definable* by the Π_1^1-formula

$$r(\vec{X}_n) \Longleftrightarrow (\forall Z)[(\forall \vec{y}_n)[\phi(\vec{y}_n, Z) \Rightarrow \vec{y}_n \in Z] \Rightarrow \vec{X}_n \in Z]$$

since it defines the property to be the least relation fulfilling ϕ. Note that if $n = 1$, the preceding formula quantifies only over monadic second-order variables such that the relation is *monadic second-order definable.*

(ii) If the definition of the relation r uses second-order induction ϕ is of the form $\phi(\vec{X}_n, \mathbf{X})$ with $\vec{X}_n$ being arbitrary (monadic) second-order variables. Then the fixpoint $F(\Gamma_\phi)$ exists if $\mathbf{X}$ represents r and $\mathbf{X}$ occurs only positively.

Morawietz (1999) shows that in general inductive second-order definable relations are undecidable by coding a Post Correspondence Problem (Post 1946).[17] But the statement above gives us one (unattractive) way to ensure the decidability of recursively defined relations. We can only allow singleton variables to appear in the atoms in all directly or indirectly recursive predicates. The new relations we introduce are then limited to $r^{\mathcal{A}} \subseteq \mathcal{T}$, i.e., sets. Unfortunately, this does not help us to define the needed binary relations and therefore is not of any immediate use.

On the other hand, there are binary inductive definitions which are decidable. Maybe the most obvious example is a definition of proper domination via recursion on immediate domination. Results from logic programming and higher order unification related to properties such as groundness or linearity of the involved programs or queries (Devienne et al. 1994; Levy 1996) suggest that we might be able to find an interesting subclass. Other interesting subclasses of definable relations are identified as the binary *matching* relations (Lautemann et al. 1995) and the binary relations recognizable by tree-walking automata (Bloem and Engelfriet 1997a,b). The results of Bloem and Engelfriet in turn are based on a paper by Klarlund and Schwartzbach (1993) who use so called “routing” expressions, i.e., regular expressions, to define paths in an MSO definable tree. Since we will need these relations later on, we briefly present the relevant results here.

Basically, the idea behind the approach of Bloem and Engelfriet is that those relations are inductively definable where the induction is such that only paths in a given tree are defined recursively. These paths can then be traversed with a tree walking-automaton. Finally the walking language of such an automaton is converted algorithmically into a non-recursive MSO formula.

The theorem is stated in Bloem and Engelfriet (1997a) as follows, REG-R is the set of the binary node relations definable with tree-walking automata, i.e, the regular tree node relations, and MSO-R the set of the MSO definable binary node relations

Theorem 5.12 (Bloem & Engelfriet).

$$\text{REG-R} = \text{MSO-R}$$

Since we are only interested in one direction of the proof, namely the one from the tree-walking automata (FSTWAs) to the MSO formulas, we will only present the necessary facts for translating a given tree-walking automaton into an MSO formula. Recall that an FSTWA is an ordinary FSA which works on an alphabet of directives which allow the traversal of trees. This means that it starts on a node, traverses a tree according to its directives and stops at a node (not necessarily different from the start node). The sets of pairs of nodes computed in this way constitute the desired relation.

This direction of the proof works by taking the *walking language*, i.e., the string of directives needed to get from one node to another one and representing it with the help of regular expressions. These regular expressions then are recursively translated into the non-recursive MSO formulas.

The recursive procedure trans which translates the regular expression denoting the walking language of any given tree-walking automaton into an MSO formula is given as follows (we use the symbol $\perp$ for *false*):

(5.3)
$$\begin{aligned}
\mathsf{trans}_{\emptyset}(x,y) &\equiv \perp \\
\mathsf{trans}_{\downarrow_i}(x,y) &\equiv \mathsf{edg}_i(x,y) \\
\mathsf{trans}_{\uparrow_i}(x,y) &\equiv \mathsf{edg}_i(y,x) \\
\mathsf{trans}_{\varphi(x)}(x,y) &\equiv \varphi(x) \wedge x = y \\
\mathsf{trans}_{W_1 \cup W_2}(x,y) &\equiv \mathsf{trans}_{W_1}(x,y) \vee \mathsf{trans}_{W_2}(x,y) \\
\mathsf{trans}_{W_1 \cdot W_2}(x,y) &\equiv (\exists z)[\mathsf{trans}_{W_1}(x,z) \wedge \mathsf{trans}_{W_2}(z,y)] \\
\mathsf{trans}_{W^*}(x,y) &\equiv \mathsf{trans}^*_W(x,y) \\
\mathsf{trans}^*_W(x,y) &\equiv (\forall X)(\forall v,w)[(v \in X \wedge \mathsf{trans}_W(v,w) \rightarrow w \in X) \wedge \\
&\qquad\qquad x \in X \rightarrow y \in X]
\end{aligned}$$

The resulting formula uses only the MSO definable tests of the original automaton, the closed sets constructed via (5.5) for the Kleene-$*$-case, and the edg_n relations defined in (5.4). No recursion is involved any more!

The edge relation simply ensures that there exists a well-formed local tree to support the needed daughter relation, i.e., there are enough left sisters.

(5.4)
$$\begin{aligned}
\mathsf{edg}_n(x,y) \overset{def}{\Longleftrightarrow} & (\exists x_1,\ldots,x_{n-1})[x \triangleleft x_1 \wedge \cdots \wedge x \triangleleft x_{n-1} \wedge x \triangleleft y \\
& \wedge x_1 \prec x_2 \wedge \cdots \wedge x_{n-1} \prec y \wedge (\forall w)[x \triangleleft w \\
& \wedge w \not\approx x_1 \wedge \cdots \wedge w \not\approx x_{n-1} \wedge w \not\approx y \rightarrow y \prec w]]
\end{aligned}$$

For the case of the recursion inherent in reflexive dominance another standard solution exists in MSO logic on finite trees. It is a well-known fact (e.g. Courcelle 1990) that the reflexive transitive closure R^* of a binary relation R on nodes is (weakly) MSO definable, if R itself is. This is done via a second-order property which holds of the sets of nodes which are closed under R:

$$(5.5) \qquad R\text{-closed}(X) \stackrel{def}{\Longleftrightarrow} (\forall x,y)[x \in X \wedge R(x,y) \rightarrow y \in X]$$

Using the closed sets, we can define the reflexive transitive closure of a relation analogously to the last case in (5.3).

5.6 Definable MSO transductions

The definition of MSO definable transductions plays no role in this second part of the book and can safely be skipped on first reading. Nevertheless, since it concerns MSO definability, we state the necessary facts here.

The following paragraphs go directly back to Courcelle (1997). For convenience, we repeat some of the previous definitions here in a slightly more general form. Recall that representation of objects with relational structures makes them available for the use of logical description languages. Let R be a finite set of relation symbols with the corresponding arity for each $r \in R$ given by $\rho(r)$. A relational structure $\mathcal{R} = \langle D_{\mathcal{R}}, (r_{\mathcal{R}})_{r \in \mathcal{R}} \rangle$ consists of the domain $D_{\mathcal{R}}$ and the $\rho(r)$-ary relations $r_{\mathcal{R}} \subseteq D_{\mathcal{R}}^{\rho(r)}$.

Example 5.13. Let A be an alphabet. A word $w \in A^*$ can be considered as a relational structure $||w|| = \langle D_{\mathcal{R}_{w,A}}, (r_{\mathcal{R}_{w,A}})_{r \in \mathcal{R}_{w,A}} \rangle$ in the following way.

$\mathcal{R}_{w,A}$ is defined to be $\{s, P_{a_1}, \ldots, P_{a_n}\}$ for $A = \{a_1, \ldots, a_n\}$ where s is binary (successor) and the P_{a_i}, $1 \leq i \leq n$, are unary (labels).

$$\begin{array}{rcl} D_{\mathcal{R}_{w,A}} & = & \begin{cases} \emptyset & \text{if } w = \varepsilon \\ \{1,2,\ldots,k\} & \text{if } w \text{ is not empty and } |w| = k \end{cases} \\ s & = & \{(1,2),(2,3),\ldots,(k-1,k)\} \\ P_{a_i} & = & \{j \in D_{\mathcal{R}_{w,A}} \mid \text{if } a_i \text{ is the } j\text{th letter of } w\} \end{array}$$

Similarly, we can code trees as relational structures by using a tree domain as the domain $D_{\mathcal{R}_{w,A}}$ of the structure and defining s as the corresponding tree order, i.e, the corresponding successor functions.

Then one can use logic directly to define tree transductions. The classical technique of interpreting a relational structure within another one forms the basis for MSO transductions. Intuitively, the output tree is interpreted on the input tree. E.g., suppose that we want to transduce the input tree t_1 into the output tree t_2. The nodes of the output tree t_2 will be a subset of the nodes from t_1 specified with a unary MSO relation ranging over the nodes of t_1. The daughter relation will be specified with a binary MSO relation with free variables x and y ranging over the nodes from t_1. We will use this concept in the second part of this book to transform lifted trees into the intended ones.

Definition 5.14 (MSO transduction). Let R and Q be two finite sets of ranked relation symbols. A (non-copying) MSO transduction of a relational structure $\mathcal{R}$ (with set of relation symbols R) into another one $\mathcal{Q}$ (with set of relation symbols Q) is defined to be a tuple $(\varphi, \psi, (\theta_q)_{q \in Q})$ consisting of an MSO formula φ defining the domain of the transduction in $\mathcal{R}$, an MSO formula ψ defining the resulting domain of $\mathcal{Q}$, and a family of MSO formulas θ_q defining the new relations Q using only definable formulas from the "old" structure $\mathcal{R}$, i.e., for α a variable assignment,

$$D_{\mathcal{Q}} = \{d \in D_{\mathcal{R}} \mid (\mathcal{R}, d) \models \psi[\alpha]\}$$

and for each $q \in Q$

$$q_{\mathcal{Q}} = \{(d_1, \ldots, d_n) \in D^n_{\mathcal{Q}} \mid (\mathcal{R}, d_1, \ldots, d_n) \models \theta_q[\alpha]\} \text{ where } n = \rho(q)$$

Note that the transduction is only defined if φ holds. Furthermore it is important to note that the transductions we have used to illustrate the transitions of the various tree transducers cannot be defined with this kind of MSO transduction. This is due to the fact that we always require the domain to be a subset of the original domain whereas the examples given previously all require a copying MSO transduction. The transductions we will implement in the third part of this book will be non-copying, though.

Looking ahead, our description of non-context-free phenomena with two devices with only regular power is an instance of the theorem that the image of an MSO definable class of structures under a definable transduction is not MSO definable in general (Courcelle 1997).

Theorem 5.15 (Courcelle). *The image of an MSO definable class of structures is not MSO definable in general.*

What is of further interest to us is that there is a relation between the MSO definable transductions and the macro tree transducers introduced in Section 4.4.2 on page 56.

In Engelfriet and Maneth (1999) it is proven that a special class of MTTs is equivalent to the MSO definable tree translations. The restrictions on MTTs necessary for the proof are that they are *finite-copying* and that they have a *regular look-ahead*. A full, technical presentation of these notions is beyond the scope of this monograph. The interested reader is referred to the original literature. Intuitively, regular look-ahead means that every rule of an MTT is associated with an FSTA which is called upon to verify the applicability of the rule. The class of tree transductions realized by MTTs with and without a regular look-ahead are equivalent (Engelfriet and Vogler 1985). The restriction to be finite-copying intuitively consists of the fact that every subtree can only be processed a bounded number of times. This is true for copying via the input tree as well as the for copying via the parameters which makes the technical presentation quite involved. Alternatively, one can also show that the MTTs are only of *linear size increase* since those have been shown to be MSO definable as well (Engelfriet and Maneth 2001). Since we can always construct both the MTTs and the MSO transductions separately, we ignore these points and silently assume that we can construct an MSO transduction for every MTT.

5.7 Terminology

To sum up the presentation of the concepts concerning MSO-based model-theoretic syntax, I will briefly recapitulate the parlance introduced in the preceding sections to provide an overview of the terminology which links MSO logic directly with the underlying finite-state automata and therefore forms the basis of the following chapter on applications of the compilation technique.

- A constraint is *satisfiable* iff it results in an automaton recognizing a non-empty language, i.e., if the resulting minimized automaton has at least one final state which is reachable by some number of transitions from the initial state.

- A constraint is *valid* iff it results in the trivial non-empty automaton, i.e., if the resulting minimized automaton has only one state which is initial and final.

- The following tests are decidable: $w \in \mathcal{L}$, $\mathcal{L} = \emptyset$, $\mathcal{L} = \Sigma^*$, $\mathcal{L}_1 \subset \mathcal{L}_2$, $\mathcal{L}_1 = \mathcal{L}_2$

- A (maximally) binary branching *tree* is a subset T of the domain of N_2. A *labeled tree* is a tuple $\langle T, F_1, \ldots, F_k \rangle$ where T stands for the nodes marking the tree and the F_i denote the k variables/features labeling the tree.

- A *grammar* in this setting is a definition of a $k+1$-ary relation on N_2 designating all and only the well-formed labeled trees.

- The *recognition problem* is just the emptiness problem for the conjunction of the grammar formula/automaton with a formula/automaton characterizing the input. This point will be elaborated in Section 6.1 on page 85.

- Simplifying somewhat, the *parsing problem* can bee seen as the conjunction of the grammar formula/automaton with a formula/automaton characterizing the input. Naturally, for the extraction of a parse tree from that forest, one has to compute the actual intersection of the two tree sets. We will show in the next chapter how to do this efficiently.

Chapter 6

Applications

In this chapter we take a look at how we can use the techniques developed in the preceding sections for natural language processing. This chapter focuses on exploring the "real world use" of the MSO logic to tree automaton compilation. Therefore it can easily be skipped by the reader more interested in the formal, two-step approach following in the third part of this book.

There are two perspectives one can take on the equivalence of MSO logic and tree automata. First, one can think of the decidability proof as suggesting a way of doing (MSO) theorem proving. This is the way things are done in computer science applications such as hardware and system verification. However, one can also think of things the other way around, and take MSO logic as a specification language for automata. So we can make use of the logic-automaton correspondence either as a way of proving theorems using automata or as a way of manufacturing automata to MSO specifications.

An appealing – but naive – idea for using the translation from formulas into automata is to use the resulting efficient finite-state automata directly for parsing. This presupposes that the automaton can be compiled at all. Unfortunately, so far it has not been possible, using existing tools and machines with large memory to compile an entire P&P grammar. Nevertheless, we will show how to use tree automata for parsing before we proceed with a more modest application, namely to compile and use only modules of the theory. Those two sections are primarily concerned with the efficiency of the compilation. A further application addresses the problem of the limited expressibility of $\mathcal{L}^2_{K,P}$ – in particular the fact that free-indexation which is often employed in GB accounts of long-distance dependencies is undecidable – from a practical viewpoint, i.e., we try to approximate a full theory by guessing the necessary number of indeces. Finally, we briefly mention other possibilities for using the techniques.

6.1 Parsing with tree automata

As discussed in Cornell (2000), one can use tree automata directly for parsing. Let us recapitulate his discussion here.

One might think that we can directly use tree automata for parsing of context-free languages with all the benefits of the more standard FSA approaches to parsing. However, the main feature of tree automata is that they recognize (parse) trees. But those are what we want to construct in parsing! While this approach might seem circular, we will show in the following paragraphs a solution for parsing with tree automata which strongly resembles the known approaches to context-free grammars. The idea is essentially that a tree automaton may recognize *all* trees over a certain signature which allows the necessary underspecification to allow a meaningful parsing process via intersection of automata in the spirit of Lang (1992).

What we need to parse with MSO grammars – apart from the FSTA recognizing the well-formed trees according to a given MSO specification – is a tree automaton recognizing a particular input string.[18] Therefore we construct an automaton where the leaves are formed by the words we want to recognize. At this point we do not care which structure the tree has, all we need is the appearance of the string at the leaves.

More formally, given a many sorted or ranked alphabet Σ and a string $w \in \Sigma_0^*$, there exists a subset T_Σ^w of T_Σ such that w is the yield of all $t \in T_\Sigma^w$, there is no $t \in T_\Sigma - T_\Sigma^w$ which yields w and there is a tree automaton $\mathfrak{Y}^w$ recognizing T_Σ^w.

We construct the tree automaton $\mathfrak{Y}^w = \langle Q^w, \Sigma, \delta^w, q_0, F^w \rangle$ as follows. Let $w = w_1 \dots w_n$ with $|w| = n$. Intuitively, we will have states corresponding to leave nodes indicating that we read a particular word from the input and states which correspond to interior nodes which care only about the branching factor and the right order of the appearing subtrees. The automaton will have complex states with a semantics borrowed from standard approaches to parsing of context-free grammars. In the simple case, we will indicate with state (i, j) that we read word w_i (which implies that $j = i + 1$) or, in the case of a nonterminal node that we found a subtree spanning $w_i \dots w_j$. For the empty word we have to add states (i, i) for all $0 \leq i \leq n$. That means, we need the following set of states Q^w:

$$Q^w = \{(i, j) \mid 0 \leq i \leq j \leq n\} \cup \{q_0\}.$$

The transitions are set up such that, for the elements $w_i \in \Sigma_0$, $\delta^w(q_0, w_i) =$

$(i-1,i)$. Note that w_i might equal w_j although $i \neq j$. Thus the automaton is nondeterministic. But since bottom-up tree automata are closed under determinization, we can ignore this issue here. The transitions are defined as follows: For all $\sigma \in \Sigma^n$, $n > 0$,

$$(q_1,\ldots,q_n,\sigma) = \begin{cases} (i,j) & \text{if } q_1 = (i,j_1), q_2 = (j_1,j_2),\ldots,q_n = (j_{n-1},j) \\ undef & \text{otherwise} \end{cases}$$

As can easily be seen, all the transitions do is to ensure the correct branching and the appropriate sequent of daughter states. Finally, we have to specify the final state(s). The run of the automaton was successful if we found a state spanning the entire string, i.e., $F^w = \{(0,n)\}$.

This layout gives us the following refined definition of the parsing problem using tree automata:

Algorithm 6.1 (parsing with tree automata). Let Σ be a many sorted or ranked alphabet. Given a tree automaton $\mathfrak{G}$ representing a grammar and therefore recognizing a subset of T_Σ and a string w over Σ_0^*, we construct the yields-automaton $\mathfrak{Y}^w$ as specified above and intersect it with $\mathfrak{G}$ to yield the parse-forest automaton $\mathfrak{P}^w$, i.e., $\mathfrak{G} \cap \mathfrak{Y}^w = \mathfrak{P}^w$. The resulting automaton $\mathfrak{P}^w$ recognizes all and only the well-formed trees yielding w, i.e., it compactly represents the parse forest for w.

Since we have to construct a new yields-automaton for every input, this approach is too inefficient to be used in "real" applications. Fortunately, we can interleave the construction of the yields automaton and the parsing process – the intersection construction.

The intersection construction uses pairs of states of the input automata as its own states. What we find in our case are states which look remarkably like the items used in standard chart parsing approaches, e.g., initial states have the form $(\sigma_{w_i},(i-1,i))$. If we just drop the slightly complicated notation, i.e., the extra set of braces, we get tuples of the form $\langle w_i, i-1, i\rangle$ which are exactly the items used in CYK-parsing. Then the construction of the parse forest automaton $\mathfrak{P}$ with the interleaved construction of the yields-automaton is strongly reminiscent of CYK parsing, see Table 6.1 on the next page.

The given algorithm is a generalization of the one given in Cornell (2000) to arbitrarily branching tree automata. Note that we still presuppose that the grammar automaton $\mathfrak{G}$ is deterministic. By using the leaves of the parse

Table 6.1: Interleaving the Intersection and Yield-Automaton Construction

```
% Initialize
P ← ∅
I ← ∅
δ^𝔓 ← ∅
n ← length(w)
for i = 1 to n do
    I ← I ∪ {⟨w_i, i−1, i⟩}
end for
% Process the agenda
while I ≠ ∅ do
    remove ⟨B, i, j⟩ from I
    P ← P ∪ {⟨B, i, j⟩}
    for all σ ∈ Σ_m, m > 0 do
        for all ⟨B^1, k, i_1⟩, ⟨B^2, i_1, i_2⟩, ..., ⟨B^{m−1}, i_{m−1}, i⟩ ∈ P do
            A ← δ^𝔊(B^1, ..., B^{m−1}, B, σ)
            if ⟨A, k, j⟩ ∉ P ∪ I then
                add ⟨A, k, j⟩ to I
            end if
            add (⟨B^1, k, i_1⟩, ..., ⟨B^{m−1}, i_{m−1}, i⟩, ⟨B, i, j⟩, σ) = ⟨A, k, j⟩ to δ^𝔓
        end for
    end for
end while
```

tree, i.e., the input string, to initialize our agenda I we get a bottom-up construction of the parse automaton $\mathfrak{P}$. Essentially, this follows from using the reachable-states construction. In the algorithm, the symbol '$\leftarrow$' is used for an assignment. So, in the algorithm, we take an element from the agenda, add it to the productions of the parse automaton $\mathfrak{P}$ and infer new items from the agenda through possible transitions already in the parse automaton $\mathfrak{P}$ and grammar automaton $\mathfrak{G}$.

The removal of useless states – a state is useless if no final state can be reached from it – usually practiced in FSNLP to keep the automata as small as possible, can serve as a top-down analogue to the top-down guidance used in Earley-based approaches to parsing. It remains an open problem to specify the corresponding algorithms.

We have shown in this section how one can directly use tree automata for parsing. Thus, given a tree automaton representing a grammar, however it was specified, we can use it together with the algorithm above to parse sentences. But it is still an open question whether a grammar automaton for a P&P theory can be compiled at all. In the next section, we turn to a more modest proposal, namely how we can use parts of the grammar independently.

6.2 Compiling grammatical principles to FSTAs

In this section, we consider our most modest proposal, namely to do automaton construction and theory verification on subparts of the grammar. The question of which grammatical properties can be compiled in a reasonable time is largely empirical. The software tool MONA for the compilation of MSO formulas into both FSAs and tree automata (Klarlund and Møller 1998 has been used to investigate this question.

As an example of the application of this tool, we compiled an automaton from the X-Bar Theory presented in Rogers's monograph. Note that this is a non-trivial part of the overall P&P-theory formalized there (cf. Rogers 1998).

In many variants of P&P-theories this module of the grammar is essentially a set of simple phrase structure rules defining possible d-structures, over which transformations will later operate. Rogers's formalization is of a monostratal theory, however, in which well-formedness conditions on chains take the place of movement transformations. As a result, the X-Bar theory Rogers presents is far from trivial, since it must describe the kinds of structures that arise after transformations have applied. As a result it amounts to some five pages of MSO formulas which serve as input to MONA, see Appendix B.1 on page 194.

Additional complications arise in the MSO specification of X-Bar theory because, in the underlying grammatical theory, there are three layers of structure: nodes of the tree are "segments" which are grouped into "categories" (sets of nodes which have been "split" by adjunctions here refering to a purely structural notion having little or nothing to do with morphosyntactic categories like noun, verb, preposition, etc.). Then categories are assigned "bar-level" features. So bar-levels, being features, are sets of categories, which in turn are sets of segments. However, it is easy to avoid this third-order notion by associating features with the segments in such a way as to assure that every segment of a category has features identical to those which, in the grammatical theory, are to be assigned to the category. Furthermore we have to keep track of which nodes are *trace* positions in their chains, which nodes by contrast are still in their *base* positions, and which phrases are *adjuncts*, i.e., attached to a segment of a non-trivial category.

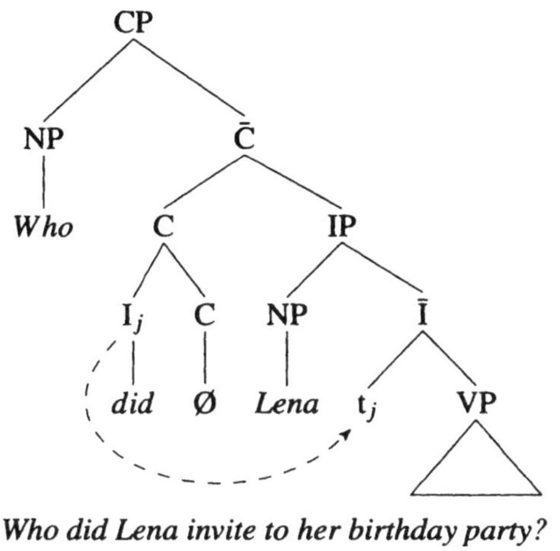

Figure 6.1: An example for the need for categories

Figure 6.1, which is a slightly modified figure from Rogers's book, depicts a motivation of the need for these complex categories. We want that I_j c-commands its trace t_j. But under the standard node-based definition this is simply not true. The solution taken by Rogers (following the GB tradition and in particular Rizzi) is to say that I_j is not dominated by the category labeled with C, i.e., both of the nodes labeled with C and therefore the next possible category dominating both I_j and t_j is $\bar{C}$ which gives us the desired c-command relation.

In general an adjunction structure resulting in the formation of categories has the following schematic form, see Figure 6.2 on the following page (again taken from Rogers). The XPs form a category resulting from adjoining two YPs of which the lower one itself has an adjoint ZP. We use the feature *Adj* to pick out the adjoint nodes, i.e., in this case the maximal YP nodes and the ZP node. The mother node of the entire tree labeled XP might or might not be labeled with *Adj* depending on whether it is used as an adjunct or not.

The main content of X-Bar theory is a set of conditions on the distribution of the bar-level features, and a principle which states that every category has a "head", another category immediately below it with which it shares essential features like grammatical category (noun, verb, etc.). A node is allowed to be labeled with *Bar0* if it has exactly one lexical child category whose features it inherits. It is labeled *Bar1* if its category immediately dominates a node (its head) which is labeled *Bar0* and all its other (non-head) children are labeled

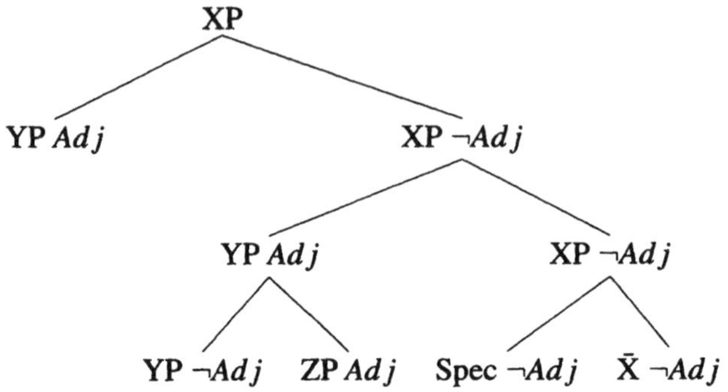

Figure 6.2: Adjunction structures

Bar2. Finally, a node is labeled *Bar2* if it is a trace (i.e., is assigned to the set *Trace*) or its category immediately dominates some corresponding category belonging to *Bar1* and all its non-head children are in *Bar2*. The X-Bar module encodes these three definitions and principles limiting the distribution of adjuncts (i.e., of the Adj feature) such that no node is marked as adjoined unless it is the immediate child of a non-minimal node of a non-trivial category and that we cannot adjoin to any arbitrary node, e.g., not to traces.

We recapitulate Rogers's definition very closely to be able to show where the problems occur. Please recall that his formulas are formalizing the notions from *Relativized Minimality* by Rizzi (1990). Therefore we do not discuss the pros and cons of the linguistic analyses, but concentrate on the presentation of the technical realization. Recall again that Rogers takes the representational approach, i.e., move-α is encoded in well-formedness conditions of chains. In parts the presentation is reminiscent of the introductory example given in Section 3.2.3 on page 39.

The very first definition is somewhat artificial, it just ensures that certain features have to be equal for any two given nodes. This is achieved by simply listing the features in a conjunction.

$$\mathsf{F.Eq}(x,y) \stackrel{def}{\Longleftrightarrow} (x \in N \Leftrightarrow y \in N) \wedge (x \in V \Leftrightarrow y \in V) \wedge \ldots$$

A component is a connected path through a tree such that all its nodes are labeled identically with respect to the features defined by F.Eq and by ensuring that the feature marking adjoint nodes are distributed properly. This is defined such that for any two nodes in the component which are directly related by immediate dominance, there exists another unique daughter which is an adjunct. The definition for Path(X) was given in (5.2) on page 63.

$$\begin{aligned}\mathsf{Comp}(X) \overset{def}{\Longleftrightarrow} & \ \mathsf{Path}(X)\\ & \wedge (\forall x,y)[(x \in X \wedge y \in X) \Rightarrow \mathsf{F.eq}(x,y)]\\ & \wedge (\forall x,x')(\exists y)(\forall z)[(x \in X \wedge x' \in X \wedge x \triangleleft x') \Rightarrow\\ & \qquad (x' \notin Adj \wedge x \triangleleft y \wedge y \not\approx x' \wedge y \in Adj \wedge\\ & \qquad\quad (x \triangleleft z \Rightarrow (z \approx x' \vee z \approx y)))]\end{aligned}$$

A category is just a maximal component.

$$\mathsf{Cat}(X) \overset{def}{\Longleftrightarrow} \mathsf{Comp}(X) \wedge (\forall Y)[(X \subseteq Y \wedge Y \not\subseteq X) \Rightarrow \neg\mathsf{Comp}(Y)]$$

Naturally we have to make sure that all adjuncts are indeed in the right configuration, i.e., there exists a category which contains a node dominating it and a further node which is a sister. Each node labeled with Adj is the child of a node from a non-trivial category.

$$(\forall x)[x \in Adj \Rightarrow (\exists y,z,Y)[x \not\approx z \wedge y \triangleleft x \wedge y \triangleleft z \wedge \mathsf{Cat}(Y) \wedge y \in Y \wedge z \in Y]]$$

We overload the definition of Cat in the sense that we also have a binary predicates Cat(X,x) if x is a member of the category X and Cat(x,y) if two nodes belong to the same category.

$$\begin{aligned}\mathsf{Cat}(X,x) &\overset{def}{\Longleftrightarrow} \mathsf{Cat}(X) \wedge x \in X\\ \mathsf{Cat}(x,y) &\overset{def}{\Longleftrightarrow} (\exists X)[\mathsf{Cat}(X,x) \wedge \mathsf{Cat}(X,y)]\end{aligned}$$

Now we are in the position to recast the primitives of the MSO language (dominance, precedence, etc.) in terms of categories as basic objects. A node from a category dominates another node in case all nodes of the category properly dominate it. It follows immediately that a category does not dominate nodes which are adjoined to it.

$$\mathsf{D}(x,y) \overset{def}{\Longleftrightarrow} (\forall x')[\mathsf{Cat}(x,x') \Rightarrow x' \triangleleft^{+} y]$$

For the definition of precedence we define two auxiliary predicates encoding the notions of exclusion and inclusion. A node x stands in the exclusion relation to another node y if no node of x's category stands in the (reflexive) dominance relation to y.

$$\mathsf{Excl}(x,y) \overset{def}{\Longleftrightarrow} (\forall x')[\mathsf{Cat}(x,x') \Rightarrow \neg(x' \triangleleft^{*} y)]$$

A node x includes another one y in case x does not exclude y.

$$\mathsf{Incl}(x,y) \overset{def}{\Longleftrightarrow} \neg\mathsf{Excl}(x,y)$$

A node x now precedes another one y if both of their categories exclude each other and if x precedes y in the old sense.

$$\mathsf{Prec}(x,y) \overset{def}{\Longleftrightarrow} \mathsf{Excl}(x,y) \wedge \mathsf{Excl}(y,x) \wedge x \prec y$$

Two nodes stand in the immediate dominance relation if they stand in the dominance relation and no category falls properly between them. Here adjunction plays a crucial role since a category must neither dominate the nodes adjoined to it nor the ones adjoined to its children. For a full discussion of this issue, see Rogers (1998)

$$\begin{aligned}\mathsf{ID}(x,y) \overset{def}{\Longleftrightarrow} \mathsf{D}(x,y) \wedge \neg(\exists z)[(&\mathsf{Excl}(z,x) \wedge \mathsf{D}(z,y)) \\ &\vee (z \in Adj \wedge \mathsf{Excl}(z,x) \wedge \mathsf{Incl}(z,y))]\end{aligned}$$

Now we can state the definition of c-command between categories. It is not much different from the definition given in (3.3) on page 37 only that we do not demand asymmetry and directedness.

$$\mathsf{C\text{-}Com}(x,y) \overset{def}{\Longleftrightarrow} \neg\mathsf{D}(x,y) \wedge \neg\mathsf{D}(y,x) \wedge (\forall z)[\mathsf{D}(z,x) \Rightarrow \mathsf{D}(z,y)]$$

And finally the definition for asymmetric directed c-command is identical to the one given in (3.3). It shows that with this admittedly complicated machinery, we can hide the complexities of the definitions completely.

$$\mathsf{AC\text{-}Com}(x,y) \overset{def}{\Longleftrightarrow} \mathsf{C\text{-}Com}(x,y) \wedge \neg\mathsf{C\text{-}Com}(y,x) \wedge \mathsf{Prec}(x,y)$$

Before we can turn to the actual definition of the X-Bar principles, we need some more auxiliary definitions to facilitate the presentation. Not all of them are defined for categories. The first predicate is self-explanatory.

$$\mathsf{Sibling}(x,y) \overset{def}{\Longleftrightarrow} x \not\approx y \wedge (\exists z)[z \triangleleft x \wedge z \triangleleft y]$$

As usual, we want only one head in any given local tree. It is marked with the feature Hd.

$$x \in Hd \Rightarrow (\forall y)[\mathsf{Sibling}(x,y) \Rightarrow y \notin Hd]$$

A category projects its features to the category which it immediately dominates and which is its head.

$$\mathsf{Proj}(x,y) \stackrel{def}{\Longleftrightarrow} \mathsf{ID}(x,y) \wedge y \in Hd$$

This implies the sharing of the relevant features, the head-features, here encoded in F.EqProj.

$$\mathsf{Proj}(x,y) \Rightarrow \mathsf{F.EqProj}(x,y)$$

Projection is a central notion in the X-Bar theory since it relates a category with its ancestors.

Now we see how it is used in the definition of the X-Bar principles. First of all, we require that every node has either a bar level feature or is lexical.

$$(\forall x)[x \in Bar0 \vee x \in Bar1 \vee x \in Bar2 \vee \mathsf{Lexicon}(x)]$$

A node has bar level 2 if it is either a trace or it immediately dominates a category which has bar level 1 and all its non-head children are maximal, i.e., XPs.

$$\begin{aligned}(\forall x)\big[&x \in Bar2 \Rightarrow \\ &x \in Trace \wedge (\forall y)[\neg \mathsf{D}(x,y)] \vee \\ &(\exists y)[y \in Bar1 \wedge \mathsf{Proj}(x,y)] \wedge (\forall y)[(\mathsf{ID}(x,y) \wedge y \notin Hd) \Rightarrow y \in Bar2]\big]\end{aligned}$$

A node has bar level 1 if it is the projection of a lexical head and all non-head children are maximal.

$$\begin{aligned}(\forall x)\big[&x \in Bar1 \Rightarrow \\ &(\exists y)[y \in Bar0 \wedge \mathsf{Proj}(x,y)] \wedge (\forall y)[(\mathsf{ID}(x,y) \wedge y \notin \mathsf{Hd}) \Rightarrow y \in Bar2]\big]\end{aligned}$$

And finally, a node has bar level 0 if it has exactly one child which it projects and which is lexical and in base position if itself is in base position.

$$\begin{aligned}(\forall x)\big[&x \in Bar0 \Rightarrow \\ &(\exists! y)[\mathsf{ID}(x,y)] \wedge (\forall y)[\mathsf{ID}(x,y) \Rightarrow (\mathsf{Lexicon}(y) \wedge \mathsf{Proj}(x,y) \wedge \\ &\qquad (x \in Base \Leftrightarrow y \in Base))]\big]\end{aligned}$$

Figure 6.3: A problem for Rogers's X-bar theory

Rogers then goes on from there to define all the notions such as, e.g., *complementizer* or *specifier* which are used in linguistic theorizing. We stop here since we have all ingredients to make our point.

One sees immediately that such an X-Bar theory becomes quite complicated indeed, and its correctness correspondingly hard to verify by hand, although the presentation is natural enough and stays close to the linguistic statements. In fact, we did discover a minor bug in Rogers's formalization. We attempted to prove the assertion that Rogers's X-Bar theory implies the disjointness of the three bar-levels, i.e., that no node can belong to more than one bar-level. We created a predicate XBar which encoded all the definitions given above and then we coded the implication as an MSO formula, and attempted to prove it in MONA.

$$\mathsf{XBar}(T) \Rightarrow \mathsf{Disjoint}(Bar0, Bar1)$$

The attempt failed, with MONA reporting a counterexample.[19] In particular, Rogers's X-Bar theory does not imply that the *Bar0*-feature is disjoint from the *Bar1* and *Bar2* features.

The problem arises because of the fact that the distribution of features is such that they can appear anywhere they are not explicitly forbidden. In our case this means that the constraints allow for example a unary branching subtree with two nodes; a node which is labeled with both *Bar0* and *Bar1* and whose (unique) daughter is at the same time lexical and *Bar0*. In such a tree all constraints are satisfied. The mother node fulfills the *Bar1* constraint since it has a *Bar0* daughter and no other children and the *Bar0* constraint since it has a unique daughter which is lexical, see Figure 6.3. This second node is allowed since Rogers does not place a constraint on the sets denoting lexical elements. Positively expressed, this means that they are allowed to appear on internal nodes of a parse tree. To avoid this we have to add conditions forcing the lexical variables to only appear on the frontier of our parse tree.

$$(\neg\exists x,y)[\mathsf{Lexicon}(x) \wedge \mathsf{ID}(x,y)]$$

Furthermore, both to avoid errors of this type and to improve efficiency, we added a constraint which makes all our features appear only on nodes in the parse tree, i.e., we ensured that all our features are subsets of the set encoding our parse tree. The variable we use to denote the parse tree is initialized as a connected, rooted set for convenience. That constraint is not necessary, but makes the results much more readable.

The resulting corrected XBar-predicate has 11 free variables and its description consists of the aforementioned five pages of MONA formulas. We only assumed absolutely necessary features and a minimum of lexical entries (in fact only two lexical entries and 8 features). Nevertheless it represents a full module of a large scale formalization of a P&P theory, the predicate could be compiled in less than 5 min, see Table 6.2 on page 99, and it could be used in further verification tasks. This shows that – while we still do not know whether it is feasible to compile a grammar automaton – we can indeed handle interesting linguistic properties with these techniques. And, as a further advantage, we can verify even immensely complicated theories automatically and generate counter-examples which help in debugging.

6.3 Approximating P&P grammars

As stated, the set of well-formed trees defined by a P&P grammar which uses free indexation is not in general recognizable. Therefore we cannot hope in principle to construct a grammar formula which defines exactly the well-formed parse trees strongly generated by a P&P grammar using just the MSO logic–tree automaton correspondence. One question which arises immediately in a more practical and less theoretical setting is how well we can approximate a context-sensitive language with a context free grammar. There are two features of P&P grammars which help us here. First, P&P grammars are *principle-based*, so they are readily formalized in logic. The logic of WS2S is insufficient, but it should be easy to embed it in a more powerful logic which is sufficient. Then the techniques of general model theory will become available to address the question of how good an approximation we can achieve. Secondly, P&P grammars are *modular*, so it may be possible to isolate those parts of the grammar which exceed the expressive capacity of WS2S. In that case we can observe quite directly the compromises that would have to be made to stay within an MSO logic for natural language. This is indeed the case here: the power of a P&P grammar seems to come rather directly from the assumption of an unbounded supply of referential indices, which can be used to keep track of arbitrarily many simultaneously occurring long-distance dependencies. Tree automata, on the other hand, can only keep track of a bounded number of distinct objects via their (finite) set of states. Hence, no formalization of a grammar in MSO logic is possible without the assumption of a bounded number of indices.

So the problem of approximating a full P&P grammar becomes the problem of estimating in advance how many indices will be enough. Clearly, any given sentence will require a bounded number of indices, but we cannot realistically expect to recompile our entire grammar automaton for each input sentence.[20] We can, however, precompile a number of different versions of a grammar offline, each with an index theory of a different size, and then select which grammar automaton to use given the input sentence. So it makes sense to consider how one could formalize the parts of the grammar that rely on indices in such a way that they can be parameterized with the number of indices and compiled in a variety of sizes.

Furthermore there are a number of ways in which one can "engineer" a theory so that it uses a minimal number of indices. For example, any one index can be used to keep track of any number of distinct chains, as long as those chains do not overlap. Also, there is no need to make each notionally distinct index correspond to a single feature: if we have n "index variables" I_i then we can use them as bits of a complex index, meaning that we have in fact 2^n possible distinct indices. We can extend this idea by making use of other features besides special purpose index (or index-bit) features: using bar-level features for example, we can distinguish between the twelfth *Bar2* chain and the twelfth *Bar0* chain. Pursuing this strategy we end up with the approach Rogers actually employs. He uses no special purpose index variables but rather only combinations of those features which are independently required in the grammar. This reduces the number of possible alphabet symbols that an automaton must deal with.

Given such a bounded set of indices which we can use on a particular parse, we proceed to formalize the necessary conditions in our MSO tree logic. As noted above, what we use for our "indices" is formally relatively unimportant. What matters is what it means for two nodes to be co-indexed, see below. That is the definition which gives the theory its "memory resources". Note that in MSO logic free variables must be represented in both the head of the formula and the resulting automaton to preserve their satisfying assignments. In case one is not interested in the information provided by a particular variable, it can be bound existentially at the top level of the formula. Where readability is more of an issue, one can leave these "global" variables out under the assumption that they are implicit. However, since they cannot be ignored in the alphabet of the automata, we try to be more exact. Therefore, $\vec{I_n}$ stands for the n indices we have to create depending on the input, and the "definitions" we now present are really definition schemata.

$$\mathsf{Co\_Idx}(x,y,\vec{I_n}) \stackrel{def}{\Longleftrightarrow} (x \in I_1 \Leftrightarrow y \in I_1) \wedge \ldots \wedge (x \in I_n \Leftrightarrow y \in I_n)$$

After the instantiation of the schematic representation, we can compile an automaton for the corresponding memory limited grammar formula. All the predicates which depend on any predicate scheme at any point will themselves have to be schematized, of course, and realized as families of definitions which vary in the number of their arguments. As an example of these we present a formula scheme encoding a simple version of a "trace binding condition" (a simplified version of the empty category principle which uses c-command instead of local government), which simply requires that all traces have a c-commanding antecedent with which they are co-indexed. TBind will have $n+2$ arguments; n depending on the number of indices currently allowed and the chosen coding. The needed c-command definition simply says that all nodes z which properly dominate x also have to dominate y and that x must not reflexively dominate y, recall the discussion on page 37.

$$\begin{aligned}
\mathsf{C\text{-}Com}(x,y) &\stackrel{def}{\Longleftrightarrow} (\forall z)[z \triangleleft^+ x \Rightarrow z \triangleleft^+ y] \wedge \neg(x \triangleleft^* y) \\
\mathsf{TBind}(P, Trace, \vec{I_n}) &\stackrel{def}{\Longleftrightarrow} \text{\% for all traces in the parse tree} \\
&\quad (\forall x \in P)[x \in Trace \Rightarrow \\
&\quad \text{\% there exists a proper antecedent.} \\
&\quad (\exists y \in P)[\mathsf{C\text{-}Com}(y,x) \wedge \mathsf{Co_Idx}(x,y,\vec{I_n})]]
\end{aligned}$$

In this definition scheme we use a set called *Trace* to identify traces. Naturally this presupposes that we formulate more appropriate constraints on the distribution of this label in the resulting parse tree in our grammar.

In conclusion, we note that the logic-automaton connection may be fruitful for doing principle-based parsing, even in spite of the principled limitation to weakly context-free languages. In particular, it seems unlikely that, in any given corpus of input sentences, there are any which require large numbers of overlapping chains: the same drain on memory which this causes for tree automata seems to affect human language users as well (Stabler 1994). The fact that we can adjust to such memory limitations without substantially affecting the underlying grammar – all we require is a special definition of what it means to be co-indexed – is especially welcome. However, for doing theory verification these limitations remain serious: given n indices, the claim that there are only n indices is a theorem, but not a theorem of the underlying grammar. On the other hand, if there is a sentence in the language which actually does have $n+1$ overlapping chains it will be rejected by a limited grammar. So we have neither soundness nor completeness for doing theorem proving.

6.4 Some experimental results

Even supposing, as seems reasonable, that real world parsers can function with a limited supply of indices, we still have to face the extreme explosive potential of the formula-to-automaton compilation procedure. It is still an open question which formulas can be compiled on present day computers. We used MONA (Klarlund and Møller 1998) to provide some answers to the usability of these ideas in practice.

The main innovation in MONA, which seems indeed to be a real technical breakthrough, is the use of binary decision diagrams (BDDs) to compress the transition tables of the output automata. (An introduction to BDDs can for example be found in Bryant (1992).) Since an alphabet of k features contains 2^k symbols, alphabet size, and hence transition table size, is a problem which, while only elementarily complex, can actually dominate in practice the non-elementary complexity of the actual compilation procedure. The use of this technique significantly improves performance over our own prototype so that we can advance considerably with compilations than what was reported in Morawietz and Cornell (1997c). Now we can actually implement significant modules of a large scale P&P theory and verify them (recall the discussion of X-Bar theory in Sect. 6.2). But we also encountered limits on the number of indices in the compilation of various TBind predicates. In this section we summarize some of our results so far. Timings where done on a SUN Sparc 20 with 225 MB of RAM using a beta release of version 1.2 of MONA. Our results are displayed in Table 6.2.

Table 6.2: Statistics for Various Predicates

Predicate/N	Total Time	$\|A\|$	$\|\alpha\|$	$\|BDD\|$
Connected	00:00:00.090	4	25	7
Path	00:00:00.130	4	21	9
C-Com	00:00:00.170	5	40	19
TBind/2	00:00:00.230	12	832	52
TBind/4	00:00:01.610	80	76288	422
TBind/8	00:55:15.000	2304	–	13881
TBind/16	core dump after approx. 10 min			
TBind'/4	00:00:07.480	87	145963	759
TBind'/6	00:04:58.830	457	–	4901
TBind'/7	core dump after approx. 30 min			
XBar	00:04:51.080	66	18133	982

The first column of the table contains the predicate identifier and the number of indices (not the index bits). The second column contains the time needed to compile the automaton without the printing of the actual output automaton. The third column contains the number of states in the output automaton, the fourth column the number of transitions. The number of transitions has been compacted in the sense that it uses a don't care symbol, i.e., if transitions on q_1 and q_2 and both $\langle x_1, \ldots, x_{i-1}, x_i, x_{i+1}, \ldots, x_n \rangle$ and $\langle x_1, \ldots, x_{i-1}, \neg x_i, x_{i+1}, \ldots, x_n \rangle$ lead to the same state q, we have only a single transition on $\langle x_1, \ldots, x_{i-1}, \bot, x_{i+1}, \ldots, x_n \rangle$. Also note that for very large automata we cannot present the exact number of transitions any more since printing the result takes too much time and space and unfortunately MONA does not have an option to display (only) the number of transitions without printing the full automaton. The last column contains the size of the BDD used to represent the transition table. One readily observes the enormous gains this compression scheme confers by comparing this to the transition table size.

Consider the tricky "grammar engineering" question of what kind of coding to use for indices, as discussed above. In TBind, we used features to encode index bits and in TBind′ we straightforwardly used features to encode (disjoint) indices. The second approach turned out to consume considerable amounts of memory: we were only able to compile an automaton with six indices, though on a machine with 800 megabytes of RAM it is possible to compile TBind′ with at least seven indices (Nils Klarlund, p.c.). Using the index-bit encoding we could compile a version of TBind with eight indices (i.e., three index bit features) on our own machines; however, adding another bit again ran us out of memory resources.[21] The steepness of the relevant curves leads us to suspect that no present day machine will be able to compile TBind/16. The use of index bits cannot in principle reduce the memory load which long distance dependencies place on automata. This shows that MSO logic is exponentially more compact in coding the facts than tree automata.

An interesting question is whether a large machine can compile TBind′/9. More generally, the discreet encoding allows one to better approximate the capacity of available machines. Adding a bit increases the number of chains that can be represented too greatly, even though in general this encoding leads to more compact automata. The compactness gain is more than offset by the memory requirements that even one more chain places on a tree automaton's state space.

Another interesting point to observe is that the memory demands in these compilations mainly came from intermediate automata. Considering Table 6.2, one notes that the BDD size and number of states in the automata which are actually output are not overwhelmingly large. So while it requires rather large and powerful computers to manufacture automata from MSO formulas, the resulting automata can potentially be put to use on much smaller machines.

6.5 Further applications

In this section we will very briefly outline some further uses of the compilation technique presented in the preceding chapters. Since they are either speculative or deal with work which is only marginally related to the material presented in this monograph, the presentation will be sketchy at best and is only given to provide starting points for further reading.

6.5.1 MSO logic and CLP

The automaton for a grammar formula is presumably considerably larger than a parse-forest automaton, that is, the automaton for the grammar conjoined with an input description. Considering the problems we might have in extending the compilation of separate modules to an entire grammar automaton, it makes sense to search for ways to incrementally construct the parse-forest automaton for a particular input. For this, we propose the embedding of the MSO constraint language into a constraint logic programming (CLP) scheme. Intuitively, the constraint base is an automaton which represents the incremental accumulation of knowledge about the possible valuations of variables constructed by applying and solving clauses with their associated constraints. We can start with a description of the input and add further constraints incrementally rather then having to represent all constraints at once and then limiting them to an input. That is to say, we actually use the compiler *on line* as the constraint solver. Some obvious advantages include the ability to use our succinct and flexible constraint language with negation and MSO quantification. In fact, we gain even more power, since we can include inductive definitions of relations and have a way of guiding the compilation process under the control of a program.

Morawietz (1999) presented a CLP language built upon MSO logic following Höhfeld and Smolka (1988). Logic programming (LP) nicely reflects the separation of the actual logic of a program and the control of its execution (Lloyd 1984). Programs in the LP paradigm are sets of logical clauses. These programs are interpreted within Herbrand models, i.e., sets of ground atoms. One could be content with this declarative interpretation, but on the other hand, one wants to compute with them. The added operational interpretation used in most LP languages is based on SLD-resolution (Linear resolution with a Selection function for Definite clauses). Then the semantics is reformulated in procedural terms of least models and fixpoints such that the languages have provably equivalent denotational and operational semantics. Two problems with this approach – the generate and test paradigm to find the solutions and the use of uninterpreted structures – can be overcome by the addition of constraints to the standard logic programming scheme.

Intuitively, with the constraint logic programming scheme we developed a way to give definite clause specifications over MSO formulas. This extended language can be used to constrain the variables by incrementally adding suitable constraints to a constraint store. The store can be viewed as a tree automaton representing the possible valuations. In fact, the generation of the tree automaton we are interested in is controlled by the incremental construction. By doing this, we can focus on just those parts of the grammar which are relevant to the actual computation instead of having to consider – and precompile – all possibilities inherent in the grammar at once. A standard interpreter (left to right, depth first search) is sufficient for the execution of one of our programs. The answer of a search branch of such a program is a satisfiable MSO constraint represented by a tree automaton. Backtracking then allows the search for more answers. Furthermore, the embedding allows for applying a wealth of techniques developed in general for (constraint) logic programming and the corresponding interpreters to optimize the behaviour of the programs.

The CLP language was supposed to serve both the facilitation of the use of MSO formalizations in computational linguistics and the extension of the generative capacity of MSO-based grammar formalisms. The arguments on non-context-freeness of natural languages are our main motivation for the necessity of the extension. For a more detailed presentation of the necessary arguments see our discussion of verb raising phenomena in German, Dutch and Swiss German in Section 9.3 on page 124.

Unfortunately it turns out that we can write a program in the CLP language which has an SLD refutation iff a given Post correspondence system has a solution. Therefore we can state the next lemma.

Lemma 6.2. *Satisfiability in MSO logic extended by an CLP scheme is undecidable.*

Furthermore, we can achieve the same by only considering a smallest binary program (see Hanschke and Würtz (1993) for a definition) by the use of difference lists. Since smallest binary programs (on terms) are Turing equivalent (Devienne et al. 1994), it seems that our extension has the same power.

There are two directions one can take from here. Firstly, we can accept the extension as it is. In that case we have defined a general purpose programming language on trees. Compared with Prolog, the difference is that we do not interpret terms over a Herbrand universe, but sets of nodes in N_2. And secondly, we can search for (syntactic) characterizations of decidable subclasses of these inductive definitions. We pursued this last proposal in Section 5.5 and will continue to use it in the third part of this book.

6.5.2 MSO logic as an automaton specification language

In the tradition of the approaches to finite-state language processing mentioned in Section 4.1 one could also use the presented techniques simply for the specification of (tree) automata from a powerful constraint language. In FSNLP, the flexibility of finite-state devices is usually implemented in a type of finite-state calculus. Recall that FSTAs are closed under all the major operations: intersection, union, complementation, determinization and minimization. There is only one difference to FSAs, namely that FSTAs are not reversible. And, since it is possible to parse (context-free) languages using tree automata, the use of FSTAs represents a step in the hierarchy of language classes. To my knowledge there are no published results in this direction (yet). Considering the descriptive complexity of natural languages, it seems obvious that the gain in expressive power might well be worth the slight decrease in efficiency.

Another aspect of FSNLP is not so easily addressed. Most finite-state calculi also offer the possibility to specify transducers. But we have not experimented with linguistically motivated tree transductions at all. What remains is very tentative: As we will see later, one can define transductions with MSO logic. These in turn correspond to a special class of macro tree transductions (Engelfriet and Maneth 1999). This might allow an analogue construction of a calculus of tree transformations.

6.5.3 Query languages

Query languages for structured documents form an important application of the theoretical results presented above. As is shown in Neven (1999) and Neven and Schwentick (1999, 2000), MSO logic seems to provide a powerful and flexible language which can also be implemented efficiently.

A structured document is a text with an implicit structure; the main example of course being Web pages written in HTML. Each such text, while being nothing more than a text to the reader, has to be structured in itself into headers, paragraphs etc. with tags. Furthermore, there is associated information, e.g., author and creation date/time, which has to be represented as well for archiving such pages in a database. These data seem to be tree structured and could be handled with the techniques presented in this book.

XML with the corresponding Data Type Definitions (DTD) seems to be developing toward a standard to specify structured documents. As it turns out DTDs seem to correspond to regular tree languages with certain non-local information (Chidlovskii 2000).

Querying structured documents is a challenge to be achieved for intelligent document retrieval. Standard search-techniques like a simple keyword search return only occurrences of these keywords. They are not able to relate them to the structure of the underlying document. Consider the following simple example (taken from Neven 1999):

> Suppose we are looking for newspaper articles written in August 2000 where the header contains the word submarine. Searching for the keywords "August 2000" and "submarine" gives all Web pages containing these keywords at some completely arbitrary position. The simple mechanism of search engines does not allow to specify that "submarine" should occur as the header of the article and that "August 2000" should be a date. The need for new database systems and associated query languages capable of storing and manipulating such structured documents therefore emerges.

If we now consider the above mentioned fact that there is non-local information in structured documents (e.g., links), we know that MSO alone cannot be sufficient. As we will see in the next part of this book, there might be a way of accommodating a certain amount of non-locality with MTTs.

6.5.4 Hardware verification

In spite of the non elementary complexity, some very encouraging results from the areas of computer hardware and system verification (Kelb et al.

1997; Basin and Klarlund 1995, 1998; Klarlund and Møller 1998; Klarlund 1998; Jensen et al. 1997) suggest that the techniques for implementing the compilation process are in fact efficient; it is the problem space expressible in MSO tree logics that is hard. And, as we have seen, non-local dependencies seem to provide one of the few breaking points of the technique (Morawietz and Cornell 1999; Klarlund et al. 2000).

6.5.5 Other MSO languages

As we stated previously, the decidability proof for WS2S is inductive on the structure of MSO formulas and therefore we can choose our particular tree description language rather freely, knowing that the resulting logic will be decidable and that the translation to automata will go through as long as the atomic formulas of the language represent relations which can be translated (by hand if necessary) to tree automata.

For example, Niehren and Podelski (1992), Ayari et al. (1998) and Klarlund and Schwartzbach (1997) have investigated the usefulness of these techniques in dealing with feature trees which unfold feature structures; there the attributes of an attribute-value term are translated to distinct successor functions. Furthermore, in Ayari, Basin, and Podelski and Klarlund and Schwartzbach, two concepts from programming languages are integrated into an MSO specification language, namely high-level data structures such as records and recursively-defined datatypes. The integration is based on a new logic whose variables range over record-like trees and an algorithm for translating datatypes into tree automata.

One can imagine other possibilities as well: as we saw in Section 3.2.2 on page 36, the automaton for Kayne-style asymmetric, precedence-restricted c-command (Kayne 1994) is very compact, and makes a suitable primitive for a description language along the lines suggested by Frank and Vijay-Shanker (1995).

Chapter 7

Intermediate conclusion

In this second part of the book we introduced the grammar formalism of MSO logic with its decidability proof. We drew our examples from the work by Jim Rogers and explored the practical use the application of the compilation technique has.

In particular, we showed how to use the automata-based theorem proving techniques to implement linguistic processing and theory verification. The advantages are readily apparent. The direct use of a flexible and succinct description language together with an environment to test the formalizations with the resulting finite, deterministic tree automata offers a way of combining the needs of both formalization and processing. Furthermore, it becomes possible to have a descriptive complexity result for theories which were thought to be almost "resistant" to formal approaches of this kind.

We can also say that while it is theoretically not possible to write a formula covering a non-context-free theory, we can still use the independent parts of the formalization and families of definitions with respect to a particular input to answer questions of grammaticality of sentences.

On the practical side, the advent of MONA has enabled us to advance significantly with the experiments on the compilation of P&P-based grammatical theories. Although a definitive answer on the question whether an entire grammatical theory can be compiled into one automaton is still not possible, we know that we can compile non-trivial modules. But there are still many problems left, even on the processing side. The form of the formulas has a large effect on the time required by the compiler and it is important to figure out which sort of formulas can be compiled more efficiently than others. Furthermore, writing grammar formulas in WS2S or $\mathcal{L}^2_{K,P}$ is an experience akin to assembler programming, i.e., error prone and time consuming. Therefore it remains to be seen how much impact higher-level languages such as FIDO

(Klarlund and Schwartzbach 1997) and LISA (Ayari et al. 1998) have on the time required to formalize and compile P&P theories.

Unfortunately, the drawbacks of the classical approach are also immediately obvious. The staggering complexity bound and, paradoxically, the descriptive complexity result both have to be addressed. The fact remains that there simply are natural languages which require for their analysis more than context-free power. We will address these issues in the following third part of our monograph.

Part III

Two Steps Are Better Than One

Extending the Use of MSO Logic to Non-Context-Free Linguistic Formalisms

Chapter 8

Overview of the two-step approach

> Algebra may be considered, in its most general form, as the science which treats the combinations of arbitrary signs and symbols by means of defined though arbitrary laws: for we may assume any laws for the combination and incorporation of such symbols, so long as our assumptions are independent, and therefore not inconsistent with each other: in order, however, that such a science may not be one of useless and barren speculations, we choose some subordinate science as the guide merely, and not as the foundation of our assumptions, and frame them in such a manner that Algebra may become the most general form of that science, when the symbols denote the same quantities which are the objects of its calculations: ...
>
> Peacock (1830)

In the preceding parts of this book I have shown what can be achieved with the technique of compiling MSO formulas into tree automata. While the technique is very attractive in general since it allows for the specification of linguistic theories in a concise logic while retaining the computational properties of finite-state devices, there are three major remaining problems. One is the very conciseness of the logical specification which results in an exponential blow-up of the generated tree automata such that it cannot be expected that an entire grammar can be compiled into a single tree automaton. The second and third ones are related. There has been a change in the linguistic formalisms as proposed by N. Chomsky. Instead of the monostratal, representational GB theory, linguists nowadays tend to use the approach proposed in the *Minimalist Program* (Chomsky 1995). Minimalist grammars are still monostratal, but derivational. This is at least true for the versions formalized in Stabler's approaches (Stabler 1997, 1999b; Stabler and Keenan 2000). So, in the first part of the monograph, we presented a formalism which provided an operational as well as a denotational description of theories in the GB tradition. In this second part, we will show that there is a logical description of Minimalism[22] as well as of TAGs.[23] Furthermore, minimalist theories can easily generate non-context-free structures. Since there unarguably are natural languages which allow for, e.g., cross-serial dependencies which require non-context-free structures for their analysis, the generative capacity of the linguistic formalisms has to be at least adequate for those phenomena. So, our second problem is to deal with derivational approaches to syntax and the third one to accommodate the necessary increase in generative capacity.

In this third part of the book, universal algebra will play an even more prominent role for the definition of linguistic formalisms. As specified in the preliminaries, we regard a language as a set of basic items – words – with basic operations – the structure building rules – defined on them, i.e., an algebra. The "sentences" of the language are then those structures which can be generated form the basic items with the help of the operations. An algebraic term then describes the process by which an element is formed from the generators. More on viewing linguistic formalisms as algebraic theories can be found in, e.g., Janssen (2000). This unifying view enables the presentation of a general technique for coping with so-called mildly context-sensitive structures in a general way.

Mönnich (1999) forms the cornerstone of the work presented in this volume. In this paper, Mönnich showed how to treat non-context-free structures within an algebraicized variant of macro-grammars. The technique of translating the original alphabets into nominalized, derived counterparts brings them back into the realm of structures characterizable by regular tree grammars or, equivalently, MSO logic. In this book, the technique is used and augmented to account for more grammar formalisms. And we can close the gap to linguistics by reconstructing the intended structures from the derived ones with means which are again regular and MSO logic based, respectively.

The approach proposed in this monograph is presented graphically in Figure 8.1 on the next page. We start from well understood (algebraic) tree generating formalisms and lift the resulting trees by inserting a certain amount of control information. In our work, the particular tree-generating formalisms considered will be Context-Free Tree Grammars (CFTGs), Monadic Context-Free Tree Grammars (MCFTGs) and Multiple Context-Free Grammars (MCFGs). Since these have been shown to be weakly equivalent to TAGs (Mönnich 1997a; Fujiyoshi and Kasai 2000) and Minimalist Grammars (Michaelis 2001a), respectively, we can apply our two-step technique.[24]

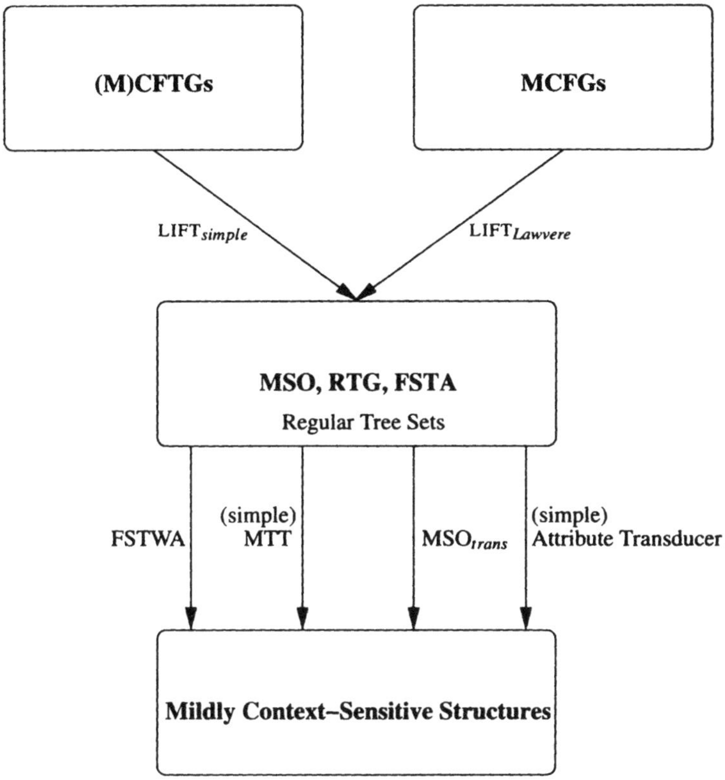

Figure 8.1: Overview of the two-step approach

These lifted trees can then be recognized/generated with formalisms having only context-free generative capacity such as Regular Tree Grammars (RTGs), MSO logic or bottom-up finite-state tree automata (FSTA). But since these trees contain the additional control information, it is necessary to transform them into the linguistically relevant ones. For this purpose we will use either tree-walking automata (FSTWA), simple macro tree transducers (MTT) or MSO definable transductions.[25] All of these transformation devices have only context-free power such that we can indeed describe mildly context-free structures with two regular steps.

Naturally, to make these techniques fully accessible to the reader, we have to present some more definitions and notations during the course of the discussion.

It has to be admitted that the use of lifting operations is not the only device that has been employed for the purpose of providing grammar formalisms with a controlled increase of generative capacity. Alternative systems that were developed for the same purpose are, e.g., tree adjoining grammars, head grammars and linear indexed grammars (cf. Vijay-Shanker and Weir 1994). Although these systems make highly restrictive claims about the structure of natural language formalisms their predictive power is closely tied to the individual strategy they exploit to extend the context-free paradigm. The great advantage of the tree oriented formalism derives from its connection with *descriptive complexity theory*. Tree properties can be classified according to the complexity of logical formulas expressing them. This leads to a perspicuous and fully *grammar independent* characterization of tree families by MSO logic. Although this characterization encompasses only regular tree sets, the lifting process of Section 10.2 on page 141 allows us to simulate the effect of CFTG-like productions with regular rewrite rules.

In the following sections we will begin to lay out the motivation and the need for this complex approach before we define the necessary tree generating formalisms. We proceed with the definitions for lifting, i.e., for the insertion of the extra control information which enables the treatment with mechanisms which have only context-free power. This allows the coding of the lifted formalisms with equivalently finite-state tree automata and MSO logic. These two codings will be presented in their own section. Finally, we will show how to transform the trees with the control information into the intended ones.

Chapter 9

Non-context-freeness of natural language

The main obstacle for the simple and direct use of MSO logic stems from the fact that theories in the minimalist tradition (Chomsky 1995) are derivational and that they allow non-context-free structures and therefore cannot be dealt with by the classical approach outlined in the previous part. In this chapter we will formally define minimalist grammars following Stabler (1997, 1999b) and tree adjoining grammars following Vijay-Shanker and Weir (1994) and Joshi and Schabes (1997). Both are formalisms which have a descriptive complexity which is higher than the one of context-free grammars. Furthermore, we will sketch a linguistic phenomenon – verb raising in a dialect of Swiss German following Shieber (1985) – which requires for its analysis non-context-free structures to illustrate the need for the machinery proposed in this part of the monograph.

9.1 Minimalist grammars

The shift in emphasis back from general interacting principles to rule-based linguistic constructions with the additional constraints of the required optimality of the ensuing derivations necessitated the definition of a new grammar type: Minimalist Grammars. In this section we will briefly introduce the formalism as it is present in the work of Stabler (1997, 1999b).

In a nutshell (and suppressing a plethora of important details), a minimalist derivation is powered by just two operations: MERGE, combining two structures in a rather straightforward way creating a new node by "projecting" one of the input structures and installing both as its sole daughters, and MOVE, which is dependent on the existence of a pair of attracting/attracted features in the structure so far constructed. It raises an element of the structure carrying the attracted feature and attaches it somewhere higher up in a *check*ing-configuration with the attracting feature, which is deleted in the process. There are two kinds of attracting features, called *strong* and *weak*, inducing immediate or delayed movement, respectively. In our case, the moved element will always be adjoined to the element carrying the attracting feature. For details we refer the reader to Chomsky (1995), especially chapter 4.

We give the formal definition of a minimalist grammar (MG) along the lines of Stabler (1997).[26] In order to keep the presentation simple, we omit the cases of *strong selection* (triggering *head movement*), and *covert movement*. Thus the definition given here comes close to the one given in Stabler (1999b), where some further restrictions are formulated as to which subtrees of a given tree may move. In fact, the example MG which will be considered below respects both the definition in Stabler (1997) as well as that in Stabler (1999b).

We begin by giving yet another definition of trees. They are rather special trees and used only in the definition of minimalist grammars. We will simply call them *expression trees*.

Definition 9.1 (Expression Trees). For a given set (of features), Feat, a five-tuple $\tau = \langle N_\tau, \triangleleft^*_\tau, \prec_\tau, <_\tau, Label_\tau \rangle$ fulfilling (E1)–(E3) is called an *expression tree (over Feat)*.

(E1) $(N_\tau, \triangleleft^*_\tau, \prec_\tau)$ is a finite, binary ordered tree (domain). N_τ denotes the non-empty set of nodes. $\triangleleft^*_\tau$ and $\prec_\tau$ denote the usual relations of *dominance* and *precedence* defined on a subset of $N_\tau \times N_\tau$, respectively, i.e., $\triangleleft^*_\tau$ is the reflexive and transitive closure of $\triangleleft_\tau$, the relation of *immediate dominance*.[27]

(E2) $<_\tau \subseteq N_\tau \times N_\tau$ denotes the asymmetric relation of *(immediate) projection* which holds for any two siblings in $(N_\tau, \triangleleft^*_\tau, \prec_\tau)$, i.e., each node $x \in N_\tau$ different from the root either *(immediately) projects* over its sibling y ($x <_\tau y$) or vice versa ($y <_\tau x$).

(E3) The function $Label_\tau$ assigns a string from Feat* to every leaf of the tree $(N_\tau, \triangleleft^*_\tau, \prec_\tau)$, i.e., a leaf is labeled by a finite sequence of features from Feat.

The set of all expressions trees over Feat is denoted by Exp(Feat).

Before we define the minimalist grammars themselves, we need some further notations. Consider $\tau = (N_\tau, \triangleleft^*_\tau, \prec_\tau, <_\tau, Label_\tau) \in$ Exp(Feat) with Feat being a set of features.

Each $x \in N_\tau$ has a *head* $h(x) \in N_\tau$ – a leaf such that $x \lhd_\tau^* h(x)$ holds, and such that each $y \in N_\tau$ on the path from x to $h(x)$ with $y \neq x$ projects over its sister. The *head of a tree* τ is the head of τ's root.

A subtree υ of τ is a *maximal projection (in τ)*, if the root of υ is a node $x \in N_\tau$ such that x is the root of τ or x's sister projects over x. The maximal projection dominated by the sister of the head of τ is the *complement (of τ)*. Each maximal projection in τ which is not dominated by the mother of the head of τ is a *specifier (of τ)*.

τ *has feature* $f \in \mathsf{Feat}$ if τ's head-label starts with f. τ is *simple* (a *head*) if it consists of exactly one node, otherwise τ is *complex* (a *non-head*).

Let r_τ be the root of τ. Suppose υ and $\varphi \in \mathsf{Exp}(\mathsf{Feat})$ to be subtrees of τ with roots r_υ and r_φ, respectively, such that $r_\tau \lhd_\tau r_\upsilon$ and $r_\tau \lhd_\tau r_\varphi$. Then we take $[_<\upsilon,\varphi]$ (or $[_>\varphi,\upsilon]$) to denote τ in case that $r_\upsilon <_\tau r_\varphi$ and $r_\upsilon \prec_\tau r_\varphi$ (or $r_\varphi \prec_\tau r_\upsilon$).

Definition 9.2 (Stabler 1997). A 4-tuple $G = \langle \mathsf{Non\text{-}Syn}, \mathsf{Syn}, \mathsf{Lex}, \mathcal{F} \rangle$ that obeys (M1)–(M4) is called a *minimalist grammar (MG)*.

(M1) Non-Syn is a finite set of *non-syntactic features* partitioned into a set Phon of *phonetic features* and a set Sem of *semantic features*.

(M2) Syn is a finite set of *syntactic features* partitioned into the sets Base, Select, Licensees and Licensors such that for each *(basic) category* x $\in$ Base the existence of =x $\in$ Select is possible, and for each -x $\in$ Licensees the existence of +X $\in$ Licensors is possible. Moreover, the set Base contains at least the category c.

(M3) Lex is a finite set of expressions over Feat = Non-Syn $\cup$ Syn such that for each tree $\tau = \langle N_\tau, \lhd_\tau^*, \prec_\tau, <_\tau, \mathit{Label}_\tau \rangle \in \mathsf{Lex}$ the function Label_τ assigns to each leaf in $\langle N_\tau, \lhd_\tau^*, \prec_\tau \rangle$ a string from

$$\mathsf{Select}^*\mathsf{Licensors}_\varepsilon\mathsf{Select}^*\mathsf{Base}_\varepsilon\mathsf{Licensees}^*\mathsf{Phon}^*\mathsf{Sem}^* \subseteq \mathsf{Feat}^*.$$ [28]

(M4) The set $\mathcal{F}$ consists of the structure building functions MERGE and MOVE as defined in (me) and (mo), respectively.

(me) The function MERGE is a partial mapping from two expression trees to a new expression tree, i.e., from Exp(Feat) $\times$ Exp(Feat) to Exp(Feat).

A pair of expressions $\langle \upsilon, \varphi \rangle$ belongs to Dom(MERGE) if υ has feature $^{=}$x and φ has category x for some x $\in$ Base.[29] Then,

$$\text{MERGE}(\upsilon,\varphi) = \ [_{<}\upsilon',\varphi'] \quad \text{if } \upsilon \text{ is simple and has feature } {}^{=}\text{x},$$

where υ' and φ' are expressions resulting from υ and φ, respectively, by deleting the feature the respective head-label starts with. And

$$\text{MERGE}(\upsilon,\varphi) = \ [_{>}\varphi',\upsilon'] \quad \text{if } \upsilon \text{ is complex and has feature } {}^{=}\text{x},$$

where υ' and φ' are expressions as in case (me.1).

(mo) The function MOVE is a partially defined mapping from an expression tree into a new expression tree, i.e., from Exp(Feat) to Exp(Feat). An expression υ belongs to Dom(MOVE) in case that υ has feature +X $\in$ Licensors, and υ has exactly one subtree φ that is a maximal projection and has feature -x $\in$ Licensees. Then,

$$\text{MOVE}(\upsilon) = \ [_{>}\varphi',\upsilon'] \quad \text{if } \upsilon \text{ has feature +X}$$

Here υ' results from υ by deleting the feature +X from υ's head-label, while the subtree φ is replaced by a single node labeled ε. φ' is the expression resulting from φ just by deleting the licensee feature -x that φ's head-label starts with.

Note that, by (me), a simple tree (head) selects another tree as its complement to the right, whereas a complex tree selects another tree as a specifier to the left.

Intuitively, MERGE and MOVE take trees with matching feature pairs as their input and produce new trees as their output with the "clashing" feature pair removed. Recall that each node is labeled with a string of features. Consider the simplified schematic presentation of MERGE and MOVE in Figure 9.1 on the next page. The input to MERGE are two trees whose root nodes are labeled with the feature pair $^{=}$a and a. Then we can remove those features and create a new tree which is headed by the tree which had the label $^{=}$a. This is indicated by the symbol $<$ on the new root.

The input to move, on the other hand, is a single tree whose root is labeled with a feature +F and which contains a subtree whose root has an accessible -f feature. We can move this subtree into a specifier position and remove the feature pair.

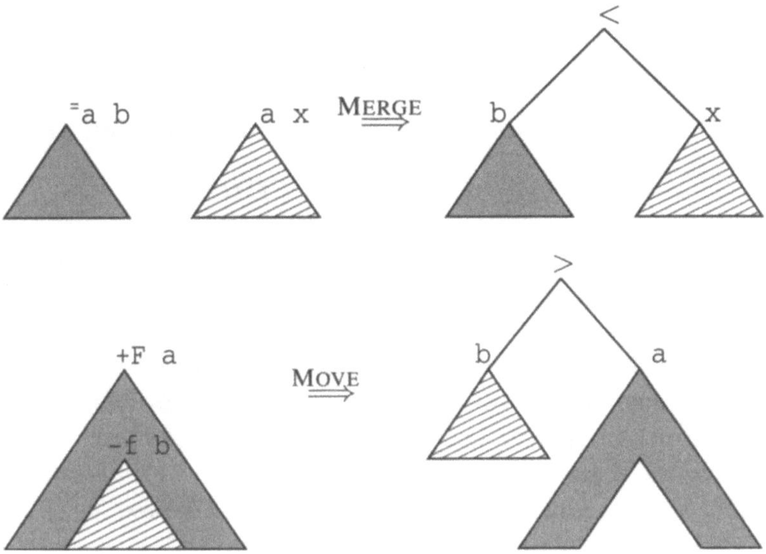

Figure 9.1: Schematic presentation of MERGE and MOVE

To illustrate MGs and their generative power, we give as an example a simple MG G_{ww} for the copy language over $\{1,2\}^*$.

Example 9.3. Let G_{ww} be an MG with Sem $= \emptyset$, Phon $= \{1,2\}$, Base $= \{\texttt{c}, \texttt{a}_1, \texttt{a}_2, \texttt{b}, \texttt{c}_1, \texttt{c}_2, \texttt{d}\}$, Licensors $= \{\texttt{+L}_1, \texttt{+L}_2\}$, Licensees $= \{\texttt{-l}_1, \texttt{-l}_2\}$, Select $= \{{}^{=}\texttt{a}_1, {}^{=}\texttt{a}_2, {}^{=}\texttt{b}, {}^{=}\texttt{c}_1, {}^{=}\texttt{c}_2, {}^{=}\texttt{d}\}$, and with Lex consisting of the following 10 simple expressions, where $i \in \{1,2\}$,[30]

$$\alpha_i = \texttt{a}_i\texttt{-l}_1 i \qquad \gamma_i = {}^{=}\texttt{b+L}_1\texttt{c}_i\texttt{-l}_1 i \qquad \zeta_1 = {}^{=}\texttt{b+L}_1\texttt{d}$$

$$\beta_i = {}^{=}\texttt{a}_i\texttt{b-l}_2 i \qquad \delta_i = {}^{=}\texttt{c}_i\texttt{+L}_2\texttt{b-l}_2 i \qquad \zeta_2 = {}^{=}\texttt{d+L}_2\texttt{c}$$

Then, e.g., for $i \in \{1,2\}$,

$$\text{MOVE}(\text{MERGE}(\zeta_2, \text{MOVE}(\text{MERGE}(\zeta_1, \text{MERGE}(\beta_i, \alpha_i))))) \in \mathsf{Exp}(\mathsf{Feat})$$

and the string language generated is $\mathcal{L}(G_{ww}) = \{\, ww \mid w \in \{1,2\}^* \}$.

Let $G = (\mathsf{Non\text{-}Syn}, \mathsf{Syn}, \mathsf{Lex}, \mathcal{F})$ be an MG. Then $CL(G) = \bigcup_{k \in \mathbb{N}} CL^k(G)$ is the *closure of* Lex *(under the functions in* $\mathcal{F}$*)*. For $k \in \mathbb{N}$ the sets $CL^k(G) \subseteq \mathsf{Exp}(\mathsf{Feat})$ are inductively defined by

$$CL^0(G) = \mathsf{Lex}$$

$$CL^{k+1}(G) = CL^k(G) \cup \{\text{MERGE}(\upsilon,\varphi) \mid (\upsilon,\varphi) \in \text{Dom}(\text{MERGE}) \cap CL^k(G) \times CL^k(G)\} \cup \{\text{MOVE}(\upsilon) \mid \upsilon \in \text{Dom}(\text{MOVE}) \cap CL^k(G)\}$$

Every $\tau \in CL(G)$ is called an *expression in G*. Such a τ is *complete (in G)* if its head-label is in $\{c\}\mathsf{Phon}^*\mathsf{Sem}^*$ and each other of its leaf-labels is in $\mathsf{Phon}^*\mathsf{Sem}^*$. Hence, a complete expression has category c, and this instance of c is the only instance of a syntactic feature within all leaf-labels.

The *(phonetic) yield* $Y(\tau)$ of an expression $\tau \in \mathsf{Exp}(\mathsf{Feat})$ is the string created by concatenating τ's leaf-labels "from left to right" and stripping off all non-phonetic features. $L(G) = \{Y(\tau) \mid \tau \in CL(G)$ with τ is complete$\}$ is the *(string) language (derivable by G)* and is called a *minimalist language*.

A derivation of the admittedly very simple string '11' is given in Figure 9.2 on the facing page where we instantiate the example expression tree given in Example 9.3 with $i = 1$. Note that the very first MERGE has been omitted. As can be seen, even this simple string entails a fairly complicated derivation with two movements.

Michaelis (2001a) proves the fact that each MG is weakly equivalent to a linear context-free rewriting system (LCFRS) or a multiple context-free grammar (MCFG) by giving an algorithm for the transformation.[31] We will not reproduce the proof here. However, the core idea is that for the set of trees appearing as intermediate steps in converging derivations of G, one can define a finite partition. The equivalence classes of this partition are formed by sets of trees where the features triggering movement appear in identical structural positions. Each nonterminal in a corresponding MCFG represents such an equivalence class, i.e., an infinite set of trees. The reader interested in more details of the transformation is referred to the original paper and furthermore to Michaelis et al. (2001), where the translation is exemplified with the grammar given in Example 9.3 on the page before. Because of Michaelis' proof, we can state the following theorem.

Theorem 9.4 (Michaelis). *Each minimalist grammar is weakly equivalent to an LCFRS (or an MCFG).*

In the following chapters we will silently presuppose that it is enough to deal with MCFGs since we can transform any given MG appropriately.

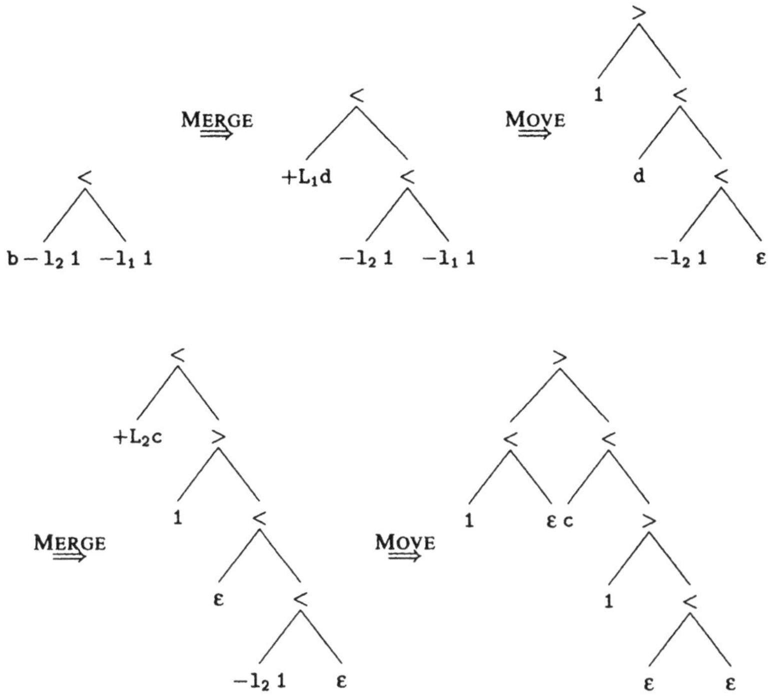

Figure 9.2: An example derivation of the MG G_{ww} given in Example 9.3 on page 119

9.2 Tree adjoining grammar

Tree Adjoining Grammar (TAG, Joshi et al. 1975; Joshi 1985, 1987) is maybe the prototypical mildly context-sensitive formalism for natural languages. In fact, the desiderata Joshi poses for any formalism dealing with natural languages coined this terminology (recall the discussion in the introduction, see Section 1.1 on page 5).

Since we will also show how to cope with the formalism of Tree Adjoining Grammar, we will very briefly sketch a simplified version of the definitions given in Joshi and Schabes (1997) or Vijay-Shanker and Weir (1994).[32]

Definition 9.5 (Tree Adjoining Grammar). A Tree Adjoining Grammar (TAG) is a quintuple $G = \langle V_N, V_T, S, I, \mathcal{A} \rangle$ where V_N is a finite set of nonterminals, V_T a finite set of terminals, $S \in V_N$ the start symbol, I a finite set of initial trees and $\mathcal{A}$ a finite set of auxiliary trees.

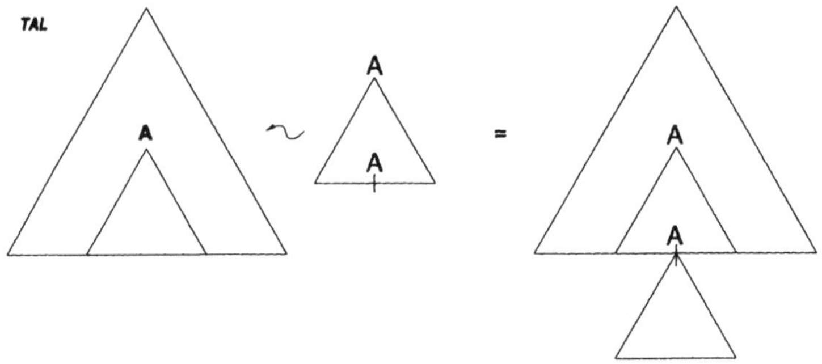

Figure 9.3: Schematic presentation of adjunction in TAGs

Initial trees are such that all interior nodes (including the root node) are labeled with nonterminals and all nodes on the frontier are labeled with terminal or nonterminal symbols; the nonterminals being marked for substitution. The same holds for the auxiliary trees with one exception. There exists one distinguished leaf-node which is labeled with the same nonterminal as the root node. This node is called the foot node. Furthermore, the nodes can be marked to allow or forbid adjunction. For simplicity, we only indicate nodes where no adjunction is allowed by putting a bar on top of them.

New trees are built from the sets I and $\mathcal{A}$ via adjunction or substitution. Adjunction is defined such that an auxiliary tree is spliced into an existing tree such that it basically "expands" a nonterminal. Consider the schematic representation of adjunction in Figure 9.3. The subtree rooted in the node labeled with the nonterminal A is taken out of the leftmost tree. The new auxiliary tree is inserted in its place (if the root and foot are also labeled with the identical nonterminal A) and the original subtree is appended at the foot node.

There also exists a simpler operation in TAGs, called *substitution*, to generate new trees. Intuitively, in substitution, a nonterminal is replaced by a tree with a matching nonterminal at its root. Since we do not need the formal definitions here, the reader is referred to the literature cited above for details. The corresponding tree and string languages are defined straightforwardly.

An example for a TAG generating the non-CF language $a^n b^n c^n d^n$ is given below:

Example 9.6. Let $G_{TAG} = \langle\{S\}, \{a,b,c,d\}, S, \{\alpha\}, \{\beta\}\rangle$ be a TAG. The only initial tree α and the only auxiliary tree β are given as follows:

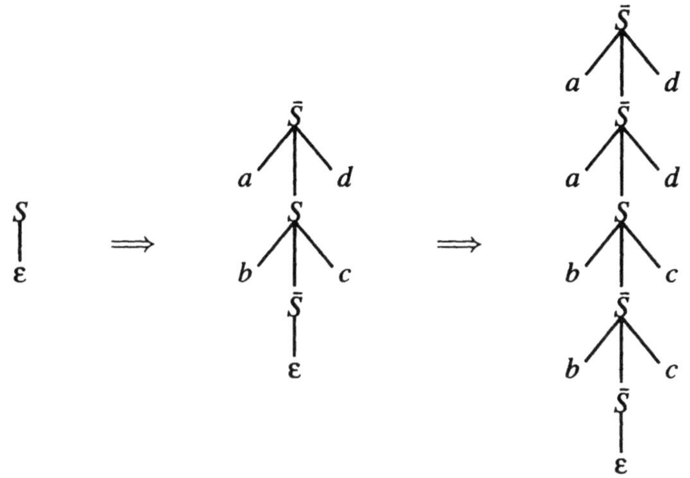

Figure 9.4: An example derivation of the TAG G_{TAG} given in Example 9.6

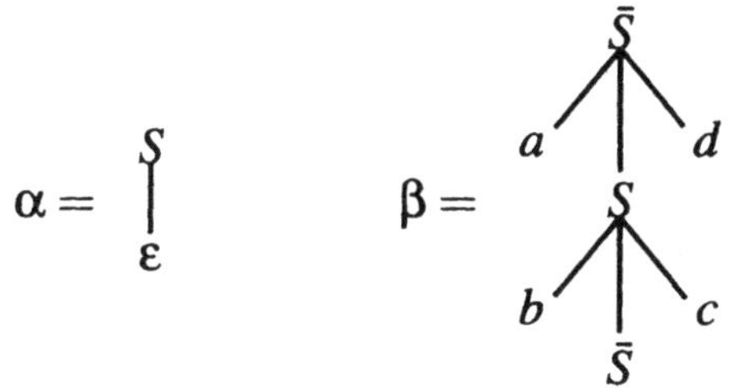

A derivation yielding *aabbccdd* has only two steps, both adjoin the auxiliary tree in the only possible position, see Figure 9.4.

It can be shown that TAGs can only generate string languages with dependencies up to four, i.e., $a^n b^n c^n d^n$ can be generated, but there is no TAG which generates $a^n b^n c^n d^n e^n$.

Interestingly, it has been shown by Mönnich (1997a) and Fujiyoshi and Kasai (2000) that TAGs are weakly equivalent to a restricted form of CFTGs: monadic context-free tree grammars ((M)CFTGs). Therefore, our techniques are immediately applicable. To a large extent, the intuition behind the proof is fairly simple. Since CFTGs can insert multiple subtrees in a single step, but TAGs only a single one, all we have to do is limit the appearing operative nonterminals of the CFTG to unary or monadic ones. This will become clearer after the formal definition and the intuitive explanation of CFTGs in Definition 10.1 on page 135. For the moment, we just state the theorem.

Theorem 9.7 (Mönnich; Fujiyoshi & Kasai). *The languages generated by TAGs are weakly equivalent to those generated by monadic CFTGs.*

Since the proof is constructive, i.e., there exists an algorithm to transform any given TAG into an equivalent monadic CFTG, we will tacitly assume in the following chapters that it is enough to deal with (M)CFTGs.

9.3 Linguistic motivation: verb raising

Calvin: "I like to verb words."

Hobbes: "What?"

Calvin: "I take nouns and adjectives and use them as verbs. Remember when 'access' was a thing? Now it's something to *do*. It got verbed. Verbing weirds language."

Hobbes: "Maybe we can eventually make language a complete impediment to understanding."

Bill Watterson, in the newspaper cartoon *Calvin and Hobbes*

As mentioned in the introduction, the exercise in formal coding is made necessary by the fact that natural language sports at least some constructions which lead to (i) non-CF string languages, or (ii) to non-CF, or better, non-recognizable structures, even though the resulting string languages are formally context-free. Let us note here that it is not the goal of this section to attempt a linguistically relevant discussion of cross-serial dependencies. All we want to show is that a formalism for natural languages has to handle non-context-free structures and how our proposal could do it. For a serious introduction of approaches to cross-serial dependencies see Pullum and Gazdar (1982). Both of the phenomena enumerated above show up in the West-Germanic languages: the verbal complex of Züritüütsch (a dialect of Swiss German as spoken around Zürich) is an example of (i), while (ii) is exhibited – for different reasons – by the corresponding constructions of Dutch and Standard German (Huybregts 1976, 1984):

(9.1) a. *(... weil) der Karl die Maria dem Peter den Hans schwimmen lehren helfen lässt*

(German fragment as a string language:
Palindrome language – CF)

b. *(... omdat) Karel Marie Piet Jan laat helpen leren zwemmen*
(Dutch fragment as a string language:
$a^n b^n$ – CF)

c. *(... wil) de Karl d'Maria em Peter de Hans laat hälffe lärne schwüme*
(Züritüütsch fragment as a string language:
$a^n b^m c^n d^m$ – Non-CF)

(... because) Charles Mary Peter John lets help to teach to swim

(... because) Charles lets Mary help Peter to teach John to swim

Looking closely at, e.g., the Swiss German example, we notice that the DPs and the Vs of which the DPs are objects occur in cross-serial order. This is observable since the verbs mark their objects for case. It appears that there are no limits on the length of such constructions in grammatical sentences of Swiss German. This fact alone would not suffice to prove that Swiss German is not a context-free string language. It could still be the case that Swiss German *in toto* is context-free even though it subsumes an isolable context-sensitive fragment. Relying on the closure of context-free languages under intersection with regular languages (Huybregts 1984, for Dutch) and (Shieber 1985, for Swiss German) were able to show that not only the fragment exhibiting the cross-serial dependencies but the whole of the languages has to be assumed as non-context-free.

Shieber's argument runs as follows. Consider the following sentences which were taken from Shieber (1985) and which exhibit cross-serial dependencies similarly to the ones given in (9.1):

(9.2) a. *Jan säit das mer em Hans es huus hälfed aastriiche.*

b. John said that we helped Hans (to) paint the house.

(9.3) a. *Jan säit das mer d'chind em Hans es huus lönd hälfed aastriiche.*

b. John said that we let the children help Hans paint the house.

(9.4) a. *Jan säit das mer d'chind em Hans es huus haend wele laa hälfed aastriiche.*

b. John said that we have wanted to let the children help Hans paint the house.

The NPs and the Vs of which the NPs are objects occur in cross-serial order. *D'chind* is the object of *lönd*, *em Hans* is the object of *hälfe*, and *es huus* is the object of *aastriiche*. Furthermore, the verbs mark their objects for case: *hälfe* requires dative case, while *lönd* and *aastriiche* require the accusative. It appears that there are no limits on the length of such constructions in grammatical sentences of Züritüütsch. Shieber poses four claims about sentences of this type: Firstly, there are subordinate clauses where all Vs follow all NPs. Secondly, sentences where all dative NPs precede all accusative NPs and all verbs subcategorizing for dative NPs precede all verbs subcategorizing for accusative NPs are acceptable. Thirdly, the number of verbs and their corresponding NPs agree. And lastly, an arbitrary number of verbs can occur in such clauses. These facts alone would not suffice to prove that Züritüütsch is not a context-free string language. It could still be the case that the entire language of Züritüütsch is context-free even though it subsumes a context-sensitive fragment. Recall that the intersection of a context-free language with a regular language is again a context-free language.

So, Shieber intersects Züritüütsch, e.g., (9.4), with the regular language given in (9.5a) to obtain the result in (9.6). As is well known, this language is not context-free.

(9.5) a. *Jan säit das mer (d'chind)* (em Hans)* es huus händ wele (laa)* (hälfe)* aastriiche.*

b. John said that we (the children)* (Hans)* the house wanted to (let)* (help)* paint.

(9.6) *Jan säit das mer (d'chind)^n(em Hans)^{m}es huus händ wele (laa)^n(hälfe)^m aastriiche.*

And therefore it follows that the original language itself cannot have been context-free.

Züritüütsch is not an isolated case that one could try to sidestep and to classify as methodologically insignificant. During the last 15 years a core of structural phenomena has been found in genetically and typologically unrelated languages that leaves no alternative to reverting to grammatical formalisms whose generative power exceeds that of context-free grammars.[33]

Huybregts (1984) provides a similar argument for Dutch taking into account a particular fragment: in contrast to Swiss German, Dutch does not

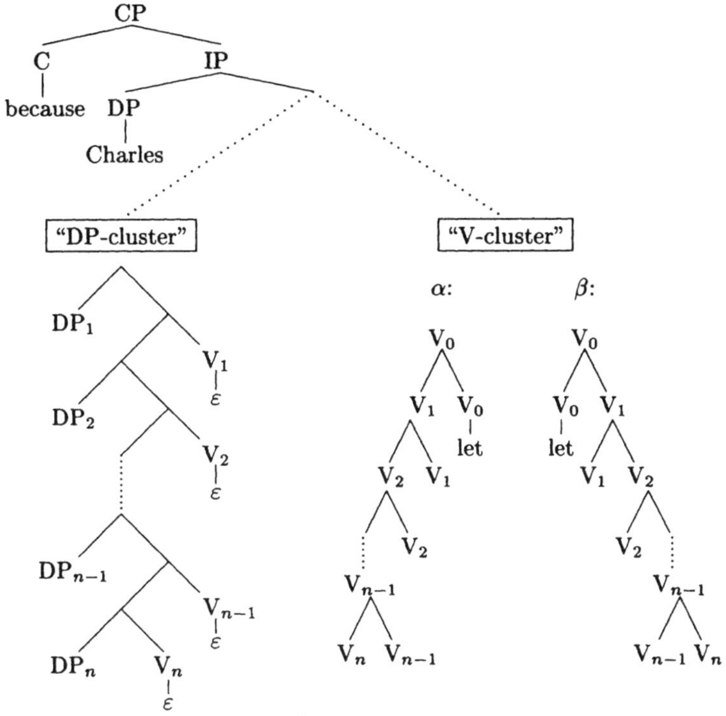

	overt CASE	*V*-cluster
German	+	α
Dutch	–	β
Züritüütsch	+	β

Figure 9.5: The structure of Germanic Verb Raising

show overt case-marking of objects. Therefore Huybregts' argument crucially relies on a given morphologized – and thus syntactical – difference between animate and inanimate pronominals. The proof of the non-context-freeness proceeds then analogously to Shieber's argument.

Abstracting from the details of the particular languages, the standard analyses of these cross-serial constructions involve the following property which is problematic from the point of view of context-freeness: In all cases they posit a bipartite structure like the one in Figure 9.5 with basically all DPs on one branch and all the verbs on the other – but with fixed syntactic and semantic relations between the branches, whether visibly marked (as in Züritüütsch, Standard German) or not (Dutch).

As is easily conceived, there is no context-free device which could directly handle the unbounded number of non-local dependencies the structural separation of the two "clusters" enforces. A relatively simple transformational device as the minimalist MERGE-MOVE machine, however, has little difficulty to combine nearness and separation in the required way.

The following assumptions suffice for a(n overly simplified) treatment of our example construction, generally known as verb raising (VR):

- VR is a lexical property of a certain class of verbs, e.g., *lassen-laten-laa* ("let"), *helfen-helpen-hälffe* ("help")... but not of, e.g., *schwimmen-zwemmen-schwüme* ("swim");
- VR-verbs take VP-complements;
- VR-verbs (optionally) have a strong V-feature, like the one standardly postulated for the inflectional head I;
- PF serializes complex V_0/I_0 as head-last (German) or head-first (Dutch / Züritüütsch).

The minimalist MERGE-MOVE machine achieves the complex result by a sequence of very simple discrete steps and so VR comes as close to being a consequence of formal universals as a basically idiosyncratic phenomenon will ever be.

We will show briefly how one could generate the bipartite structures indicated in Figure 9.5 on the page before with an MG according to the definitions given in Section 9.1.

Example 9.8. For our example, we only specify the relevant lexicon of the MG G_{VR} and leave the sets of features implicit. In fact, the lexicon is fairly simple. We can express it schematically as given below. In this minimalist grammar, we do not use actual lexical elements, but rather the main categories as phonological material to facilitate the understanding of the dependencies. We need n different DPs, n different verbs (one of the form $/V_n/$ and $n-1$ of the form $/V_{n-i}/$, $1 \leq i \leq n-1$) and one inflectional element. There are two different entries for the verbs since we need a base case to start the creation of the verbal complex and a "recursive" step which is terminated with the inflectional head.

`[dp]`	$/DP_n/$	`[=dp v v-]`	$/V_n/$
`[=v +V i]`	$/I/$	`[=v +V =dp v v-]`	$/V_{n-i}/$

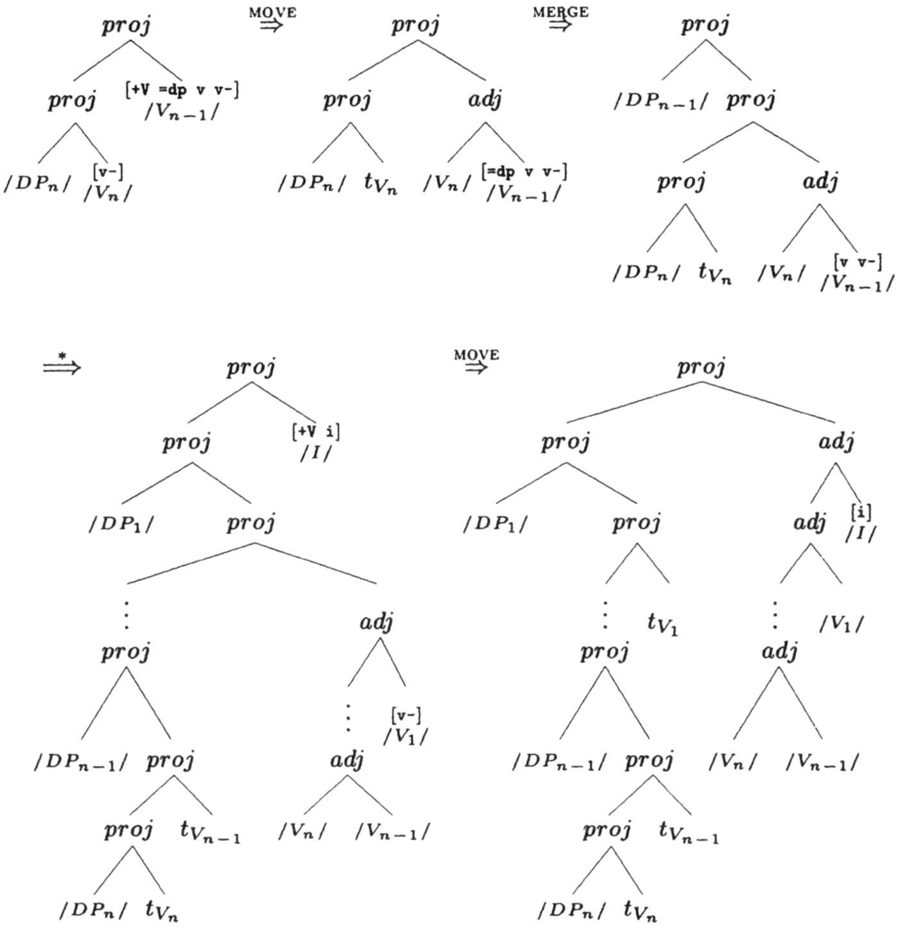

Figure 9.6: An example derivation of the MG G_{VR} given in Example 9.8

Note that we allow ourselves x- features indicating movement to the right. In Stabler's original system this type of head-movement was done within a special MERGE-step which did movement and merging of structures at the same time, triggered by X+ features. We think that it is clearer to separate the two operations.

Note that we deliberately do not use Stabler's "projection"-labels for the intermediate nodes (<,>), but rather use $proj(x,y)$ and $adj(x,y)$ as shorthands for Chomsky's *head-of-y*(x,y) and [*head-of-y*, *head-of-y*](x,y), respectively, to allow for the differences in word order. We assume that $adj(x,y)$ is "spelled-out" *xy* in German and *yx* in Dutch and Züritüütsch.

We cannot go into much detail here, but as one can see in Figure 9.6 on the preceding page, we skipped the initial merge of the lowermost verb with the lowermost DP and the next merge with the next highest verb. The resulting tree has both a v- and a +V feature available which triggers a movement. We indicate the moved category with an appropriately indexed trace. The resulting structure then demands the merging of a DP which makes a v feature available which triggers the merging of the next verb. After finitely many steps we choose an inflectional node instead of a verb for merging. It triggers the last move and leads to the final result. Clearly, the result corresponds to the schematic representation chosen for cross-serial dependencies in Figure 9.5 on page 127.

In this section, we have presented linguistic reasons why MSO logic alone can not be sufficient. But in order to concentrate on the relevant details, we will use short, artificial examples in the following sections to illustrate our proposals.

Chapter 10

The first step: Lifting

We begin the presentation of our approach with the introduction of the formalisms which are adequate for the desiderata outlined in the previous sections. This means that they have to be mildly context-sensitive, but characterizable with both logic (in particular MSO logic) and some type of automaton (in particular tree automata). Since to my knowledge no formalism exists which is immediately suitable, we present a two-step approach with the desired properties. Therefore we will introduce two types of tree grammars which can be "lifted", i.e., a certain amount of control information is explicitly coded in the trees, such that they are amenable to formalizations in terms of tree automata and MSO logic. In this chapter, I will present context-free tree grammars (CFTGs), two specializations of CFTGS, *monadic* CFTGs and regular tree grammars (RTGs) and multiple context-free grammars (MCFGs). All of these have an adequate descriptive complexity. In Michaelis (2001a,b) it is proven that MCFGs are weakly equivalent to MGs. Since the proof is constructive, we can algorithmically transform any given MG into a weakly equivalent MCFG. The weak equivalence between TAGs and CFTGs has independently been proven by Mönnich (1997a) and Fujiyoshi and Kasai (2000). Therefore both CFTGs and MCFGs form an adequate basis for the following work.

10.1 Tree grammars

The algebraic perspective allows the uniform and natural extension from strings to trees by the simple technique of generalizing from unary to multiary operators. In this section, in the same way as presented in the preliminaries (Section 2 on page 17) and the section of tree automata (Section 4.2 on page 49), grammars working on strings are generalized to grammars working on trees. Thus we have a natural counterpart to the Chomsky hierarchy: reg-

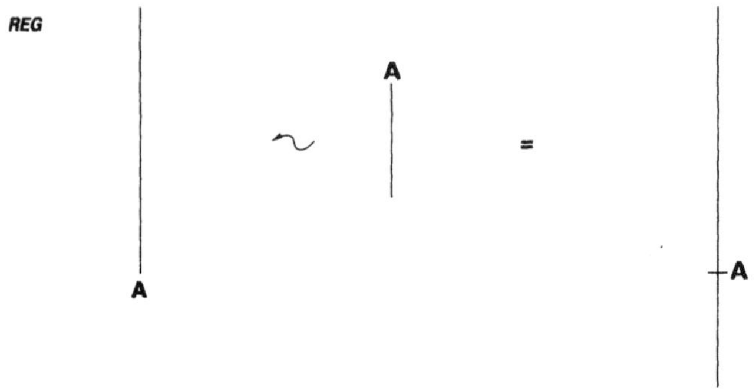

Figure 10.1: Derivation steps in Regular Grammars

ular tree grammars correspond to the known regular grammars and context-free tree grammars to the context-free grammars.[34]

We will illustrate this with a couple of (over)simplified pictures. In a regular grammar, we replace a nonterminal A simply with a string, see Figure 10.1. The nonterminal always appears at the right end of the string.[35] Therefore the replacement is simply appended at the rightmost side.

Conversely, in the tree case, the nonterminal A appears somewhere on the "right" end of the tree, i.e., the frontier, see Figure 10.2. But, as in the string case, the new tree is simply substituted for the nonterminal.

For context-free grammars, the nonterminal A can appear anywhere in the string (cf. Figure 10.3 on the facing page). But, again, the new string is simply inserted in its place. Note that basically the unary daughter of A is taken, the new string inserted at A's position and the (degenerate) subtree rooted in A's daughter is appended to the right.

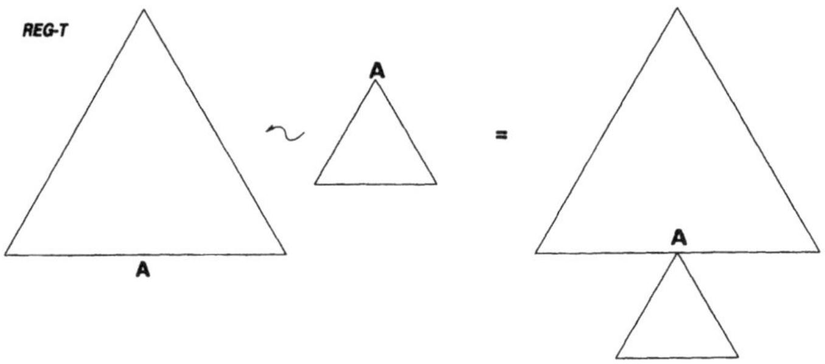

Figure 10.2: Derivation steps in Regular Tree Grammars

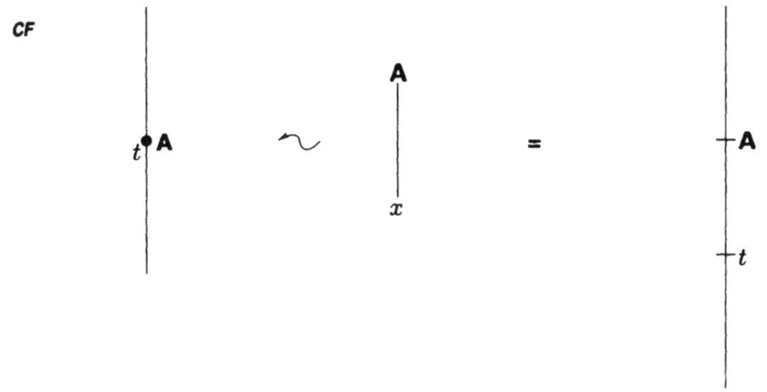

Figure 10.3: Derivation steps in Context-Free Grammars

Finally, context-free tree grammars allow the nonterminal A to appear anywhere inside of a tree, see Figure 10.4. Now A has more than one daughter. Lets say, it dominates n subtrees. In a derivation step, we have to replace A with a new tree with exactly n empty slots. These slots have to be filled with some of the n subtrees – the original daughters – of A. Please note that although the order and number of the subtrees in the example is preserved upon insertion in the new tree in Figure 10.4, this is not required by the formal definition given later. In fact, the ability to permute the daughters freely and to copy and delete subtrees is a crucial part of the generative power of context-free tree grammars. This simple figure only serves as an illustration of the basic concept. I hope that this analogy demonstrates that indeed tree grammars and their derivations arise naturally as generalizations of the more standard string grammars.

In Table 10.1 on the following page, there is an overview of the connection between the language classes from the Chomsky hierarchy together with

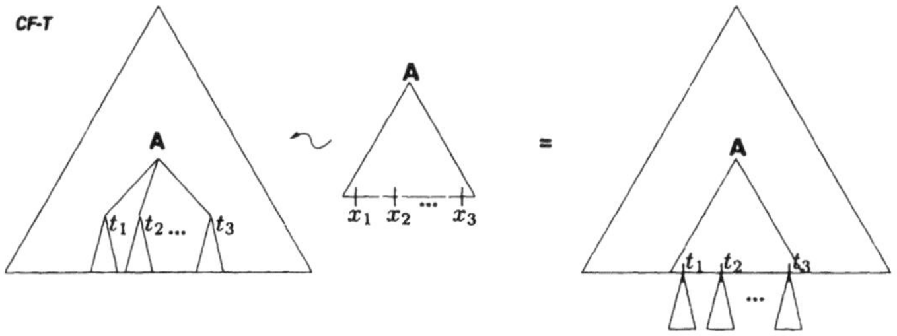

Figure 10.4: Derivation steps in Context-Free Tree Grammars

Table 10.1: Grammars, Automata and Language Classes

Language	Automata	Tree Grammar
regular	FSA	
context-free	bottom-up FSTA	RTG
mildly context-sensitive		MCFTG, MCFG
indexed		CFTG

classes of finite-state devices recognizing them and tree grammars generating them. Naturally this overview contains only those types of automata and tree grammars which we will use in the remainder of this monograph.

In the next section the grammar formalisms used will be formally defined and illustrated with examples.

10.1.1 Context-free tree grammars

We now formally introduce context-free tree grammars (CFTGs). This type of grammar is related to a type of grammars which were defined by Fischer (1968) and which were called *macro grammars*. In his setting, the use of macro-like productions served the purpose of making simultaneous string copying a primitive operation. CFTGs constitute an algebraic generalization of macro grammars (cf. Rounds 1970b).

Let us view grammars as a mechanism in which local transformations on trees can be performed. The central ingredient of a grammar is a finite set of productions, where each production is a pair of trees. Such a set of productions determines a binary relation on trees such that two trees t and t' stand in that relation if t' is the result of removing in t an occurrence of a first component in a production pair and replacing it by the second component of the same pair. The simplest type of such a replacement is defined by a production that specifies the substitution of a single-node tree t_0 by another tree t_1. Two trees t and t' satisfy the relation determined by this simple production if the tree t' differs from the tree t in having a subtree t_1 that is rooted at an occurrence of a leaf node t_0 in t. In slightly different terminology, productions of this kind incorporate instructions to rewrite an auxiliary variable as a complex symbol that, autonomously, stands for an element of a tree algebra. Recall that in context-free string grammars a nonterminal auxiliary symbol is rewritten as a string of terminal and nonterminal symbols, independently of the context in which it occurs. As long as the carrier of a tree algebra is made of constant tree terms the process of replacing null-ary variables by trees is analogous. As we will see, the situation changes dramatically if the carrier of the algebra is made of symbolic counterparts of derived operations and the variables in production rules range over these second-level entities.

Definition 10.1 (Context-Free Tree Grammar). For a singleton set of sorts $\mathcal{S}$, a *context-free tree grammar (CFTG)* for $\mathcal{S}$ is a 5-tuple $\Gamma = \langle \Sigma, \mathsf{F}, S, \mathsf{X}, \mathsf{P} \rangle$, where Σ and F are ranked alphabets of *inoperatives* and *operatives* over $\mathcal{S}$, respectively. $S \in \mathsf{F}$ is the start symbol, X is a countable set of variables, and P is a finite set of productions. Each $p \in \mathsf{P}$ is of the form $F(x_1, \cdots, x_n) \longrightarrow t$ for some $n \in \mathbb{N}$, where $F \in \mathsf{F}_n$, $x_1, \cdots, x_n \in \mathsf{X}$, and $t \in T(\Sigma \cup \mathsf{F}, \{x_1, \cdots, x_n\})$.

Intuitively, an application of a rule $F(x_1, \ldots, x_n) \rightarrow t$ "rewrites" a tree rooted in F as the tree t with its respective variables substituted by F's daughters.

A CFTG $\Gamma = \langle \Sigma, \mathsf{F}, S, \mathsf{X}, \mathsf{P} \rangle$ with $\mathsf{F}_n = \emptyset$ for $n \neq 0$ is called a *regular tree grammar (RTG)*. Since RTGs always just substitute some tree for a leaf-node, it is easy to see that they can only generate recognizable sets of trees, *a forteriori* context-free string languages (Mezei and Wright 1967). If F_n is non-empty for some $n \neq 0$, that is, if we allow the *operatives* to be parameterized by variables, however, the situation changes. CFTGs in general are capable of generating sets of structures, the *yields* of which belong to the class of context-sensitive languages known as the *indexed* languages. In fact, CFTGs characterize the class of indexed languages modulo the inside-out derivation mode (Rounds 1970b).

Because of the impossibility of mirroring the process of copying in a grammar with a completely uncontrolled derivation regime, we restrict ourselves to the following mode of derivation.

Definition 10.2. Let $\Gamma = \langle \Sigma, \mathsf{F}, S, \mathsf{X}, \mathsf{P} \rangle$ be a CFTG and let $t, t' \in T(\Sigma \cup \mathsf{F})$. t' is *directly derivable* by an *inside-out step* from t ($t \Rightarrow t'$) if there is a tree $t_0 \in T(\Sigma \cup \mathsf{F}, \{x\})$ containing exactly *one* occurrence of x, a corresponding rule $F(x_1, \ldots, x_m) \rightarrow t''$, and trees $t_1, \ldots, t_m \in T(\Sigma)$ such that $t = t_0[F(t_1, \ldots, t_m)]$ and $t' = t_0[t''[t_1, \ldots, t_m]]$. The inside-out restriction on the derivation scheme requires that the trees t_1, t_2 through t_n be terminal trees, i.e., do not contain variables or operatives. As is customary $\Rightarrow^*$ denotes the transitive-reflexive closure of $\Rightarrow$.

Accordingly, a function symbol may be replaced only if all its arguments are trees over the terminal alphabet. In the conventional case this form of replacement mechanism would correspond to a "rightmost" derivation where "rightmost" is to be understood with respect to the linear order of the leaves forming the frontier of a tree in a derivation step.

In the following definition of a tree language we now switch back to accepting only trees over the ranked alphabet Σ, i.e., we do not allow operatives to remain in the final trees.

Definition 10.3 (Inside-Out Tree Language). Let $\Gamma = \langle \Sigma, \mathsf{F}, S, \mathsf{X}, \mathsf{P} \rangle$ be a CFTG. We call $\mathcal{L}(\Gamma) = \{t \in T(\Sigma) \mid S \Rightarrow^* t\}$ the *context-free inside-out tree language* generated by Γ from S.

In the case of RTGs the analogy with the conventional string theory goes through and inside-out and outside-in derivations yield the same languages.

We will exemplify the gain in generative power of context-free tree grammars compared to RTGs – or standard context-free grammars – with an artificial construction of the string language $a^n b^m c^n d^m$ which is a subset of the actual non context-free dependencies occurring in Swiss German (see Section 9.3 on page 124). The example uses the full power of the second-order substitutions of derived operators.

Example 10.4. Let $\Gamma = \langle \Sigma_0 \cup \Sigma_2, \mathsf{F}_0 \cup \mathsf{F}_4, S, \mathsf{X}, \mathsf{P} \rangle$ be defined as follows:

$$\begin{array}{rclrclrcl} \Sigma_0 & = & \{\varepsilon, a, b, c, d\} & & & & \Sigma_2 & = & \{\bullet\} \\ \mathsf{X} & = & \{x_1, x_2, x_3, x_4\} & \mathsf{F}_0 & = & \{S\} & \mathsf{F}_4 & = & \{F\} \end{array}$$

$$\mathsf{P} = \left\{ \begin{array}{rcl} S & \longrightarrow & \varepsilon \\ S & \longrightarrow & F(a, \varepsilon, c, \varepsilon) \\ S & \longrightarrow & F(\varepsilon, b, \varepsilon, d) \\ F(x_1, x_2, x_3, x_4) & \longrightarrow & F(\bullet(a, x_1), x_2, \bullet(c, x_3), x_4) \\ F(x_1, x_2, x_3, x_4) & \longrightarrow & F(x_1, \bullet(b, x_2), x_3, \bullet(d, x_4)) \\ F(x_1, x_2, x_3, x_4) & \longrightarrow & \bullet(\bullet(\bullet(x_1, x_2), x_3), x_4) \end{array} \right\}$$

The tree language generated by the grammar in Example 10.4 can intuitively be described as a parallel derivation of a's and c's and b's and d's. Therefore, the number of occurrences of a's and c's and of b's and d's, respectively, has to be the same. By taking the yield of the tree terms, we get the language $\mathcal{L} = \{a^n b^m c^n d^m\}$.

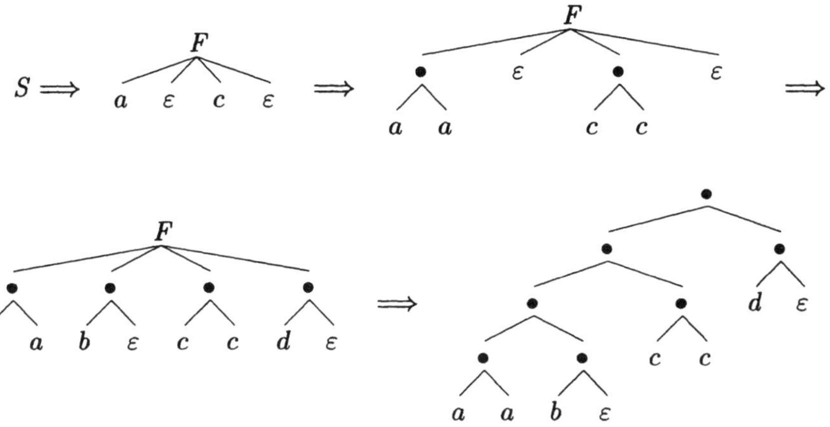

Figure 10.5: An example derivation of the CFTG Γ given in Example 10.4

In Figure 10.5 we show an example derivation of the string *aabccd*. It uses the second rule for *S*, followed by successive application of the first, second and third rule for *F*.

The definition of a CFTG given above could be canonically generalized to the case of many-sorted signatures Σ and F over some set of sorts $\mathcal{S}$. Since we will be concerned with such generalized versions of CFTGs only in their regular form, we restrict our definition to simplify our presentation. Therefore we give a "new" definition of RTGs although we already presented them as special cases of CFTGs.

Definition 10.5 (Regular Tree Grammar). For a set of sorts $\mathcal{S}$, a *regular tree grammar (RTG)* for $\mathcal{S}$ is a 4-tuple $\mathcal{G} = \langle \Sigma, \mathsf{F}, S, \mathsf{P} \rangle$, where $\Sigma = \langle \Sigma_{w,s} \,|\, w \in \mathcal{S}^*, s \in \mathcal{S} \rangle$ is a many-sorted signature of *inoperatives* and $\mathsf{F} = \langle \mathsf{F}_{\varepsilon,s} \,|\, s \in \mathcal{S} \rangle$ a (reduced) many-sorted signature of *operatives* of rank 0. Moreover, Σ and F are finite. $S \in \mathsf{F}$ is the start symbol and P is a finite set of productions. Each $p \in \mathsf{P}$ has the form $F \longrightarrow t$, where $F \in \mathsf{F}_{\varepsilon,s}$ for some $s \in \mathcal{S}$ and $t \in T(\Sigma \cup \mathsf{F})$, i.e., a term (tree) over $\Sigma \cup \mathsf{F}$, such that t is of sort s.

Let $t', t'' \in T(\Sigma \cup \mathsf{F})$ and $p = F \longrightarrow t \in P$. We say *$t'$ directly derives t'' (by the application of p)*, also denoted by $t' \Rightarrow t''$, if t' has a leaf-node F and t'' results from t' by substituting t for this node F. Let $\Rightarrow^*$ be the reflexive and transitive closure of $\Rightarrow$. The tree-language generated by $\mathcal{G}$ is the set $\mathcal{L}_T(\mathcal{G}) = \{t \in T(\Sigma) \,|\, S \Rightarrow^* t\}$.

The yield $Y(t)$ of a $t \in T(\Sigma \cup \mathsf{F})$ is the string resulting from concatenating the leaf-nodes of t "from left to right." Thus, $Y(t) \in (\bigcup_{s \in \mathcal{S}} \Sigma_{\varepsilon,s} \cup \bigcup_{s \in \mathcal{S}} \mathcal{F}_{\varepsilon,s})^*$.

The string-language generated by $\mathcal{G}$ is the set $\mathcal{L}_Y = \{Y(t) \mid t \in L_T(\mathcal{G})\} \subseteq (\bigcup_{s \in \mathcal{S}} \Sigma_{\varepsilon,s})^*$.

Since RTG-rules (even based on a many-sorted signature) still just substitute some tree for a leaf-node, it is still the case that they generate recognizable sets of trees, i.e., context-free string languages.

An example for a regular tree grammar and a corresponding derivation will be given later in the paper in the context of the discussion of lifting, see Example 10.11 on page 143.

We will show in Section 10.3.1 on page 151 the equivalence between RTGs and FSTAs which ensures the closure of the regular tree languages under the standard boolean operations. This is somewhat surprising since the regular tree languages yield the context-free string languages which are not closed under intersection. That RTGs are closed under intersection is due to the fact that we are not talking about the strings, but rather about strings together with their structure, i.e., the trees. Thus, the simple step from strings to trees enables us to use operations which were not available before.

Finally, since we need them to show how to handle TAGs, we also define monadic context-free tree grammars (MCFTGs). Since they are only a simplification of the definition we have given in Definition 10.1 on page 135, we outline only the differences here. The main difference is that MCFTGs allow only one variable to appear in each rule. As a consequence, the operatives of the CFTG are also constrained to be at most unary, i.e., they can only have at most one argument and therefore allow only one variable in their scope.

Definition 10.6 (Monadic Context-Free Tree Grammar). Let $\mathcal{S}$ be a set of sorts. A monadic context-free tree grammar (MCFTG) for $\mathcal{S}$ is a 5-tuple $\Gamma = \langle \Sigma, \mathsf{F}_0 \cup \mathsf{F}_1, \mathcal{S}, \mathsf{X}, \mathsf{P} \rangle$, i.e., a CFTG, where all the rules in P are of one of the following "unary" types where ($A, B, C, B_i \in \mathsf{F}_1 \cup \mathsf{F}_0$, $1 \leq i \leq n$, $a \in \Sigma$, $x \in \mathsf{X}$):

$$\begin{aligned} A &\longrightarrow a \\ A &\longrightarrow B(C) \\ A(x) &\longrightarrow a(B_1, \ldots, B_{i-1}, x_i, B_{i+1}, \ldots, B_n) \\ A(x) &\longrightarrow B_1(B_2(\ldots B_n(x)\ldots)) \end{aligned}$$

As an example, we present an MCFTG Γ_{TAG} for $a^n b^n c^n d^n$ generating the same language as the TAG grammar G_{TAG} given in Example 9.6 on page 122.

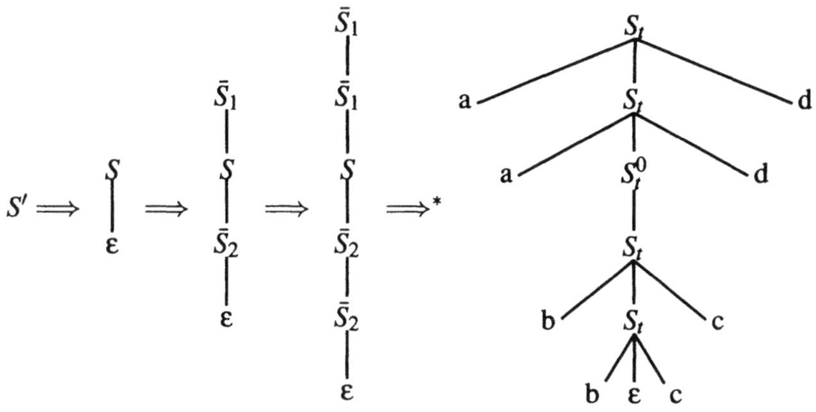

Figure 10.6: An example derivation of the MCFTG Γ_{TAG} from Example 10.7

Example 10.7. Let $\Gamma_{TAG} = \langle\{a,b,c,d,\varepsilon,S_t,S_t^0\},\{S,S',\overline{S}_1,\overline{S}_2,\overline{a},\overline{b},\overline{c},\overline{d}\},S',$ $\{x\},\mathrm{P}\rangle$ with P given as follows

$$\begin{array}{rlcrl} S' & \longrightarrow S(\varepsilon) & \quad & \overline{a} & \longrightarrow a \\ S(x) & \longrightarrow \overline{S}_1(S(\overline{S}_2(x))) & & \overline{b} & \longrightarrow b \\ S(x) & \longrightarrow S_t^0(x) & & \overline{c} & \longrightarrow c \\ \overline{S}_1(x) & \longrightarrow S_t(\overline{a},x,\overline{d}) & & \overline{d} & \longrightarrow d \\ \overline{S}_2(x) & \longrightarrow S_t(\overline{b},x,\overline{c}) & & & \end{array}$$

A corresponding derivation of the string *abbccdd* is shown in Figure 10.6. The example derivation is somewhat longer than the one given for the almost identical TAG grammar generating the same language. This is due to the fact that we need nonterminals to introduce each branching of the resulting tree separately. In the first step, we simply rewrite the start symbol into a unary branching tree with a single nonterminal which is again labeled with S and which dominates ε. In the second one, the symbol S is replaced with the term $\overline{S}_1(S(\overline{S}_2(x)))$ where the (degenerate) tree ε is simply appended in the only argument position x of $\overline{S}_2$. This step is repeated before we terminate with an application of the rule rewriting S to S_t^0. We simplified the presentation in the sense that in this last step we also applied the rules for the "barred" operatives, i.e., we replaced each $\overline{S}_i$, $i \in \{1,2\}$ with the corresponding term and each $\overline{s} \in \{\overline{a},\overline{b},\overline{c},\overline{d}\}$ with s. As one can see, the recursive step can be iterated arbitrarily often yielding the desired non-context-free language $a^n b^n c^n d^n$.

10.1.2 Multiple context-free grammars

We include the definition of multiple context-free grammars (MCFG) into this section although, strictly speaking, they are not tree grammars, but string grammars working on tuples of strings. Intuitively, each nonterminal represents a tuple of (terminal) strings and therefore has an arity. Each rule of an MCFG is basically like a context-free rule, but associated with a function which executes basic morphisms of the right arity on the tuples of strings.[36] We present this formalism here since they can be used as representations of MGs and our approach is applicable to it. Furthermore, if we view the right hand sides of the rules as a function applied to the nonterminals as arguments, we can also view them as a sort of tree grammar. Historically, MCFGs are a specialization of the generalized context-free grammars introduced by Pollard (1984) and are very similar to LCFRSs. They have the same generative capacity, although they are not restricted to be non-erasing. We follow Seki et al. (1991) in our presentation of the formal definition.

Definition 10.8. A *multiple context-free grammar* (MCFG) is defined as a five-tuple $\mathcal{G} = \langle V_N, V_T, V_F, P, S\rangle$ with V_N, V_T, V_F and P being a finite set of nonterminals, terminals, linear basic morphisms and productions, respectively. $S \in V_N$ is the start symbol. There is a function d from V_N to $\mathbb{N}$ such that $d(S) = 1$. Each $p \in P$ has the form $A \longrightarrow f(A_0, \dots, A_{n-1})$ for $A, A_0, \dots, A_{n-1} \in V_N$ and $f \in F$ a function from $(V_T^*)^k$ to $(V_T^*)^{d(A)}$ with arity $k = \sum_{i=0}^{n-1} d(A_i)$. Recall that basic morphisms are those which use only variables, constants, concatenation, composition and tupling.

The derivation-relation $\Rightarrow_{\mathcal{G}}$ for $\mathcal{G}$ is defined as follows: If $A \longrightarrow f() \in P$ then $A \Rightarrow_{\mathcal{G}} f()$, where $f() \in (V_T^*)^{d(A)}$ (i.e., f is some constant tuple of terminal strings). If $A \longrightarrow f(A_0, \dots, A_{n-1}) \in P$ and $A_i \Rightarrow_{\mathcal{G}} t_i$ for some $t_i \in (V_T^*)^{d(A_i)}$ then $A_i \Rightarrow_{\mathcal{G}} f(t_0, \dots, t_{n-1})$. The language generated by $\mathcal{G}$ is $\mathcal{L}(\mathcal{G}) = \{t \in V_T^* \mid S \Rightarrow_{\mathcal{G}}^* t\}$. As usual, $\Rightarrow^*$ stands for the reflexive transitive closure of $\Rightarrow$.

We also have to state one important result concerning the generative capacity of MCFGs. The class of languages generated by MCFGs properly includes the class of context-free languages and is properly included in the class of context-sensitive languages (Seki et al. 1991). Therefore, from this perspective, they are an adequate formalism for our purposes.

As for the other grammar formalisms, we illustrate the definition with an example grammar yielding a simple non-context-free language.

Example 10.9. Consider the following MCFG $\mathcal{G}_{MCFG} = \langle\{S, A\}, \{a_1, a_2, a_3\}, S, P\rangle$ with P as defined below:

$$P = \left\{ \begin{array}{lcl} S & \rightarrow & g(A) \\ A & \rightarrow & f() \\ A & \rightarrow & h(A) \end{array} \right\} \qquad \begin{array}{lcl} g(x,y,z) & = & xyz \\ f() & = & \langle a_1, a_2, a_3 \rangle \\ h(x,y,z) & = & \langle xa_1, ya_2, za_3 \rangle \end{array}$$

The language generated by $\mathcal{G}_{MCFG}$ is $\mathcal{L}(\mathcal{G}_{MCFG}) = a_1^n a_2^n a_3^n$. An example derivation of the string $a_1 a_1 a_2 a_2 a_3 a_3$ firstly replaces all the nonterminals and then "executes" the functions. In the first step, the function f generates a tuple $\langle a_1, a_2, a_3\rangle$ whose components are then augmented with the appropriate symbols by h and "terminated" by g.

$$\begin{aligned} S &\rightarrow g(A) \\ &\rightarrow g(h(A)) \\ &\rightarrow g(h(f())) \\ &\rightarrow g(h(\langle a_1, a_2, a_3 \rangle)) \\ &\rightarrow g(\langle a_1 a_1, a_2 a_2, a_3 a_3 \rangle) \\ &\rightarrow a_1 a_1 a_2 a_2 a_3 a_3 \end{aligned}$$

10.2 Lifting

We call the process which makes the control information inherent in term based grammar formalisms explicit lifting. The intuition here is that basic assumptions are commonly made about the interpretation of terms which are usually left implicit. We make them explicit by inserting the "control" information which allows us to code the resulting structures with regular means, i.e., regular tree grammars or finite-state tree automata.

10.2.1 Lifting CFTGs

The intuition behind the lifting process is that each term compactly encodes information such as composition, concatenation or (later on) tupling.

Any *context-free* tree grammar Γ for a singleton set of sorts $\mathcal{S}$ can be transformed into a *regular* tree grammar Γ^L for the set of sorts $\mathcal{S}^*$, which characterizes a (necessarily recognizable) set of trees encoding the instructions necessary to convert them by means of a unique homomorphism h into

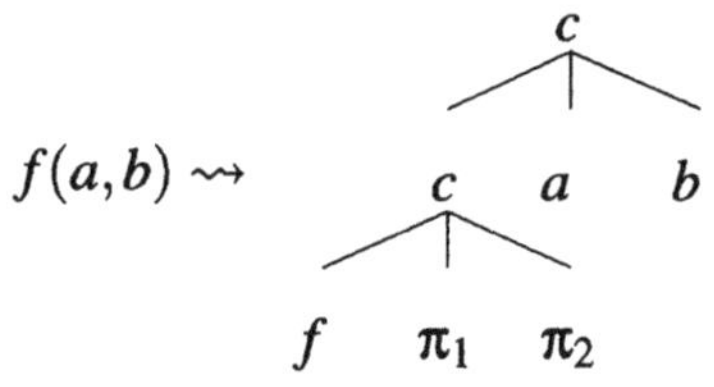

Figure 10.7: Intuition for simple lifting

the ones the original grammar generates (Maibaum 1974). This "lifting" is achieved by constructing a new, derived alphabet (an $\mathbb{N}$-sorted signature) Σ^L for a given single-sorted signature Σ, as well as by translating the terms over the original signature into terms of the derived one via a primitive recursive procedure. The lift-operation takes a term in $T(\Sigma, X_k)$ and transforms it into one in $T(\Sigma^L, k)$. Since S is a singleton, we can identify S^* with $\mathbb{N}$ (cf. Definition 2.2 on page 18). By $T(\Sigma^L, k)$ we denote the set of all trees over Σ^L which are of sort k.

Intuitively, the lifting eliminates variables and composes functions with their arguments explicitly, e.g., a term $f(a,b) = f(x_1,x_2) \circ (a,b)$ is lifted to the term $c(c(f,\pi_1,\pi_2),a,b)$, see Figure 10.7. The old function symbol f now becomes a constant, the variables are replaced with appropriate projection symbols and the only remaining non-null-ary alphabet symbols are the explicit composition symbols c.

Definition 10.10 (LIFT$_{simple}$). Let Σ be a ranked alphabet and X_k a set of variables $\{x_1, \ldots, x_k\}$, $k \in \mathbb{N}$, a finite set of variables. The *derived* $\mathbb{N}$-sorted alphabet Σ^L is defined as follows: For each $n \geq 0$, $\Sigma'_{\varepsilon,n} = \{f' \mid f \in \Sigma_n\}$ is a new set of symbols of type $\langle \varepsilon, n \rangle$; for each $n \geq 1$ and each $i, 1 \leq i \leq n$, π_i^n is a new symbol, the ith *projection symbol* of type $\langle \varepsilon, n \rangle$; for each $n, k \geq 0$ the new symbol $c_{n,k}$ is the (n,k)th *composition symbol* of type $\langle nk_1 \cdots k_n, k \rangle$ with $k_1 = \cdots = k_n = k$. The set of all $c_{n,k}$ will be denoted by C, the set of all π_i^n by Π.

$$
\begin{aligned}
\Sigma^L_{\varepsilon,0} &= \Sigma'_{\varepsilon,0} \\
\Sigma^L_{\varepsilon,n} &= \Sigma'_{\varepsilon,n} \cup \{\pi_i^n \mid 1 \leq i \leq n\} \text{ for } n \geq 1 \\
\Sigma^L_{nk_1 \cdots k_n,k} &= \{c_{n,k}\} \text{ for } n,k \geq 0 \text{ and } k_i = k \text{ for } 1 \leq i \leq k \\
\Sigma^L_{w,s} &= \emptyset \text{ otherwise}
\end{aligned}
$$

For $k \geq 0$, $\text{LIFTS}_k^\Sigma : T(\Sigma, X_k) \to T(\Sigma^L, k)$ is defined as follows:

$$\begin{aligned}
\text{LIFTS}_k^\Sigma(x_i) &= \pi_i^k \\
\text{LIFTS}_k^\Sigma(f) &= c_{0,k}(f') \text{ for } f \in \Sigma_0 \\
\text{LIFTS}_k^\Sigma(f(t_1,\ldots,t_n)) &= c_{n,k}(f', \text{LIFTS}_k^\Sigma(t_1), \ldots, \text{LIFTS}_k^\Sigma(t_n)) \\
&\quad \text{for } n \geq 1, f \in \Sigma_n \text{ and } t_1,\ldots,t_n \in T(\Sigma, X_k)
\end{aligned}$$

Note that this very general procedure allows the translation of any term over the original signature. The left hand side as well as the right hand side (RHS) of a rule of a CFTG $\Gamma = \langle \Sigma, F, X, S, P \rangle$ is simply a term belonging to $T(\Sigma \cup F, X)$, and also any structure *generated* by Γ.

Further remarks on the observation that the result of lifting a CFTG is always a RTG can be found in Mönnich (1999).

As an example, we present the lifted version $\Gamma^L = \langle \Sigma^L, F^L, S', P^L \rangle$ of the CFTG Γ given in Example 10.4 on page 136. The translation process for grammars is centered around the lift-morphism for the translation of the alphabets of the operatives and inoperatives and the RHSs of the production rules. Since the rest of the translation follows trivially from this, we dispense with a formal definition. Note that for better readability, we omit the π_i^2 from $\Sigma_{\varepsilon,2}^L$, all the 0- and 1-place composition symbols and the subscripts on all other composition symbols.

Example 10.11. Let Γ^L be an RTG defined as follows:

$$\begin{aligned}
\Sigma_{\varepsilon,0}^L &= \{\varepsilon, a', b', c', d'\} & \Sigma_{\varepsilon,2}^L &= \{\bullet'\} \\
\Sigma_{\varepsilon,4}^L &= \{\pi_1^4, \pi_2^4, \pi_3^4, \pi_4^4\} & \Sigma_{nk_1\cdots k_n,k}^L &= \{c\} \text{ (for simplicity)} \\
F_{\varepsilon,1}^L &= \{S'\} & F_{\varepsilon,4}^L &= \{F'\}
\end{aligned}$$

$$P^L = \left\{ \begin{array}{lcl}
S' & \longrightarrow & \varepsilon \\
S' & \longrightarrow & c(F', a', \varepsilon, c', \varepsilon) \\
S' & \longrightarrow & c(F', \varepsilon, b', \varepsilon, d') \\
F' & \longrightarrow & c(F', c(\bullet', a', \pi_1^4), \pi_2^4, c(\bullet', c', \pi_3^4), \pi_4^4) \\
F' & \longrightarrow & c(F', \pi_1^4, c(\bullet', b', \pi_2^4), \pi_3^4, c(\bullet', d', \pi_4^4)) \\
F' & \longrightarrow & c(\bullet', c(\bullet', c(\bullet', \pi_1^4, \pi_2^4), \pi_3^4), \pi_4^4)
\end{array} \right\}$$

We parallel the derivation for *aabccd* shown in Figure 10.5 on page 137 with this lifted grammar in Figure 10.8 on the next page.

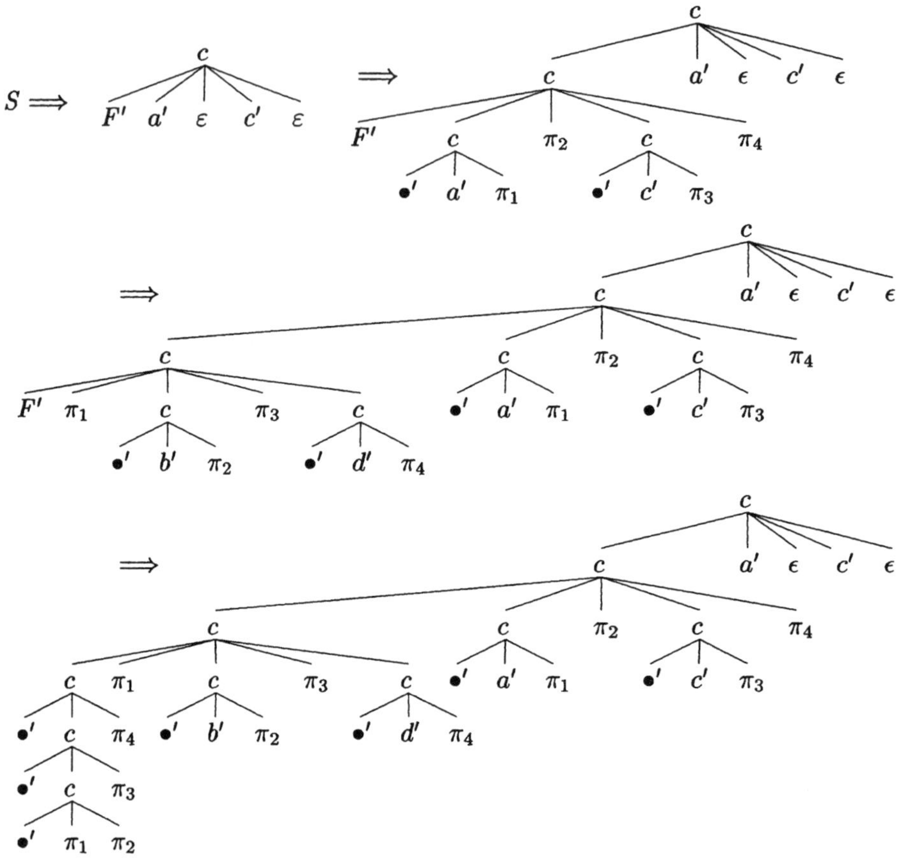

Figure 10.8: An example derivation of the lifted CFTG Γ^L given in Example 10.11

Lifting MCFTGs

Lifting MCFTGs uses the same definitions for lifting as is used for general CFTGs. To further illustrate the techniques, we present the continuation of Example 10.7 on page 138. Because the grammar is sufficiently simple, we include the subscripts on the composition symbols. Note that we now have only null-ary operatives, though we do have extra composition and projection symbols.

Example 10.12. Let $\Gamma^L_{TAG} = \langle\{a,b,c,d,\varepsilon,S_t,S_t^0\},\{S,S',\overline{S}_1,\overline{S}_2,\overline{a},\overline{b},\overline{c},\overline{d}\},S',$ $\mathsf{P}\rangle$ with P given as follows

$$
\begin{aligned}
S' &\longrightarrow c_{(1,0)}(S, \varepsilon) \\
S &\longrightarrow c_{(1,1)}(\overline{S}_1, c_{(1,1)}(S, c_{(1,1)}(\overline{S}_2, \pi_1^1))) \\
S &\longrightarrow c_{(1,1)}(S_t^0, \pi_1^1) \\
\overline{S}_1 &\longrightarrow c_{(3,1)}(S_t, a, \pi_1^1, d) \\
\overline{S}_2 &\longrightarrow c_{(3,1)}(S_t, b, \pi_1^1, c)
\end{aligned}
$$

We parallel the derivation given in Figure 10.6 on page 139 with the new grammar as given in Figure 10.9 on the following page. Note that nonterminals are now simply replaced by entire subtrees and no extra insertions take place.

10.2.2 Lifting MCFGs

Now we turn to the translation of MCFGs to RTGs. Each rule of a given MCFG is recursively transformed into a RTG-rule by coding the implicit operations of projection, tupling and composition as nonterminals or terminals. This becomes possible simply by viewing the terms appearing in the rules of the MCFG as elements of a free $\mathbb{N}\times\mathbb{N}$-sorted Lawvere algebra. The resulting RTG then "operates on" this Lawvere algebra. Recall that we are using a simple example MCFG with maximally one nonterminal on the RHSs and therefore do not have to build tuples from tuples.

Intuitively, again, we have to make the implicit operations which are "hidden" in the standard presentation of the MCFG-rules explicit. Simply using a tuple, e.g., the pair $\langle a,b\rangle$, means that we need an explicit tupling operator $(\;)$ to combine a and b. In the same spirit, as outlined above, using x_0x_1 means that the values of the two variables are concatenated with an implicit concatenation operator. And finally, applying a function to some arguments is a composition c of the function with its arguments. Note that thereby the function becomes a constant, i.e., we reify the function. In this sense, a term such as $f(a,b)$ becomes more complex: $c(c(f,(\;)(x_1,x_2)),(\;)(a,b))$. The next step is to translate these single-sorted terms into the corresponding many-sorted Lawvere algebra.[37]

For $1 \le i \le 3$, let π_i^3 denote the i-th projection which maps a 3-tuple of strings from V_T^* to its i-th component, i.e., a 1-tuple. Therefore the corre-

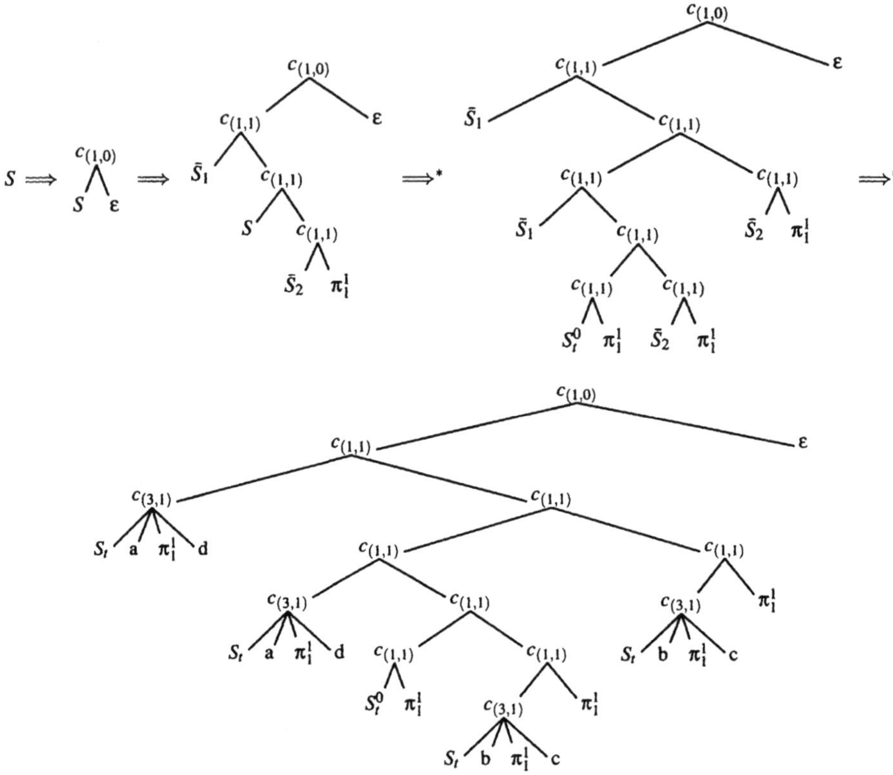

Figure 10.9: An example derivation of the lifted MCFTG Γ^L_{TAG} given in Example 10.12

sponding Lawvere arity of π_1^3, π_2^3 and π_3^3 is $(3,1)$. Let '•' denote the usual binary operation of concatenation defined for strings from V_T^*, i.e., '•' maps a 2-tuple to a 1-tuple. Thus '•' is of Lawvere arity $(2,1)$. Similarly, the corresponding (Lawvere) arity of terminals is $(0,1)$ and of nonterminals $(0,a)$, where a stands for the arity of the nonterminal.

In the following paragraphs, we will sketch the translation T from non-terminal rules of the example MCFG to RTG-rules. T takes each rule $X \longrightarrow f(Y)$, where $X, Y \in V_N$ and $f \in V_F$, of the MCFG including the corresponding definition of the mapping $f(x_1, \ldots, x_k)$ with $k \geq 0$ and transforms it into a RTG-rule as follows. We create a mother node labeled with the appropriate binary composition $c_{(j,k,l)}$ such that the left daughter contains the "lifted" version of $f(x_1, \ldots, x_k)$ under $\text{LIFT}_{Lawvere}$ and the right daughter the translation of the nonterminal Y (a formal definition of $\text{LIFT}_{Lawvere}$ follows below). Both nonterminals X and Y are used "unchanged", but annotated with the corresponding Lawvere arity resulting in the following schematic presentation of the translation: $X_{(j,l)} \longrightarrow c_{(j,k,l)}(\text{LIFTL}(f(x_1,\ldots,x_k)), Y_{(j,k)})$, where f is a mapping from k-tuples to l-tuples of terminal strings.

Note that having more than one nonterminal on the RHS of an MCFG-rule leads to an RTG-rule which requires an additional tupling node above the corresponding nonterminals in the second argument of the composition. This tupling node has to contain the information how to compose the tuples resulting from the computation of the nonterminals, e.g., if the tuple is of length four and dominates two nonterminals, the first nonterminal could contribute one, two or three components and correspondingly the second nonterminal three, two or one component. Suppose we indicate this splitting with a superscript. So, there is no unique tupling node of a certain type anymore, but a family of tupling operators of each type which can be differentiated via their superscripts, i.e., for a given MCFG rule $X \longrightarrow f(Y_1,\ldots,Y_n)$ the resulting RTG rule looks as follows

$$X_{(j,l)} \longrightarrow c_{(j,k,l)}(\text{LIFTL}(f(x_1,\ldots,x_k)), (\ )^s_{(j,k)}(Y_{(j,k_1)},\ldots,Y_{(j,k_n)}))$$

for $k = k_1 \cdots k_n$. Looking ahead, the superscript is needed to guide the tree-walking automaton into the right branch of the lifted tree. This presupposes that we also have more detailed projection symbols which can actually refer to the components of a particular tuple such that the tree-walking automaton computing a π-link can actually determine the correct filler. All of this can be implemented via a nondeterministic traversal of the relevant daughters of such a special tupling node. Since there is no insight gained by an exact specification of the necessary schematic representation, we omit this – in our case trivial – tupling node and all the ensuing complications in the example for better readability.

After this intuitive presentation of the translation of MCFG rules, we formally define the translation $\text{LIFT}_{Lawvere}$ of the functions as follows:[38]

Definition 10.13 ($\text{LIFT}_{Lawvere}$). Let $\mathcal{S}$ be a set or sorts, $\Sigma = \{\Sigma_{w,s} \mid \langle w,s\rangle \in \mathcal{S}^*\times\mathcal{S}\}$ be an $\mathcal{S}^*\times\mathcal{S}$-indexed set and $X_k = \{x_1,\ldots,x_k\}$, $k \in \mathbb{N}$, a finite set of variables. The *derived* $\mathcal{S}^*\times\mathcal{S}$-sorted alphabet Σ^L (indexed by $(\mathcal{S}^*\times\mathcal{S})^*\times(\mathcal{S}^*\times\mathcal{S}))$ is defined as follows: For each $w \in \mathcal{S}^*, s \in \mathcal{S}$, $\Sigma'_{\varepsilon,\langle w,s\rangle} = \{f' \mid f \in \Sigma_{w,s}\}$ is a new set of symbols of sort $(\varepsilon,\langle w,s\rangle)$; for each $w = w_1\cdots w_n \in \mathcal{S}^*$ and each $i, 1 \leq i \leq n$, π^w_i is a new symbol of sort $(\varepsilon,\langle w,w_i\rangle)$, the ith *projection symbol*;

for each $u,v,w \in \mathcal{S}^*$ the new symbol $c_{(u,v,w)}$ is the *composition symbol* of sort $(\langle u,v\rangle\langle v,w\rangle, \langle u,w\rangle)$ and for each $u,v \in \mathcal{S}^*$ the new symbol $(\ )_{(v,u)}$ is the *tupling symbol* of sort $(\langle v,u_1\rangle \cdots \langle v,u_n\rangle, \langle v,u\rangle)$.

$$\begin{aligned}
\Sigma^L_{\varepsilon,\langle w,s\rangle} &= \Sigma'_{\varepsilon,\langle w,s\rangle} \\
\Sigma^L_{\varepsilon,\langle w,w_i\rangle} &= \{\pi^w_i \mid 1 \le i \le n\} \quad \text{for } w = w_1 \cdots w_n \in \mathcal{S}^* \\
\Sigma^L_{\langle v,u_1\rangle\cdots\langle v,u_n\rangle,\langle v,u\rangle} &= \{(\ )_{(v,u)}\} \quad \text{for } v,u,u_i \in \mathcal{S}^* \text{ and} \\
&\qquad\qquad u = u_1 \cdots u_n, 1 \le i \le n, n \in \mathbb{N} \\
\Sigma^L_{\langle u,v\rangle\langle v,w\rangle,\langle u,w\rangle} &= \{c_{(u,v,w)}\} \text{ for } u,v,w \in \mathcal{S}^*
\end{aligned}$$

For $k \ge 0$, $\langle w,s\rangle \in \mathcal{S}^* \times \mathcal{S}$, $\mathrm{LIFTL}^{\Sigma}_{w,s} : T(\Sigma(X_k),s) \to T(\Sigma^L, \langle w,s\rangle)$ is defined as follows:

$$\begin{aligned}
\mathrm{LIFTL}^{\Sigma}_{w,s}(x_i) &= \pi^w_{i\,(w,w_i)} \\
\mathrm{LIFTL}^{\Sigma}_{w,s}(f) &= f'_{(\varepsilon,s)} \text{ for } f \in \Sigma_{\varepsilon,\langle\varepsilon,s\rangle} \\
\mathrm{LIFTL}^{\Sigma}_{w,s}(\langle t_1,\ldots,t_n\rangle) &= (\ )_{(v,u)}(\mathrm{LIFTL}^{\Sigma}_{w,s}(t_1),\ldots,\mathrm{LIFTL}^{\Sigma}_{w,s}(t_n)) \\
&\qquad \text{where each } \mathrm{LIFTL}^{\Sigma}_{w,s}(t_i), 1 \le i \le n, \text{ is of sort} \\
&\qquad (v,u_i),\ u = u_1 \ldots u_n \text{ and } t_1,\ldots,t_n \in T(\Sigma(X_k),s) \\
\mathrm{LIFTL}^{\Sigma}_{w,s}(f(t_1,\ldots,t_n)) &= c_{(u,v,w)}(f'_{(v,w)}, (\ )_{(u,v)}(\mathrm{LIFTL}^{\Sigma}_{w,s}(t_1),\ldots,\mathrm{LIFTL}^{\Sigma}(t_n))) \\
&\qquad \text{where each } \mathrm{LIFTL}^{\Sigma}_{w,s}(t_i), 1 \le i \le n, \text{ is of sort} \\
&\qquad (u,v_i) \text{ and } f \in \Sigma_{\varepsilon,\langle v,w\rangle}, v = v_1 \ldots v_n, \text{ and} \\
&\qquad t_1,\ldots,t_n \in T(\Sigma(X_k),s)
\end{aligned}$$

Again, we continue an example. The grammar $\mathcal{G}'_{MCFG}$ is the result of applying the lifting algorithm to $\mathcal{G}_{MCFG}$ given in Example 10.9 on page 141. For readability, we give the typing information separately and not immediately in the definition of $\mathcal{G}'_{MCFG}$.

Example 10.14. The grammar $\mathcal{G}'_{MCFG} = \langle\{S,A\},\{a_1,a_2,a_3\},S,P\rangle$ resulting from the lifting process has the productions given below. The productions rely on the fact that the nonterminals and new symbols have the following Lawvere types

S, a_1, a_2, a_3	:	$(0,1)$	$\pi_1^3, \pi_2^3, \pi_3^3$	:	$(3,1)$
A	:	$(0,3)$	c	:	of various types
$\bullet$	:	$(2,1)$	$(\;)$	:	of various types

Then the three rules can be displayed graphically as follows:

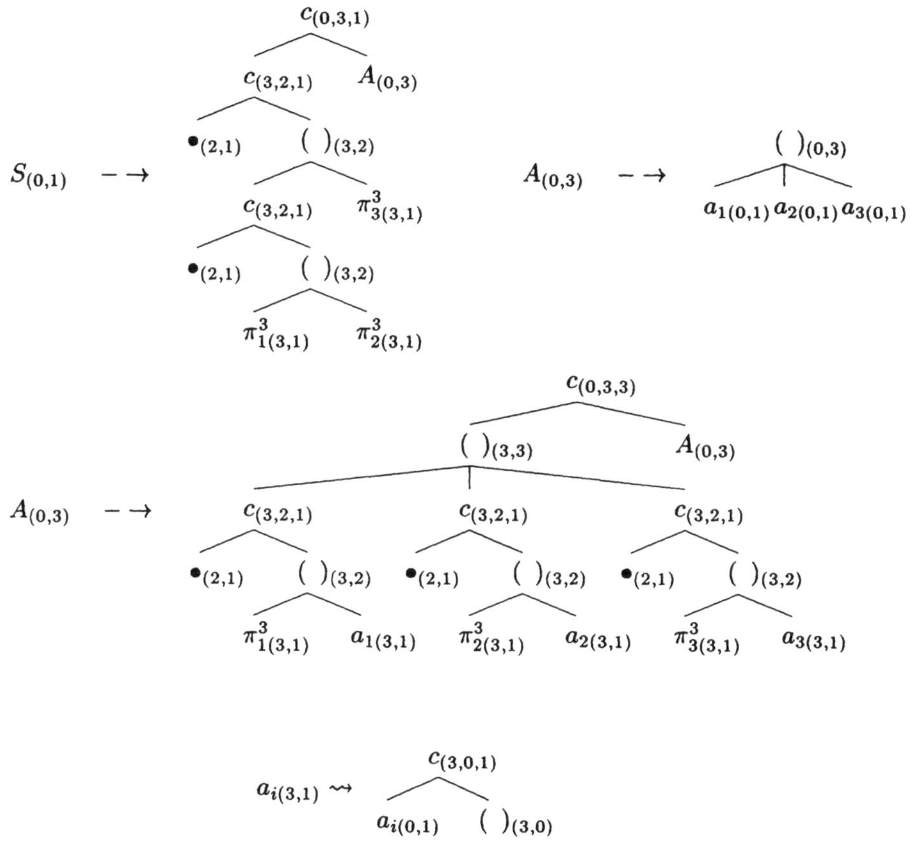

These rules contain the simplification indicated with the $\rightsquigarrow$ symbol in the last line. Whenever a terminal of type $(3,1)$ appears, it stands for the given complex tree.

In Figure 10.10 on the following page, we find an example derivation of the lifted grammar $\mathcal{G}'_{MCFG}$ parallel to the derivation given in Example 10.9 on page 141 for the MCFG $\mathcal{G}_{MCFG}$. This derivation also contains the simplification described above.

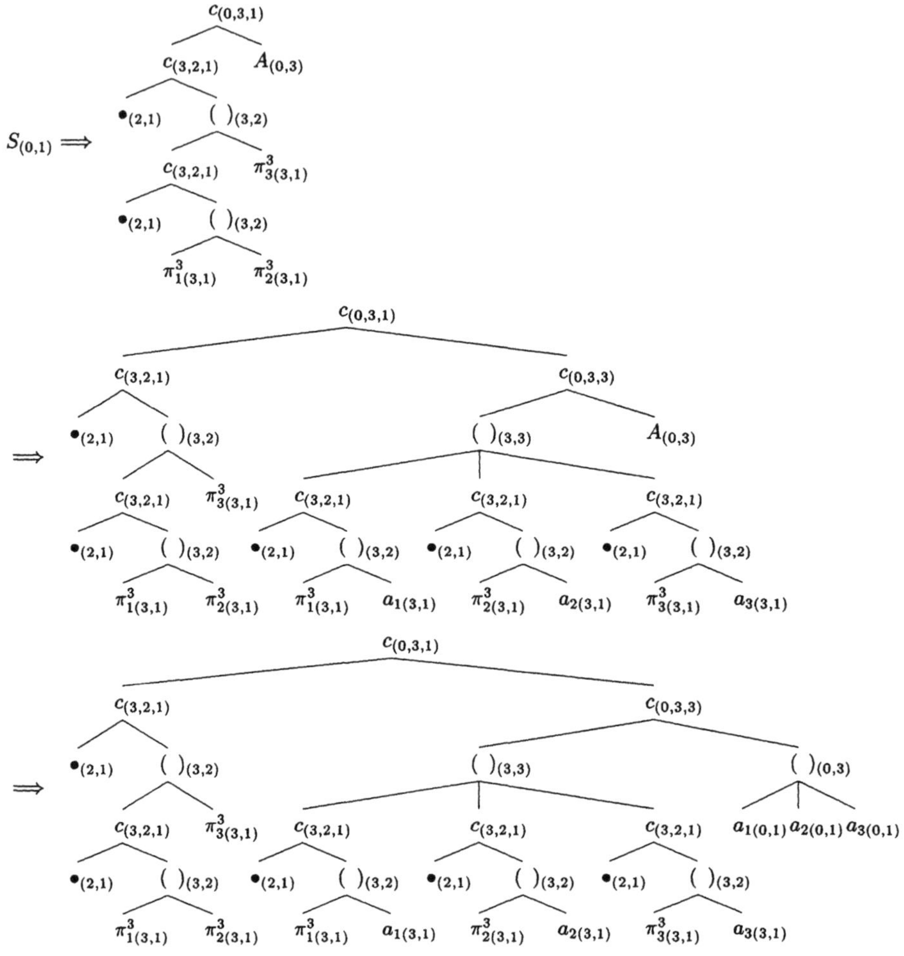

Figure 10.10: An example derivation of the lifted MCFG $\mathcal{G}'_{MCFG}$ given in Example 10.14

10.3 Coding the lifted structures

In the previous section we have shown how to code the non-context-free structures with regular tree grammars via lifting. In the last part of this chapter, we will show how to code RTGs themselves with FSTAs and from there with MSO logic. Or, more precisely, we will show how to construct an FSTA which recognizes the tree language of a given RTG. Furthermore, we will give an MSO formula which characterizes the same set of trees as well.

10.3.1 Tree automata

Since Γ^L in (10.11) generates a regular set of trees, we can construct a tree automaton $\mathfrak{A}_{\Gamma^L} = \langle Q, \Sigma, \delta, q_0, Q_f \rangle$ to recognize this set.

Construction of a tree automaton from a given lifted context-free tree grammar $\Gamma^L = \langle \Sigma^L, F^L, S', P^L \rangle$, i.e., an RTG, is straightforward. Intuitively, since tree automata recognize only local trees in each transition, we have to use auxiliary transitions for RHSs of lifted macro productions with trees of depth greater than one in order to recognize the correct trees incrementally. So, what we are doing is decomposing the RHSs into trees of depth one which can then be recognized by a transition, i.e., a preliminary step involves transforming Γ^L into a normal form $\Gamma^{NF} = \langle \Sigma^L, F^{NF}, S', P^{NF} \rangle$ via the introduction of auxiliary rules and new nonterminals. In our example, the lifted tree grammar is not in the desired normal form, but it is easy to see how to change this. For example, the production $F' \longrightarrow c(F', c(\bullet', a', \pi_1^4), \pi_2^4, c(\bullet', c', \pi_3^4), \pi_4^4)$ is transformed into the following three new productions:

$$\begin{aligned} F' &\longrightarrow c(F', C_a, \pi_2^4, C_c, \pi_4^4), \\ C_a &\longrightarrow c(\bullet', a', \pi_1^4) \text{ and} \\ C_c &\longrightarrow c(\bullet', c', \pi_3^4). \end{aligned}$$

The full translation of the other productions into the corresponding normal form is left to the reader. The resulting rules and nonterminals are reflected both in the new transitions and in the states we need. In the following, we assume without loss of generality, that the trees on the RHSs of the lifted macro productions are of depth one.

Recall that, according to the definition above, a tree automaton operates on a ranked alphabet $\Sigma = \langle \Sigma_n \mid n \in \mathbb{N} \rangle$. Therefore, in our case, we use the inoperative symbols of the lifted grammar to construct Σ, but we reduce the explicit many-sorted type information by defining Σ_n as $\{\sigma \in \Sigma^L \mid rank(\sigma) = n\}$. For the set of states Q, we need distinguishable states for each of the terminals, nonterminals and projection symbols appearing in RHSs of the rules. Furthermore, we need a new initial state q_0, i.e., $Q = \{q_\sigma \mid \sigma \in \Sigma^L_{\varepsilon,s} \cup F^{NF}\} \cup \{q_0\}$.[39] In the automaton, the state which corresponds to the start symbol S' of the grammar becomes the single final state, i.e., $Q_f = \{q_{S'}\}$.

Since our tree automata work bottom up, we have to start the processing at the bottom by having transitions from the new initial state to a new state encoding that we read a particular symbol on the frontier of the tree. So,

$$\mathfrak{A}_{\Gamma^L} = \langle Q, \Sigma, \delta, q_0, \{q_{S'}\} \rangle$$

$$\delta : \bigcup_{1 \leq n \leq 5} Q^n \times \Sigma \rightarrow Q$$

$$\begin{array}{lcl@{\qquad}rcl}
(q_0, \varepsilon) & \rightarrow & q_\varepsilon & (q_{\bullet'}, q_{a'}, q_{\pi_1}, c) & \rightarrow & q_{C_a} \\
(q_0, a') & \rightarrow & q_{a'} & (q_{\bullet'}, q_{c'}, q_{\pi_3}, c) & \rightarrow & q_{C_c} \\
(q_0, b') & \rightarrow & q_{b'} & (q_{\bullet'}, q_{b'}, q_{\pi_2}, c) & \rightarrow & q_{C_b} \\
(q_0, c') & \rightarrow & q_{c'} & (q_{\bullet'}, q_{d'}, q_{\pi_4}, c) & \rightarrow & q_{C_d} \\
(q_0, d') & \rightarrow & q_{d'} & (q_{\bullet'}, q_{\pi_1}, q_{\pi_2}, c) & \rightarrow & q_{C_2} \\
(q_0, \pi_1) & \rightarrow & q_{\pi_1} & (q_{\bullet'}, q_{C_2}, q_{\pi_3}, c) & \rightarrow & q_{C_3} \\
(q_0, \pi_2) & \rightarrow & q_{\pi_2} & (q_{\bullet'}, q_{C_3}, q_{\pi_4}, c) & \rightarrow & q_{F'} \\
(q_0, \pi_3) & \rightarrow & q_{\pi_3} & (q_{F'}, q_{\pi_1}, q_{C_b}, q_{\pi_3}, q_{C_d}, c) & \rightarrow & q_{F'} \\
(q_0, \pi_4) & \rightarrow & q_{\pi_4} & (q_{F'}, q_{C_a}, q_{\pi_2}, q_{C_c}, q_{\pi_4}, c) & \rightarrow & q_{F'} \\
(q_0, \bullet') & \rightarrow & q_{\bullet'} & (q_{F'}, q_\varepsilon, q_b, q_\varepsilon, q_d, c) & \rightarrow & q_{S'} \\
(q_0, \varepsilon) & \rightarrow & q_{S'} & (q_{F'}, q_a, q_\varepsilon, q_c, q_\varepsilon, c) & \rightarrow & q_{S'}
\end{array}$$

Figure 10.11: The tree automaton for Γ^L

together with the transitions encoding the productions, we have to construct two kinds of transitions in δ:

- transitions from the initial state on all subtrees reading a terminal symbol σ, i.e., elements of all the Σ_i from Γ, to the corresponding state; i.e., $q_0 \times \sigma \rightarrow q_\sigma$;

- transitions recognizing the internal structure of the local trees appearing in RHSs, i.e., from the states corresponding to the leaves of a tree on a RHS to the nonterminal D of the left hand side, i.e., for each lifted tree grammar production of depth one $D \longrightarrow c(d_1, \ldots, d_n)$ we have to construct a transition in the automaton which looks as follows: $q_{d_1} \times \cdots \times q_{d_n} \times c \rightarrow q_D$.

Accordingly, the tree automaton corresponding to the RTG Γ^L given in Example 10.11 on page 143 looks as given in Figure 10.11. As the reader can easily check, the automaton recognizes the same set of trees.

10.3.2 MSO logic

Alternatively, we can also code RTGs with MSO logic. The standard way of doing this requires that we first construct the corresponding tree automaton.

In Thomas (1990) tree automata are converted to formulas in MSO logic by basically encoding their behaviour. Under the assumption that we have a state set $Q = \{0, \ldots, m\}$ with the initial state $q_0 = 0$, the (closed) Σ_1^1-formula $\varphi_{\mathfrak{A}_{\Gamma L}}$ given there adapted to our signature and for maximally 5-ary tree automata looks as given below. P_a stands for the predicate labeling a node with the symbol a and $\mathsf{leaf}(x) \overset{def}{\Longleftrightarrow} (\neg\exists y)[x \triangleleft y]$.

Intuitively, the sets X_i label the tree where the automaton assumes state i. The first two lines of the formula say that we cannot have a node which is in two states and that X_0 is our "initial" set; the second one licenses the distribution of the sets according to the transitions and the last one says that we need a root node which is in a "final" set.

$$\begin{aligned}
\varphi_{\mathfrak{A}_{\Gamma L}} \overset{def}{\Longleftrightarrow} (\exists X_0, \ldots, X_m)[& \bigwedge_{i \neq j} (\neg\exists y)[y \in X_i \wedge y \in X_j] \wedge \\
& (\forall x)[\mathsf{leaf}(x) \rightarrow x \in X_0] \\
\bigwedge_{1 \leq l \leq 5} (\forall x_1, \ldots, x_l, y)[& \bigvee_{\substack{(i_1, \ldots, i_l, \sigma, j) \in \delta \\ 1 \leq k \leq l}} x_k \in X_{i_k} \wedge y \triangleleft x_k \wedge y \in X_j \wedge y \in P_\sigma] \\
& \bigvee_{i \in Q_f} (\exists x \forall y)[x \triangleleft^* y \wedge x \in X_i]
\end{aligned}$$

In Kolb et al. (1999a) we also propose a way of directly coding the behaviour of the RTG with logical formulas. Since this does not contribute any new insights, the interested reader is referred to the paper for further information.

We refrain from giving more examples of both the construction of FSTAs and MSO formulas from RTGs in the interest of brevity. We think that the constructions are simple enough that nothing is lost by the omission. Nevertheless, we later use a similar formula $\varphi_{\mathfrak{A}_{\mathcal{G}'_{MCFG}}}$ for the tree automaton $\mathfrak{A}_{\mathcal{G}'_{MCFG}}$ coding the behaviour of the lifted example MCFG $\mathcal{G}'_{MCFG}$.

10.4 Summing up the first step

We can summarize the preceding chapter outlining the first step as follows: Various forms of tree grammars have been motivated to be adequate representations of (some) natural language formalisms. Due to the needed descriptive complexity, the formalisms are not characterizable by MSO logic. Therefore we introduced the step of lifting. lifting modifies the generated structures by inserting explicit control information into the trees such that they are characterizable with regular means: the lifted structures of both CFTGs and MCFGs can be coded equivalently with RTGs, FSTAs and MSO logic. Therefore we have one formalism with the desired duality of an equivalent operational and denotational semantics.

Chapter 11

The second step: Reconstruction

Unfortunately, the terminal trees of a lifted tree grammars presented in Figure 10.8 on page 144, Figure 10.9 on page 146 and Figure 10.10 on page 150 generated/recognized by the grammars Γ^L, Γ^L_{TAG} or G'_{MCFG} given in the Examples 10.11, 10.12 and 10.14 or the tree automaton in Figure 10.11 on page 152, don't seem to have much in common with the structures linguists want to talk about, i.e., the structures generated by the "original" grammars which are presented in Figure 10.5 on page 137, Figure 10.6 on page 139 or Example 10.9 on page 141.

However, the lifted structures contain the intended structures. As mentioned before, there is a mapping h from these explicit structures onto structures interpreting the compositions (the c's), tuplings (the $(\ )$'s) and the projections (the π's) the way the names we have given them suggest, *viz.* as compositions, tuplings and projections, respectively, which are, in fact, exactly the intended structures.

On the denotational side, we will implement the mapping h with an MSO definable tree transduction (as defined in Section 5.6 on page 80) and operationally with both tree-walking automata (defined in Section 4.3 on page 53) and Macro Tree Transducer (see Section 4.4.2 on page 56) to transform the lifted structures into the intended ones. Each of the following sections will address the approaches reconstructing lifted CFTGs, MCFTGs and MCFGs.

Let us restate our goal then: Rogers (1998) has shown the suitability of an MSO description language $L^2_{K,P}$ for linguistics which is based upon the primitive relations of immediate ($\triangleleft$), proper ($\triangleleft^+$) and reflexive ($\triangleleft^*$) dominance and proper precedence ($\prec$). We will show how to define these relations with an MSO transduction, an FSTWA or an MTT thereby implementing the unique homomorphism mapping the terms into elements of the corresponding context-free tree language, i.e., the trees linguists want to talk about.

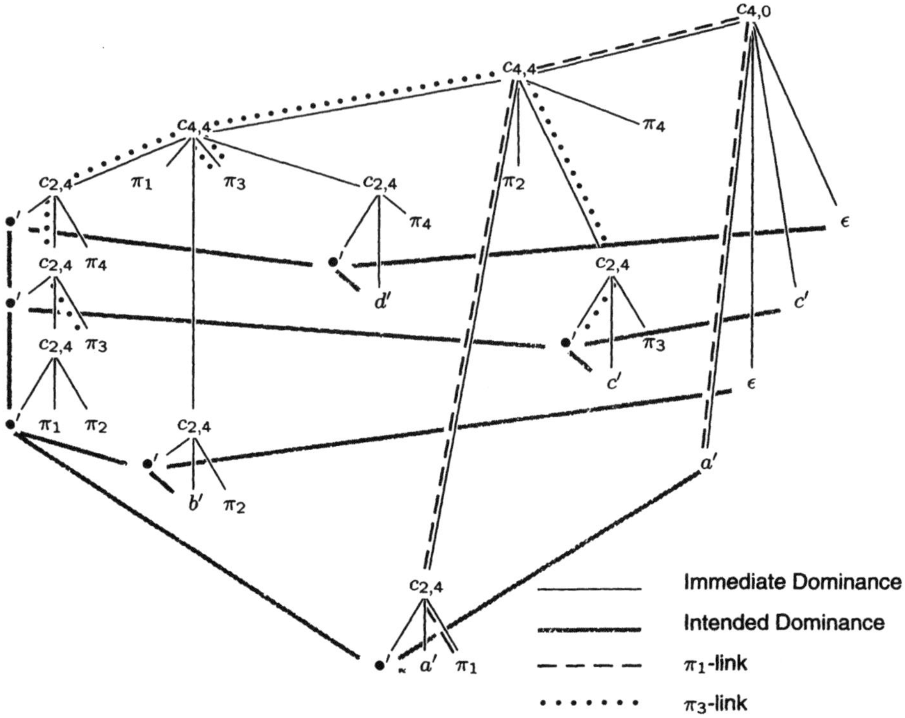

Figure 11.1: Intended relations on a lifted structure: CFTGs

Put differently, it should be possible to define a set of relations $R^I = \{\blacktriangleleft, \blacktriangleleft^+, \blacktriangleleft^*$ *(dominance)*, *c-command*, $\lhd$ *(precedence)*,...$\}$ holding between the nodes $n \in N^L$ of the explicit or lifted tree T^L which carry a *"linguistic"* label L in such a way, that when interpreting $\blacktriangleleft^* \in R^I$ as a tree order on the set of *"linguistic"* nodes and $\lhd \in R^I$ as the precedence relation on the resulting structure, we have a "new" description language on the intended structures.

11.1 Reconstructing lifted (M)CFTGs

As mentioned, we will use both an MSO definable tree transduction built upon tree-walking automata and an MTT to transform the lifted structures into the intended ones. The core of this transduction will be the definition of the new relations via tree-walking automata. In what follows, we will confine ourselves almost exclusively to the dominance relation from which most linguistically relevant relations can be derived.

To do so, it is helpful to note a few general facts (illustrated in Figure 11.1 on the facing page with another rendering of the last tree of the derivation given in Figure 10.8 on page 144):

1. Our trees – that no longer contain substitutable elements from F_0 – feature three families of labels: the "linguistic" symbols, i.e., the lifted inoperatives of the underlying macro-grammar, $\mathsf{L} = \text{lift}(\bigcup_{n\geq 0}\Sigma_n)$; the "composition" symbols $\mathsf{C} = \{c_{n,k}\}, n,k \geq 0$; and the "projection" symbols Π.

2. All non-terminal nodes in T^L are labeled by some $c_{n,k} \in \mathsf{C}$. This is due to the fact that the "composition" symbols are the only non-terminals of a lifted grammar. No terminal node is labeled by some $c_{n,k}$.

3. The terminal nodes in T^L are either labeled by some "linguistic" symbol or by some "projection" symbol $\pi_i \in \Pi$.

4. Any "linguistic" node properly dominating anything in the intended tree is on some left branch in T^L, i.e., it is the left-most daughter of some $c_{n,k} \in \mathsf{C}$. This lies in the nature of composition: $c_{n,k}(x_0, x_1, \ldots, x_n)$ evaluates to $x_0(x_1, \ldots, x_n)$.

5. For any node p labeled with some "projection" symbol $\pi_i \in \Pi$ in T^L there is a unique node μ (labeled with some $c_{n,k} \in \mathsf{C}$ by (2.)) which properly dominates p and whose i-th sister will eventually evaluate to the value of π. Moreover, μ will be the first node properly dominating p which is on a left branch. This crucial fact is arrived at by easy induction on the construction of Γ^L from Γ. The intuition of the induction is as follows. The construction of Γ^L involves making each operative nonterminal into a leftmost daughter. The variables of that operative are instantiated (in the unlifted version) by applying the rule to some existing tree(s). The fillers for the variables (and therefore the projection symbols) will be found in those trees. So, we have to find the topmost element of a RHS (which will be a composition symbol) and the fillers will be somewhere in its sisters.

By (4.) it is not hard to find possible dominees in any T^L. It is the problem of determining the actual "filler" of a candidate-dominee which makes up the complexity of the definition of $\blacktriangleleft$. There are three cases to account for:

6. If the node considered carries a "linguistic" label, it evaluates to itself;

7. if it has a "composition" label $c_{n,k}$, it evaluates to whatever its function symbol – by (4.) its leftmost daughter – evaluates to;

8. if it carries a "projection" label π_i, it evaluates to whatever the node it "points to" – by (5.) the ith sister of the first C-node on a left branch dominating it – evaluates to. Two examples for π-links can be found in Figure 11.1 on page 156.

Note that cases (7.) and (8.) are inherently recursive such that a simple MSO definition cannot be found.

11.1.1 Reconstruction with FSTWAs

In general, recursive definitions in MSO may lead to undecidability and are therefore disallowed. Fortunately, as we presented in Section 5.5 on page 75, there are certain techniques to ensure that some relation R which would most naturally be defined recursively has a valid MSO definition. Still, special care has to be taken to establish that the relations defined are well-behaved in this respect. In our case this caveat applies to $\blacktriangleleft$ as well as to its reflexive transitive closure $\blacktriangleleft^*$.

In Figure 11.1 on page 156 the π_1-link and the π_3-link are examples of such a path from the projection symbol to the corresponding filler.

Following Bloem and Engelfriet (1997a), we will use a *(basic) tree-walking automaton with node-label tests* to specify the *intended* (immediate) dominance relation on lifted trees (indicated in Figure 11.1 on page 156 with slightly thicker grey lines), thus showing in passing that it is a regular tree node relation.

To keep the automaton small and perspicuous, we consider the case with ternary (binary) branching in the explicit (intended) trees and macros with at most four parameters. This is probably the only linguistically relevant case. The extension to the general case, however, is trivial, as long as branching is bounded by some $n < \omega$.

We define $\mathfrak{A}_{\blacktriangleleft} = (Q, \Delta, \delta, I, F)$ with states Q, directives Δ, transitions δ and the initial and final states $I \subseteq Q$ and $F \subseteq Q$, respectively, as given graphically in Figure 11.2 on the facing page. Construction of the automaton is based upon the careful analysis of the trees involved which has been given above. We have to "undo" the lifting process by associating the old function symbols, i.e., the intended interior nodes, via the composition symbols with

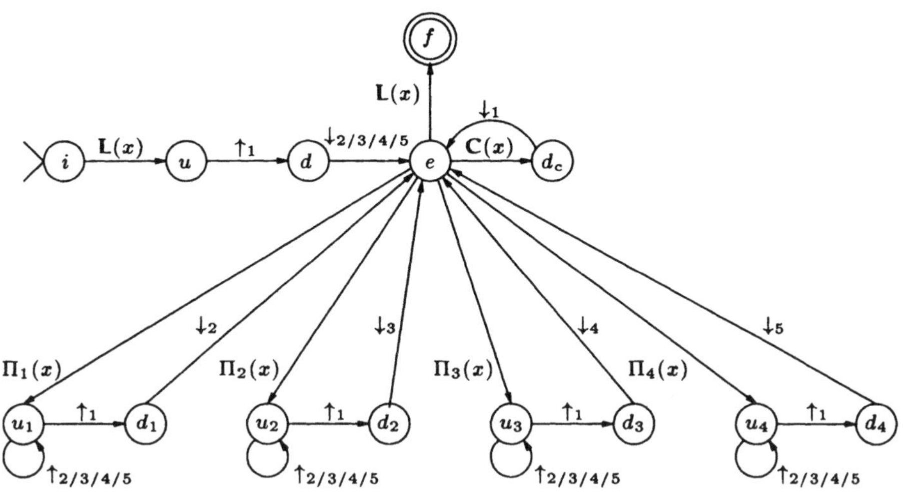

Figure 11.2: The FSTWA for dominance on intended structures: CFTGs

their respective daughters. Basically, the facts we presented in (6.) through (8.) above are implemented.

The automaton works as follows (we annotate the text with the states the automaton is in): First of all (start state *i*), if we can read a "linguistic" label on the node we started in (state *u*) and if that node is the first (leftmost) daughter (state *d*), we go to one of its sisters (state *e*). Then depending on the case we are in, we can again "read" a linguistic label and halt (state *f*), or read a composition symbol (state d_c) and find the leftmost daughter (state *e*), or read a projection symbol (one of the states u_1 to u_4) and find the corresponding node by walking upward until we are on a leftmost daughter (one of the states d_1 to d_4) and then finding the second, third, forth or fifth sister respectively (state *e*). The automaton is universal in the sense that the only variable part it contains is the number of projection functions we have to deal with, i.e., the number of the needed "triangles" in the lower part of the automaton.

As indicated in Section 4.3 on page 53, $\mathfrak{A}_{\blacktriangleleft}$ specifies, for any tree t, the node relation

$$\blacktriangleleft_t \quad = \quad R_t(\mathfrak{A}_{\blacktriangleleft}) = \quad \{(x,y) \mid \text{there is a successful run of } \mathfrak{A} \text{ on } t \text{ starting in an initial state at node } x \text{ and ending at node } y \text{ in a final one}\}.$$

However, there is another interpretation of such a tree-walking automaton.

Viewed as an ordinary FSA over the alphabet Δ, $\mathfrak{A}$ recognizes a regular (string-) language, the *walking language* W; in our case the walking-language

$$W_{\blacktriangleleft} = \mathsf{L}(x) \cdot \uparrow_1 \cdot (\downarrow_2 \cup \downarrow_3 \cup \downarrow_4 \cup \downarrow_5) \cdot (W_{\mathsf{C}} \cup W_{\Pi_1} \cup W_{\Pi_2} \cup W_{\Pi_3} \cup W_{\Pi_4})^* \cdot \mathsf{L}(x)$$

with

$$\begin{aligned} W_{\mathsf{C}} &= \mathsf{C}(x) \cdot \downarrow_1 \\ W_{\Pi_i} &= \Pi_i(x) \cdot (\uparrow_2 \cup \uparrow_3 \cup \uparrow_4 \cup \uparrow_5)^* \cdot \uparrow_1 \cdot \downarrow_{i+1} \end{aligned}$$

which is finally translated into an MSO-formula $\mathsf{trans}_{W_{\blacktriangleleft}}(x,y)$.[40] The rather tedious process, carried through in Appendix C.1 on page 207, proceeds inductively via the translation steps given in (5.3) on page 79.

Therefore the resulting formula uses only the MSO definable tests of the original automaton, the closed sets constructed via (5.5) on page 80 for the Kleene-$*$-case, and the edg_n relations (here with $1 \leq n \leq 5$) defined in (5.4).

$$x \blacktriangleleft y \overset{def}{\Longleftrightarrow} \mathsf{trans}_{W_{\blacktriangleleft}}(x,y)$$

Recall that for the case of the recursion inherent in reflexive dominance a standard solution exists via a second-order property which holds of the sets of nodes which are closed under the relevant relation. We repeat the original definition (5.5) here for convenience.

$$R\text{-}\mathsf{closed}(X) \overset{def}{\Longleftrightarrow} (\forall x,y)[x \in X \wedge R(x,y) \rightarrow y \in X]$$

Now, for any node n, the intersection of all such closed sets which contain n is exactly the set of m, such that $R^*(n,m)$. Since we are dealing with the (finite) trees generated by a context-free grammar, this construction can be safely exploited for our purposes; $\blacktriangleleft^*$ and $\blacktriangleleft^+$ can be defined as follows:

Reflexive Dominance:

$$x \blacktriangleleft^* y \overset{def}{\Longleftrightarrow} (\forall X)[\blacktriangleleft\text{-}\mathsf{closed}(X) \wedge x \in X \rightarrow y \in X]$$

Proper dominance:

$$x \blacktriangleleft^+ y \overset{def}{\Longleftrightarrow} x \blacktriangleleft^* y \wedge x \not\approx y$$

To further exemplify the constructions using tree-walking automata, we also give the one dealing with the TAG example (see Example 10.12 on page 144) in Figure 11.4 on page 162. But first consider the tree displayed in

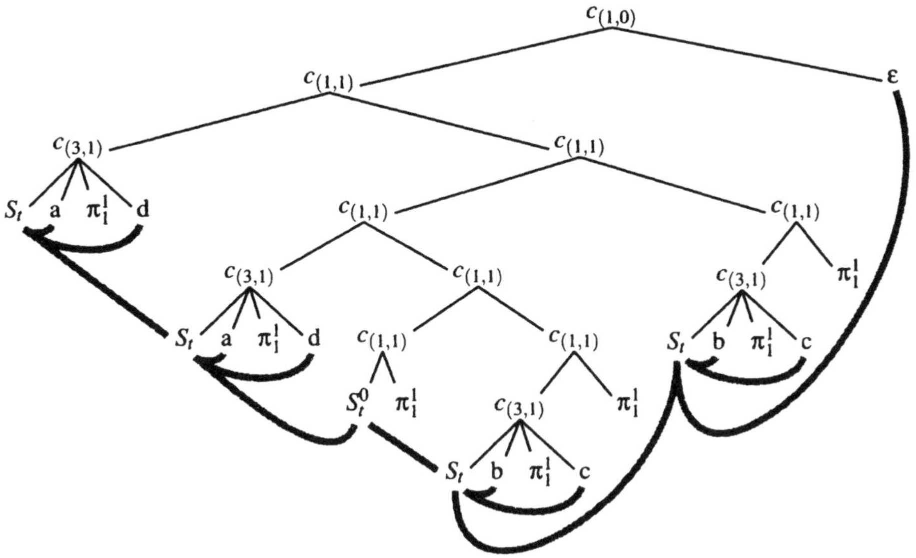

Figure 11.3: Intended relations on a lifted structure: MCFTGs

Figure 11.3 which again contains the last tree of the derivation given in Figure 10.9 on page 146. The intended tree is indicated with the thicker, mostly curved lines. Note that the order of the lines does not reflect the order of the nodes in the tree. Precedence has to be defined separately. The deliberations parallel to (1.)–(8.) are left as an exercise to the reader. In fact, all that is needed is a limitation to one projection function and a reduction of the number of possible daughters and correspondingly the tree-walking automaton is much simpler. All we have to do here is to reconstruct the daughters of the function symbols by going up and down again and possibly resolving the single (recursive) case of finding the filler for the projection symbol.

We must also give a tree-walking automaton for the intended precedence relation, similar to the automaton for dominance. We will do this only for this simplest case of MCFTGs since the argument and the construction of the automaton involved are fairly complex. The use of MCFTGs allows us to ignore the interactions between several variables on one level. Note furthermore that the RTGs in all the examples we have given are *linear* RTGs, i.e., they use each variable only once in any RHS. If the automata were not linear, then the copying of nodes makes it very hard to unravel the intended relationships. Consequently, we can present the definition for precedence as follows.

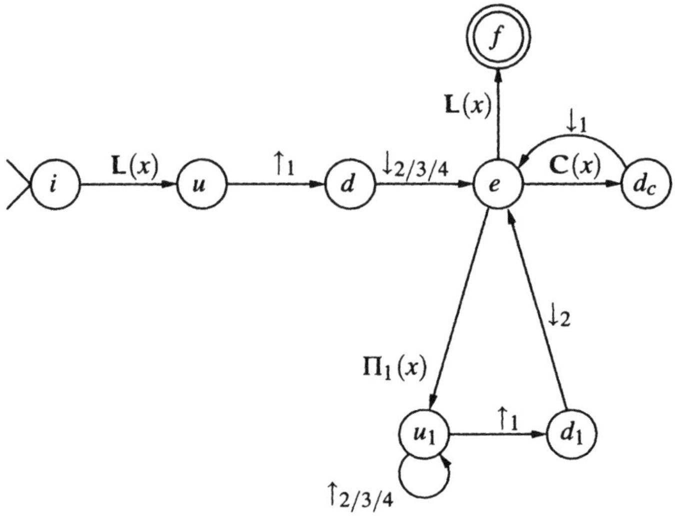

Figure 11.4: The FSTWA for dominance on intended structures: MCFTGs

The first step is defined with an FSTWA which encodes the *immediate* precedence relations between sisters. Then we define precedence following the same reasoning as before, namely as *proper* precedence, based upon the definition of immediate precedence.

Looking at the example in Figure 11.3 on the page before, what can we observe concerning precedence? The linguistically labeled terminals seem to appear in the right order such that precedence reduces to sisterhood. But what happens with the intended interior nodes? And how should we treat the projection nodes? The nonterminals have to be inserted for the "right" projection symbols and then precedence is reducible to sisterhood. But finding the correct projection symbol for a filler is non-trivial.

The FSTWA given in Figure 11.5 on the facing page basically consists of two parts: the first part deals with those cases where the nodes which are labeled with a linguistic label are already sisters (i.e., the intended terminal nodes), or have a node labeled with a projection node as sister (i.e., they precede a nonterminal). Between them we simply have an immediate precedence relation which, in the case of a projection node, has to be found via a further traversal of the tree. In Figure 11.5 on the next page those nodes are identified by going up a non-leftmost branch, and then by descending to the non-leftmost sisters. If the node found bears a linguistic label, we are done.

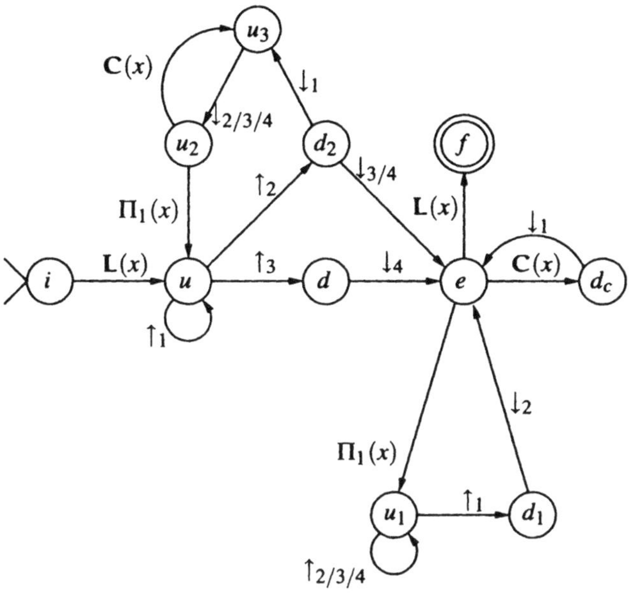

Figure 11.5: The FSTWA for precedence on intended structures: MCFTGs

If it bears a projection symbol, we proceed analogously to the definitions for dominance, i.e., go up until we find a leftmost node and then go down to the right branch.

The situation is complicated by the fact that every node with a linguistic label at the same time is a potential filler for a projection node.[41] Basically, we have to reverse the process which finds a filler for a projection node. But since a projection line can consist of several projection nodes, how do we know when to stop? The FSTWA ensures that the possible projection nodes to the fillers are found by recursively looking up and then down a tree. Starting from the nodes bearing a linguistic label which are on a leftmost branch it has to look upwards on leftmost branches until it finds the first right branch. At this point it must descend again into the subtree to find the projection node. This is achieved by repeatedly going down non-leftmost branches as long as there are composition nodes and testing for a projection node. If we find one, we can start computing its sisters. If it doesn't have any, it starts the entire process recursively. The resulting relation will be indicated by $\lhd_{imm}$ and the corresponding formula generated with the process outlined previously $\text{trans}_{W_{\lhd_{imm}}}$.

We are now in a position to finish the definition of precedence by using the definition of immediate precedence. As usual, two nodes stand in the precedence relation if they either stand in the immediate precedence relation or if they are dominated by nodes which stand in the immediate precedence relation:

$$x \lhd y \overset{def}{\Longleftrightarrow} (\exists u, v)[u \blacktriangleleft^* x \wedge v \blacktriangleleft^* y \wedge \mathsf{trans}_{W_{\lhd_{imm}}}(u, v)]$$

Finally, we turn to the possible complications with the specification of other automata defining the intended precedence relation. Basically there are two sources of problems. The first problem appears when we have more than one projection function, i.e., more than one variable in the original, unlifted grammar. Then we have far more cases to cover in finding the potential projection node corresponding to the filler we are considering since nodes can be permuted by the projection functions. This does not represent a major obstacle, but requires a finer analysis of the possible structures involved and therefore complicates the automaton. What becomes necessary is a definition which takes the intended dominance relations into account. We can paraphrase it as follows. Generally we have to separate two cases. If x and y are terminal nodes, they stand in the precedence relation if for some internal node z dominating x and y (in the intended tree) and for the paths X and Y used by the FSTWA to connect z with x and y (in the lifted tree), respectively, the first leaf node on X precedes the first leaf node on Y. This admittedly complicated condition is necessary because the FSTWA might connect z with, e.g., x via a projection node. Then, this intermediate leaf is the one which determines the intended precedence relation. And, as a further condition, we need that if x and y are internal nodes of the intended tree, they stand in the precedence relation if every terminal node which x dominates precedes (in the lifted tree) every terminal node that y dominates. Naturally, we also need the appropriate "mixed" cases between terminal and nonterminal nodes.

The second problem is more severe. In case we are not dealing with a *linear* RTG, i.e., there are variables which appear more than once on the RHS of an unlifted rule, we must be even more careful because now a filler can have more than one antecedent, i.e., there is more than one projection node which evaluates to it. This leads to the conclusion that suddenly one node immediately precedes two other nodes which cannot be desired. So far, we have no solution worked out. We know that a solution exists, because, looking ahead, we can also reconstruct the intended structures with an MTT which implies both dominance and precedence. One possible solution is copying the node as often as it is needed.[42] Another solution might be to take each individual run of the automaton into consideration which complicates matters considerably. But since this is speculation and not necessary for any of the examples, we ignore this particular problem.

We will not present any further tree-walking automata for the definition of the intended precedence relation since the basic technique has been introduced very carefully using the FSTWAs recognizing the dominance relation between the intended nodes.

11.1.2 Reconstruction with MSO transductions

Now we can turn to the definition of the transduction via MSO logic. Since we prepared it with the presentation of the needed tree-walking automata, almost no work remains to be done.

Using the defined formula for $\blacktriangleleft$ the specific MSO transduction we need to transform the lifted structures into the intended ones simply looks as follows:

$$(\varphi, \psi, (\theta_q)_{q \in Q})$$

$$Q = \{\blacktriangleleft, \blacktriangleleft^*, \blacktriangleleft^+, \lhd, \ldots\}$$

$$\begin{aligned}
\varphi &\equiv \varphi_{\mathfrak{A}_{\Gamma L}} \\
\psi &\equiv \mathsf{L}(x) \\
\theta_{\blacktriangleleft}(x,y) &\equiv \mathsf{trans}_{W_{\blacktriangleleft}}(x,y) \\
\theta_{\blacktriangleleft^*}(x,y) &\equiv (\forall X)[\blacktriangleleft\text{-}\mathsf{closed}(X) \wedge x \in X \rightarrow y \in X] \\
\theta_{\blacktriangleleft^+}(x,y) &\equiv x \blacktriangleleft^* y \vee x \not\approx y \\
\theta_{\lhd}(x,y) &\equiv x \lhd y \\
\theta_{\mathsf{labels}} &\equiv \text{taken over from } R
\end{aligned}$$

As desired, the domain of the transduction is characterized by the MSO formula for the lifted trees (see Section 10.3). The domain, i.e., the set of nodes, of the intended tree is characterized by the formula ψ which identifies the nodes with a "linguistic" label. Building on this domain, we define the other primitives of our description language analogous to $L^2_{K,P}$ with the given FSTWAs.[43]

Note that while standardly "linguistic" relations like *c-command* or *government* would be defined in terms of *dominance*, our approach allows the alternative route of taking, in the spirit of Frank and Vijay-Shanker (1998), *c-command* as the primitive relation of linguistic structure by defining, in a similar, though – since Chomsky's (1985) distinction between *segments* and *categories* has to be accommodated – somewhat more complicated fashion, an FSTWA which computes the intended *c-command* relation directly, without recourse to dominance.

11.1.3 Reconstruction with MTTs

As stated previously, there is a *unique* morphism h from the "lifted" terms over the derived alphabet Σ^L into the terms over the tree substitution algebra.

The morphism h in the case of lifted CFTGs is defined inductively as follows:

$$\begin{aligned} h(f') &= f(x_1,\ldots,x_n) \text{ for } f \in \Sigma_n \\ h(\pi_i^n) &= x_i \\ h(c(t,t_1,\ldots,t_n)) &= h(t)[h(t_1),\ldots,h(t_n)] \end{aligned}$$

where $t[t_1,\ldots,t_n]$ denotes the result of substituting t_i for x_i in t for $t \in T(\Sigma,X_k)$, $t_i \in T(\Sigma,X_m)$.[44]

Let Σ^L be a lifted alphabet as before. The unique morphism h can be performed by a simple macro tree transducer $M = \langle Q,\Sigma^L,\Sigma,q_0,P\rangle$, where $Q = \{q_n \mid n \text{ the rank of some element in } \Sigma^L\}$, q_0 is the initial state and P is a finite family of rules.

The MTT which we construct to carry out the transformation effected by the unique homomorphism h combines in a particularly perspicuous way the actions of a top-down finite tree transducer – based upon the syntactic structure of the lifted alphabet Σ^L – and the production aspect of the underlying CFTG via its (i.e., the MTT's) dependence on the local context (parameters).

How can we construct the necessary productions to recover the intended trees? We take an intuitive approach to explaining the construction of the needed MTT which is strongly dependent on another careful inspection of the tree in Figure 11.1 on page 156.

In general, in the first argument we will have a tree during a transduction. So in the rules, we have to take care of all symbols which can appear as mothers of (possibly trivial) trees with the number of variables corresponding

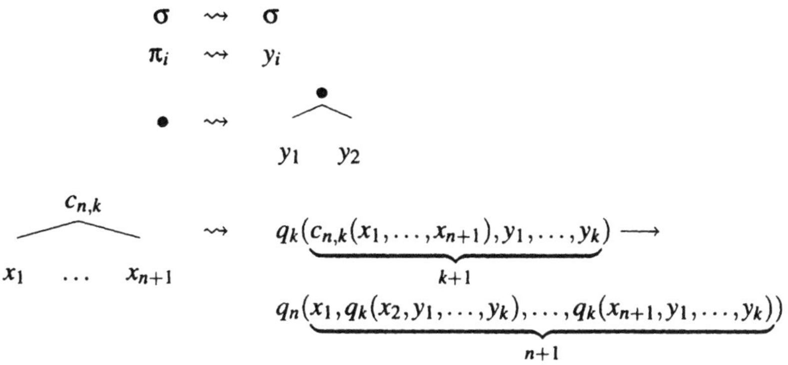

Figure 11.6: Intuition behind the construction of the MTT: CFTGs

to their arities in the first argument of any left hand side. We try to depict the intuition behind the construction of the MTT graphically in Figure 11.6.

After careful inspection of the tree language generated by the lifted RTG Γ^L, the simplest case is certainly when we are faced with a constant from Σ_0^L. In this case all we have to do is to map it back to the corresponding element from Σ, regardless of the parameters, if there are any. In case we encounter a projection symbol we simply have to return the corresponding parameter. This presupposes that we stored the "right" information there.

Furthermore, all rules with a symbol whose "unlifted" version was not a constant will have as many parameters as are needed to compute the corresponding function, e.g., '$\bullet$' is binary and therefore needs two parameters (see the last rule in Example 11.1 on the following page). The resulting rule has, on the right hand side, simply the "executed" function.

For the rules headed by a composition symbol $c_{n,k}$ we need as many parameters as are prescribed by k. This is due to the fact that while generally the relevant information in the lifted trees is on the leftmost branch, we nevertheless need the other daughters to be able to unravel the projections. Basically, we follow a depth-first strategy on the leftmost component of the lifted trees. But we are passing the necessary context computed in parallel (i.e., the evaluation of the computation of the other, non-leftmost daughters) down into that computation as well.

Similarly, we also get the necessary states from the arities of the composition symbols. The rules then simply pass the state and the parameters of the left hand side of the rule to the arguments of the alphabet symbol while continuing to work on the first argument. As an example consider an $n+1$

branching fork whose mother is labeled with $c_{n,k}$. Then we have to construct a rule which has on the left hand side state q_k with arity $k+1$. It has as its first argument a term with functor $c_{n,k}$ and arguments $x_1,\ldots,x_{n+1}$. The other arguments are the parameters y_1 to y_k. The right hand side has state q_n of arity $n+1$ with the first argument simply being x_1 and the other arguments being $q_k(x_i,y_1,\ldots,y_k)$, $1<i\leq n+1$.

Example 11.1. For our concrete example, the set of rules P of the MTT $M_{\Gamma L}$[45] look as given below (and graphically in Figure 11.7 on page 170):[46]

$$\begin{aligned}
q_0(c_{4,0}(x_1,x_2,x_3,x_4,x_5)) &\longrightarrow \\
&q_4(x_1,q_0(x_2),q_0(x_3),q_0(x_4),q_0(x_5)) \\
q_0(\sigma') &\longrightarrow \sigma \qquad\qquad \text{for } \sigma\in\{a,b,c,d,\varepsilon\} \\
q_4(c_{4,4}(x_1,x_2,x_3,x_4,x_5),y_1,y_2,y_3,y_4) &\longrightarrow \\
&q_4(x_1,q_4(x_2,y_1,y_2,y_3,y_4),q_4(x_3,y_1,y_2,y_3,y_4), \\
&\quad q_4(x_4,y_1,y_2,y_3,y_4),q_4(x_5,y_1,y_2,y_3,y_4)) \\
q_4(P_i,y_1,y_2,y_3,y_4) &\longrightarrow y_i \qquad\qquad \text{for } P_i=\pi_i \\
q_4(\sigma',y_1,y_2,y_3,y_4) &\longrightarrow \sigma \qquad\qquad \text{for } \sigma\in\{a,b,c,d,\varepsilon\} \\
q_4(c_{2,4}(x_1,x_2,x_3),y_1,y_2,y_3,y_4) &\longrightarrow \\
&q_2(x_1,q_4(x_2,y_1,y_2,y_3,y_4),q_4(x_3,y_1,y_2,y_3,y_4)) \\
q_2(\bullet',y_1,y_2) &\longrightarrow \bullet(y_1,y_2)
\end{aligned}$$

As one can see, the only remaining tree forming symbol which remains on the right hand sides is the concatenation '•'. So, we are indeed back in our "old" alphabet Σ. The parameters serve just as memory slots to pass the necessary information for undoing the projections and explicit compositions further down into the tree.

From the preceding motivating discussion and the display of the rules in Example 11.1 it should be clear that the states of the MTT do not play any role beyond requiring the right number of arguments.

Generally, an MTT works in a depth-first fashion on the leftmost daughters. But it starts fresh copies of itself on the other daughters whose results are then fed back to the "main" computation via the parameters. Specifically, applying this MTT to the tree in Figure 11.1 on page 156 yields the final tree from the derivation displayed in Figure 10.5 on page 137. To get the reader started, let us consider the first rule in Example 11.1 beginning the transduction on the root of the tree displayed in Figure 11.1 on page 156. We start in state q_0 and our root is indeed labeled with $c_{4,0}$. Then we continue in state q_4 with its leftmost daughter and pass as parameters the results of computing q_0 of the other daughters. Since in this case they are elements from Σ_0^L, we can simply use the appropriate constants from Σ in further computations. The rest of the computation leading to the final result is straightforward and left as an exercise.

The reader interested in further details of the working of the MTT on a given lifted RTG can find a simple Prolog program in Appendix D on page 209 which, given both an MTT and a lifted RTG, produces trees and their intended counterparts via iterative deepening.

Again, we exemplify the constructions further by also giving the one dealing with the TAG example Γ_{TAG}^L (see Example 10.12 on page 144) in Figure 11.8 on page 171. First reconsider the tree displayed in Figure 11.3 on page 161. The intended tree (displayed as the last tree in Figure 10.6 on page 139) can again be reconstructed with an MTT, see the grey lines in the figure. The intuition for the construction of the MTT has not changed compared to the case of CFTGs, it has only gotten simpler. Since we are only dealing with one projection, the necessary bookkeeping can be reduced drastically. The necessary transitions for the concrete MTT $M_{\Gamma_{TAG}^L}$ are given graphically in Figure 11.8 on page 171. There is only one nonterminal of arity three: S_t which gets the necessary daughters via the context parameters y_1 to y_3 (see the last rule in the left column). The same holds for the unary nonterminal S_t^0. As usual, the alphabet symbols are simply transduced into themselves. What remains is to handle the compositions. Again, we continue the traversal on the leftmost branch and start "new" transducer on the other daughters so that their result will be available to the "main" computation in the parameters. Via this construction we generate the arguments for the interior nodes of the intended tree. It is left as an exercise to the reader to use the MTT $M_{\Gamma_{TAG}^L}$ to transduce the example tree in Figure 11.3 on page 161.

11.2 Reconstructing lifted MCFGs

After the presentation of the various ways of reconstructing the intended trees out of lifted (M)CFTGs, we now repeat the process with the lifted MCFGs. Again, we will specify an MSO transduction built upon tree-walking automata as well as an MTT to recover the linguistically relevant trees.

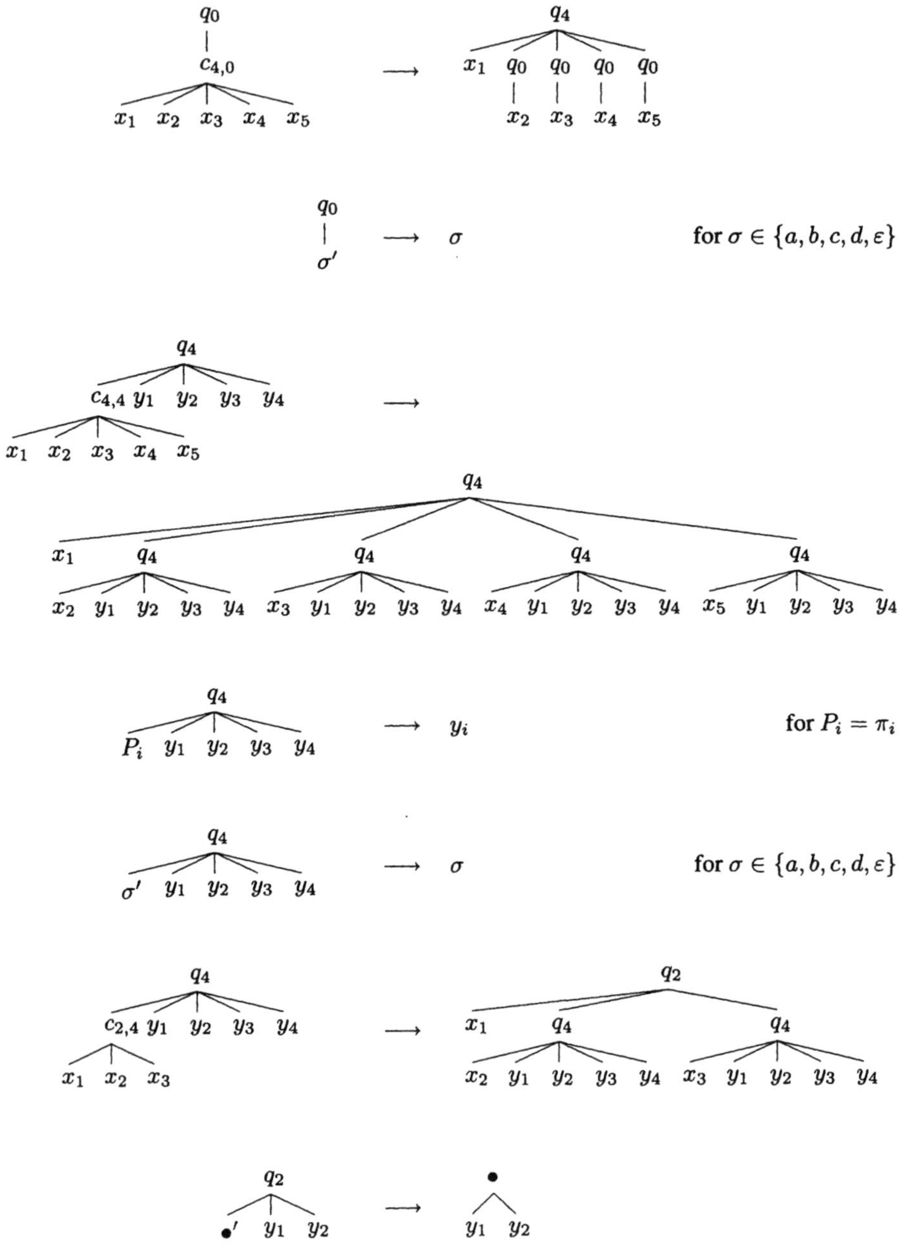

Figure 11.7: The rules of the example MTT $M_{\Gamma L}$

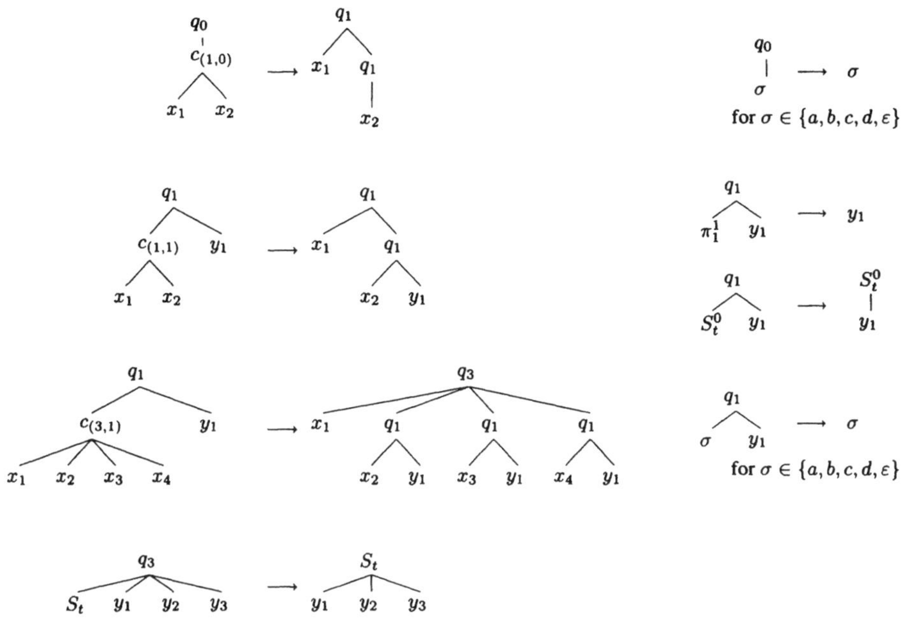

Figure 11.8: The rules of the example MTT $M_{\Gamma^L_{TAG}}$

Since the MSO transduction itself is in a certain sense universal, we will not refer back to our particular example to present it. The only variable part is the number of different projection constants appearing in the RTG, i.e., π^3_1, π^3_2 and π^3_3 and the FSTWAs needed to implement the various primitives from the description language.

Again, the core of the transduction is a tree-walking automaton defining the binary relation of immediate dominance ($\triangleleft$) on the nodes belonging to the intended structures. It is based on another, but very similar, set of simple observations. The reader is encouraged to check them against the example tree t generated by $\mathcal{G}'_{MCFG}$ given in Figure 11.9 on the following page.[47] Naturally they are very similar to the ones given previously for CFTGs. Since they are not identical, but follow the same reasoning, they serve as further illustration of the idea behind the reconstruction of the intended trees. Note, that we again indicated the dominance relations of the intended tree with thicker lines. Further work is required to also get the intended precedence relations. In fact, with the exception of the intended children of the intended root, the left-to-right order of the displayed lines is backwards.

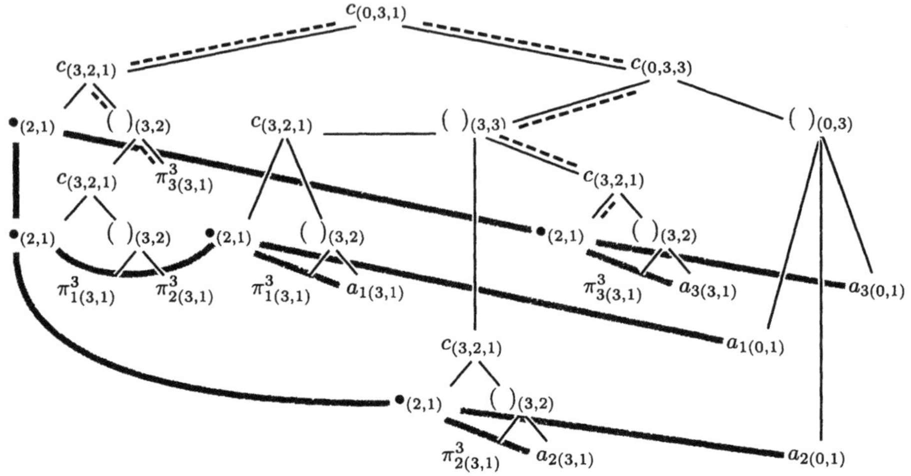

Figure 11.9: Intended relations on a lifted structure: MCFGs

1. This time, our trees feature four families of labels: the "linguistic" symbols L, i.e., the lifted symbols of the underlying MCFG; the "composition" symbols $C = \{c_{(u,v,w)}\}$; the "tupling" symbols $(\ )_{(v,u)}$ and the "projection" symbols $\Pi = \{\pi^k_i\}$.

2. Now, all nonterminal nodes in t are labeled by some $c_{(u,v,w)} \in C$ or a "tupling" symbol. Note that no terminal node is labeled by some $c_{(u,v,w)}$.

3. The terminal nodes in t are either labeled by some "linguistic" symbol as before, a "tupling" symbol of the form $(\ )_{(k,0)}$, i.e. the "empty" tuple, or by some "projection" symbol π^k_i.

4. Again, any "linguistic" node properly dominating anything in the intended tree is on some left branch in t, i.e., it is the left daughter of some $c_{(u,v,w)} \in C$. But now it furthermore is the sister of a tupling symbol whose daughters have to be evaluated to find the the intended daughters.

The following point is also similar to the one we presented in the discussion on the reconstruction of structures generated from lifted CFTGs. But now we also have to cope with the tupling symbols which accounts for the differences and the greater complexity of the observations.

5. For any node ν labeled with some "projection" symbol $\pi^u_i \in \Pi$ in t there is a unique node μ (labeled with some $c_{(u,v,w)} \in C$) which properly dom-

inates ν and which dominates a node labeled with a "tupling" symbol (which does not dominate ν) whose i-th daughter will eventually evaluate to the value of π_i^k. Moreover, μ will be the first node properly dominating ν which is reachable via a transition up a "left" branch ($\uparrow_1$) and bears a composition symbol. This fact is again arrived at by induction on the construction of $\mathcal{G}'_{MCFG}$ from $\mathcal{G}_{MCFG}$. The idea behind the proof is similar to the one presented previously. We are again reconstructing the application of a rule containing variables to an existing tree.[48] The difference now is that the unique node dominating the inserted tree appears no longer on a leftmost branch but as the right daughter of the topmost node such that we have to reformulate the conditions accordingly. And, naturally, we also have to account for the tupling nodes which appear interspersed in the tree.

By (4.) it is not hard to find possible dominees in any t. It is the problem of determining the actual "filler" of a candidate-dominee which makes up the complexity of the definition of $\blacktriangleleft$. There are three cases to account for:

6. If the node considered carries a "linguistic" label, it evaluates to itself;

7. if it has a "composition" label $c_{(u,v,w)}$, it evaluates to whatever its leftmost daughter evaluates to;

8. if it carries a "projection" label π_i^k, it evaluates to whatever the node it "points to" – by (5.) the ith daughter of a "tupling" node which is dominated by the first C-node on a left branch dominating it – evaluates to.

Again, note that cases (7.) and (8.) are inherently recursive. But the use of tree-walking automata ensures the definability. In Figure 11.9 on the preceding page the π_3^3-link marked with the dashed line is an example of such a path from the projection symbol to the corresponding filler.

11.2.1 Reconstruction with FSTWAs

According to the observations made above, a tree-walking automaton is defined to relate those nodes x and y which stand in the intended immediate dominance relation, i.e., $x \blacktriangleleft y$. The automaton is given graphically in Figure 11.10 on the following page. It starts on any node with a "linguistic" label (denoted here by L) which means for the given example $\bullet, a_1, a_2, a_3$. Then it has to go up the first branch, read a composition symbol and descend

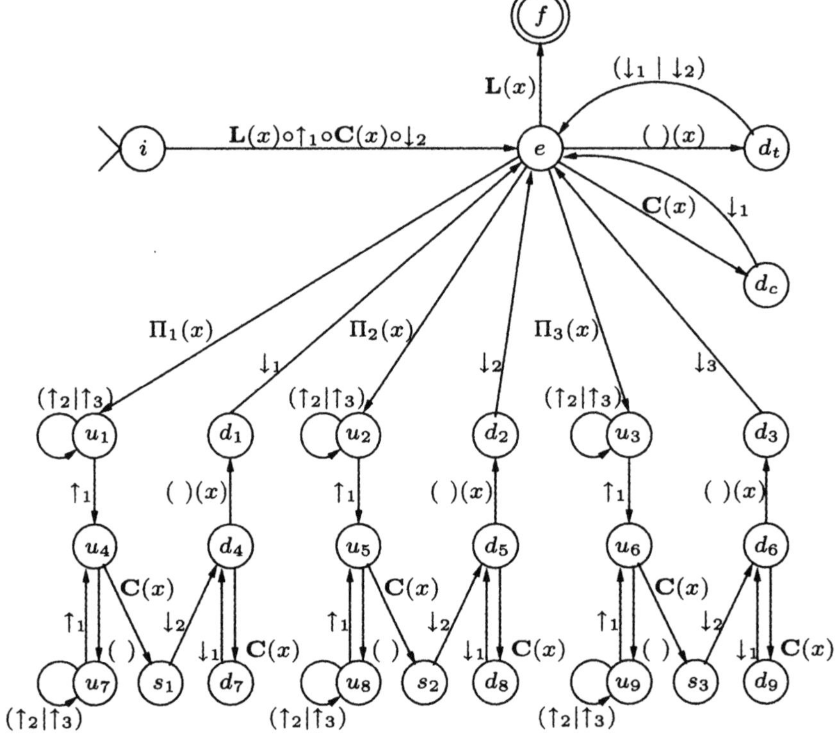

Figure 11.10: The FSTWA for dominance on intended structures: MCFGs

to its sister. If it reads a "linguistic" node, the automaton stops. If it reads a composition symbol, the automaton goes to the left daughter and tries again. If it reads a tupling symbol, the automaton proceeds with its daughters (again, see the thicker, grey lines in Figure 11.9 on page 172). On finding a projection symbol, it searches for the appropriate "filler" by going upwards until it is on a leftmost branch which is labeled with a composition symbol. Then it walks to the second sister or further down the leftmost branch until it hits a tupling node to whose appropriate daughter it descends to find the filler. The whole process is recursive, i.e., on finding another projection symbol, the automaton again tries to find an appropriate filler (see the π_3^3-link in Figure 11.9 on page 172.)

However, viewed as an ordinary finite-state automaton over the alphabet of directives Δ, the FSTWA recognizes a regular (string-) language, the *walking language*

$$W_{\blacktriangleleft} = \mathsf{L}(x) \cdot \uparrow_1 \cdot \mathsf{C}(x) \cdot \downarrow_2 \cdot (W_{(\ )} \cup W_{\mathsf{C}} \cup W_{\Pi_1} \cup W_{\Pi_2} \cup W_{\Pi_3})^* \cdot \mathsf{L}(x)$$

with

$$\begin{aligned} W_{(\ )} &= (\ )(x) \cdot (\downarrow_1 \cup \downarrow_2) \\ W_{\mathsf{C}} &= \mathsf{C}(x) \cdot \downarrow_1 \\ W_{\Pi_i} &= \Pi_1(x) \cdot (\uparrow_2 \cup \uparrow_3)^* \cdot \uparrow_1 \cdot ((\ )(x) \cdot (\uparrow_2 \cup \uparrow_3)^* \cdot \uparrow_1)^* \cdot \\ &\qquad \mathsf{C}(x) \cdot \downarrow_2 \cdot (\mathsf{C}(x) \cdot \downarrow_1)^* \cdot (\ )(x) \cdot \downarrow_i \end{aligned}$$

which can be translated recursively into an MSO formula $\mathsf{trans}_{W_{\triangleleft}}$ defining the relation $\triangleleft$ (see Bloem and Engelfriet 1997a).

11.2.2 Reconstruction with MSO transductions

Finally, the MSO transduction $(\varphi, \psi, (\theta_q)_{q \in Q})$ with $Q = \{\blacktriangleleft, \blacktriangleleft^*, \blacktriangleleft^+, \triangleleft, \ldots\}$ we use to transform the lifted structures into the intended ones is identical to the one given for CFTGs and looks as follows:

$$\begin{aligned} \varphi &\equiv \varphi_{\mathfrak{A}_{G'_{MCFG}}} \\ \psi &\equiv \mathsf{L}(x) \\ \theta_{\blacktriangleleft}(x,y) &\equiv \mathsf{trans}_{W_{\blacktriangleleft}}(x,y) \\ \theta_{\blacktriangleleft^*}(x,y) &\equiv (\forall X)[\blacktriangleleft\text{-closed}(X) \wedge x \in X \rightarrow y \in X] \\ \theta_{\blacktriangleleft^+}(x,y) &\equiv x \blacktriangleleft^* y \vee x \not\approx y \\ \theta_{\triangleleft}(x,y) &\equiv \mathsf{trans}_{W_{\triangleleft}}(x,y) \\ \theta_{\text{labels}} &\equiv \text{taken over from } R \end{aligned}$$

As desired, the domain of the transduction is characterized by the MSO formula $\varphi_{\mathfrak{A}_{G'_{ww}}}$ for the lifted trees. The domain, i.e., the set of nodes, of the intended tree is characterized by the formula ψ which identifies the nodes with a "linguistic" label which stand indeed in the new dominance relation to some other node. From there we can define the other primitives of a tree description language as previously discussed.

11.2.3 Reconstruction with MTTs

For the specification of the MTT, we come again back to the *unique* morphism h from the "lifted" terms over the derived alphabet Σ into the terms over the tree substitution algebra.

Since we are now working in a Lawvere-Algebra with the additional operation of tupling, the homomorphism has to be augmented accordingly. The morphism h for the case of the reconstruction of lifted MCFGs is defined inductively as follows:

$$\begin{aligned} h(f') &= f(x_1,\ldots,x_n) \text{ for } f \in \Sigma_{w,s}, |w| = n \\ h(\pi_i^u) &= x_i \\ h((\;)_{(u,v)}(t_1,\ldots,t_u)) &= (h(t_1),\ldots,h(t_u)) \\ h(c_{(u,v,w)}(t_1,t_2)) &= h(t_1)[h(t_2)] \end{aligned}$$

where $t[t_1,\ldots,t_k]$ denotes the result of substituting t_i for x_i in t for $t \in T(\Sigma, X_k)$, $t_i \in T(\Sigma, X_m)$.

Again, this unique morphism h can be performed by a simple macro tree transducer $M = \langle Q, \Sigma, V_T \cup \{\bullet\}, q_0, P\rangle$, where $Q = \{q_u \mid \text{for all } c_{(u,v,w)} \in \Sigma$ where the leftmost daughter is not a tupling node $\} \cup \{q_u^i \mid$ for all $c_{(u,v,w)} \in \Sigma$ where the leftmost daughter is a tupling node $(\;)_{(r,s)} \in \Sigma, i \in \{1,\ldots,s\}\} \cup \{q_v^i \mid$ for all $(\;)_{(v,u)} \in \Sigma, i \in \{1,\ldots,u\}\}$,[49] q_0 is the initial state and P is a finite family of rules. Recall, that we use only a simple example with just one nonterminal on the RHS of the MCFG-rules. This simplifies the "lifted" trees as well as the MTT we have to define.

We take – yet again – an intuitive approach to explaining the construction of the needed MTT which now is strongly dependent on inspection of the tree in Figure 11.9 on page 172 and the homomorphism h given above.

Before we proceed, we briefly review some notation for the states introduced above. In this slightly more complicated case, the states have both sub- and superscripts. The subscripts convey information about the number of parameters and the superscripts hint at computations which will return the particular arguments of a tupling operation. Furthermore, we will also use variables with both super- and subscripts. In this case, the superscripts indicate the type of the mother node of the tree which has to be substituted, whereas the subscripts just give us new variables of the same type. This typing of the variables is – strictly speaking – not necessary since one can either assume that the input trees of the MTT have been generated with an appropri-

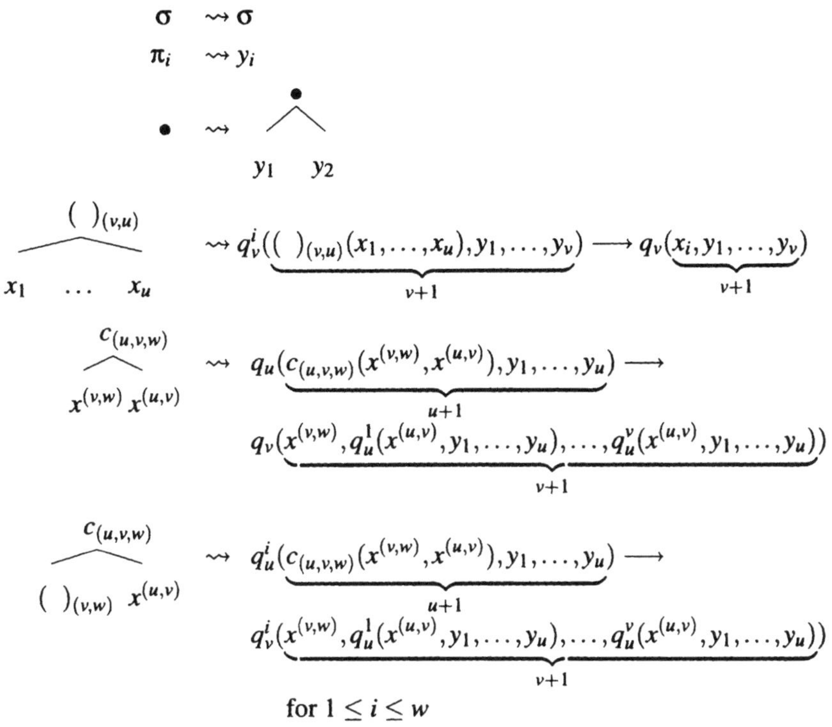

Figure 11.11: Intuition behind the construction of the MTT: MCFGs

ate RTG and therefore are well-typed; or, alternatively, that we could change the definition of the MTT to an MTT with regular look-ahead. Then the look-ahead – implemented with a tree automaton – ensures the well-typing of the input.

Again, in the first argument of a rule from P we will have a simple input tree during a transduction. So in the rules, we have to take care of all symbols which can appear as mothers of (possibly trivial) trees with the number of variables x_i corresponding to their arities in the first argument of any left hand side (LHS). We try to depict the intuition behind the construction of this kind of MTT graphically in Figure 11.11.

It is not surprising that after another careful inspection of the tree language generated by the lifted RTG $\mathcal{G}'_{ww}$, the simplest case is again the one where we are faced with a constant, i.e., with an element from Σ with rank 0 which is simply mapped back to the corresponding element from V_T, regardless of the parameters, if, indeed, there are any. Similarly, in the case that we encounter a projection symbol, we simply return the corresponding parameter with the desired information.

Repeating the argumentation from above, all rules with a constant symbol whose "unlifted" version was not a constant – in this case only the concatenation symbol '•' – need as many parameters as are needed to compute the corresponding function, e.g., again, '•' is binary and therefore needs two parameters (see the third rule in Example 11.2 on the next page). The resulting rule has, on the RHS, simply the "executed" function.

The more complicated cases involve branching nodes in the tree. Those are labeled with either a tupling or a composition symbol introduced by the lifting process. Let us turn to the easier case of tupling first.

Our first step involves constructing the rules for nodes labeled with a tupling symbol by inspecting the sort information in the subscript. Furthermore, the state on the LHS is marked with a superscript indicating along which branch of the tuple we have to descend, i.e., which argument/daughter of the tupling node we are currently evaluating. Given a symbol $(\ )_{(v,u)}$, we construct a transition with state q_v^i of arity $v+1$ which has as arguments a term labeled with $(\ )_{(v,u)}$ which has an appropriate number u of daughters x_j, and v parameters on the LHS. On the RHS, we start a "fresh" transducer (state q_v) on argument x_i of the term and the parameters, therefore q_v is also of arity $v+1$.

For the rules headed by a composition symbol $c_{(u,v,w)}$ as many parameters on the LHS as are prescribed by u and as many parameters on the RHS as prescribed by v are needed. Analogously to the case of reconstructing lifted CFTGs, this is due to the fact that while generally the relevant information in the lifted trees is on the leftmost branch (recall the facts (1) to (8) on page 173), we nevertheless need the other daughters to be able to unravel the projections. We also follow a depth-first strategy on the leftmost component of the lifted trees while still passing the necessary context (i.e., the evaluation of the computation of the other daughters) down into that computation. As for CFTGs, we construct the necessary states from the arities of the composition symbols. The rules then simply pass the state and the parameters of the LHS of the rule to the arguments of the alphabet symbol while continuing to work on the first argument. As an example consider a fork whose mother is labeled with $c_{(u,v,w)}$. Then we have to construct a rule which has on the LHS state q_u with arity $u+1$. Its first argument is a term with functor $c_{(u,v,w)}$ and two appropriately typed arguments $x^{(v,w)}$ and $x^{(u,v)}$. The other arguments are the parameters y_1 to y_u. The RHS has state q_v of arity $v+1$ with the first argument simply being the first daughter of the composition symbol, i.e., $x^{(v,w)}$, and the other arguments being $q^i_u(x^{(u,v)}, y_1, \ldots, y_u)$, $(i \leq v)$, with the interpretation that we have no parameters if $u < 1$. Furthermore, we have to supplement the state on the LHS with superscripts according to the typing information if the leftmost, i.e., the head-daughter carries a tupling symbol. More concretely, if the head-daughter of $c_{(u,v,w)}$ is $(\;)_{(v,w)}$ we need w transitions with superscripts ranging from 1 to w, i.e., q^i_u where $i \in \{1, \ldots, w\}$. And then, if the state on the LHS had a superscript, that is to say, we are working on the computation of a value of an element of a tuple, we simply pass this superscript on to the state on the RHS.

For our continued example, the set of rules P of the MTT $M_{G'_{MCFG}}$ is shown graphically in Figure 11.12 on page 181. Note that we are dealing with the trees as given in Figure 11.9 on page 172, i.e., a simplified version. The Prolog implementation given in Appendix D.2.3 on page 215 uses the unabbreviated definition, though.

Example 11.2. Non-graphically, the set of rules P of the MTT $M_{G'_{MCFG}}$ appear as given below:[50]

$$q_0(c_{(0,3,1)}(x_1^{(3,1)}, x_1^{(0,3)})) \longrightarrow$$
$$q_3(x_1^{(3,1)}, q_0^1(x_1^{(0,3)}), q_0^2(x_1^{(0,3)}), q_0^3(x_1^{(0,3)}))$$

$$q_0(\sigma) \longrightarrow \sigma \qquad \text{for } \sigma \in \{a_{1(0,1)}, a_{2(0,1)}, a_{3(0,1)}\}$$

$$q_2(\bullet_{(2,1)}, y_1, y_2) \longrightarrow \bullet_{(2,1)}(y_1, y_2)$$

$$q_3(P_i, y_1, y_2, y_3) \longrightarrow y_i \qquad \text{for } P_i = \pi_i, i \in \{1,2,3\}$$

$$q_3(\sigma, y_1, y_2, y_3) \longrightarrow \sigma \qquad \text{for } \sigma \in \{a_{1(0,1)}, a_{2(0,1)}, a_{3(0,1)}\}$$

$$q_3(c_{(3,2,1)}(x_1^{(2,1)}, x_1^{(3,2)}), y_1, y_2, y_3) \longrightarrow q_2(x_1^{(2,1)}, q_3^1(x_1^{(3,2)}, y_1, y_2, y_3),$$
$$q_3^2(x_1^{(3,2)}, y_1, y_2, y_3))$$

$$q_0^i(c_{(0,3,3)}(x_1^{(3,3)}, x_1^{(0,3)})) \longrightarrow$$
$$q_3^i(x_1^{(3,3)}, q_0^1(x_1^{(0,3)}), q_0^2(x_1^{(0,3)}), q_0^3(x_1^{(0,3)})) \qquad \text{for } i \in \{1,2,3\}$$

$$q_0^i((\ )_{(0,3)}(x_1^{(0,1)},x_2^{(0,1)},x_3^{(0,1)})) \longrightarrow q_0(x_i^{(0,1)}) \text{ for } i \in \{1,2,3\}$$

$$q_3^i((\ )_{(3,3)}(x_1^{(3,1)},x_2^{(3,1)},x_3^{(3,1)}),y_1,y_2,y_3) \longrightarrow q_3(x_i^{(3,1)},y_1,y_2,y_3)$$
$$\text{for } i \in \{1,2,3\}$$

$$q_3^i((\ )_{(3,2)}(x_1^{(3,1)},x_2^{(3,1)}),y_1,y_2,y_3) \longrightarrow q_3(x_i^{(3,1)},y_1,y_2,y_3)$$
$$\text{for } i \in \{1,2\}$$

We observe again: the only remaining tree forming symbol which remains on the RHSs is the concatenation '•'. So, we are indeed back with our "old" alphabet. The parameters serve just as memory slots to pass the necessary information for undoing the projections and explicit compositions further down the tree.

Applying the given MTT for the grammar G'_{MCFG} to the tree in Figure 11.9 on page 172 yields a final tree for a derivation of the MCFG displayed in Example 9.3. Namely the one indicated by the thicker grey lines in Figure 11.9 on page 172. To get the reader started, let us consider the first rule in Example 11.2 on the preceding page beginning the transduction on the root of the tree displayed in Figure 11.9 on page 172. We start in state q_0 and our root is indeed labeled with $c_{(0,3,1)}$. Then we continue in state q_3 with its leftmost daughter and pass as parameter y_i the result of computing q_0^i of the second daughter (in this case with $i \in \{1,2,3\}$). These transductions have to be computed separately and yield the input to the "final" projection π_1^3. The rest of the computation leading to the final result is straightforward, if tedious, and left as an exercise.

Again, the interested reader can find a simple Prolog implementation in the Appendix D on page 209 which allows some simple experiments.

11.3 Summary of the two-step approach

We have shown in this third part of the book how to account for cross-serial dependencies by coupling a logical domain specification followed by a logically definable transduction and a bottom-up finite-state tree automaton with a tree transformation induced by a macro tree transducer. The result is, of course, not restricted to cross-serial dependencies. Any type of structural relationship that is amenable to a formal analysis by means of CFTGs can be

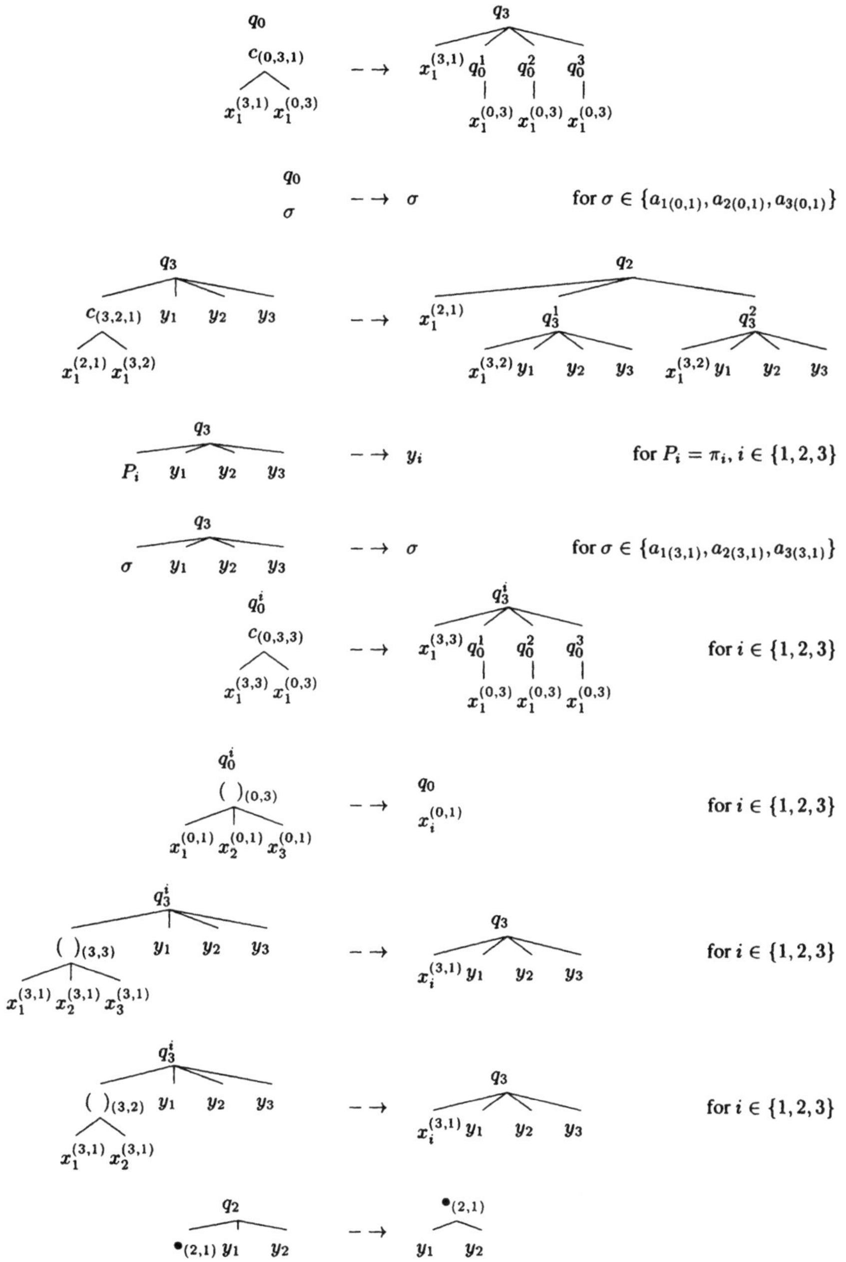

Figure 11.12: The rules of the example MTT $M_{G'_{MCFG}}$

described according to the same operational or logical procedure. The original context-free tree language is first translated into its explicit presentation. A corresponding tree automaton/closed MSO formula then isolates the explicit tree family within the realm of all possible finite trees on the lifted signature. The MTT/MSO transduction finally serves to reestablish the intended structural relations.

One drawback of the approach, namely that there is no principled connection between tree grammars as we presented them and linguistic formalisms which can handle non-context-free phenomena is addressed as well. On the one hand, we presented *monadic* CFTGs which are equivalent to TAGs. And, on the other hand, we took the result of Michaelis' translation of MGs into MCFGs as the input to our two-step approach. In particular, we have shown how to define a RTG by lifting the corresponding MCFG-rules into terms of a free Lawvere theory. This gives us again both a regular (via tree automata and macro tree transducers) and a logical description (via MSO logic and an MSO definable transduction) of the intended syntactic trees. Equivalently, we provide both an operational and a denotational account of Stabler's version of Minimalism without having to go via derivation trees.

In the wake of the celebrated result of Peters and Ritchie (1973) on the generative strength of Transformational Grammars a great number of research activities were inspired by the so-called *universal base hypothesis*. One version of this hypothesis can be paraphrased as claiming that there exists a fixed grammar *G* that plays the role of the base component of a Transformational Grammar of any natural language. Adapting this methodological point to our result it can be stated as follows: Empirical linguistic phenomena that can be accommodated within the framework of MGs are amenable to a regular analysis followed by a fixed universal transduction.

Comparing this statement of the result of the paper with the characterization of context-free graph languages by Engelfriet and van Oostrom (1996), we want to stress the point that our regular description of CFTG, MCFTG and MCFG languages does not provide a characterization of this language family in the technical understanding of an equivalence between these languages and languages defined by a regular tree language/closed MSO formula and a macro tree transducer/MSO transduction. For a recent result on the equivalence between regular tree languages followed by an MSO definable tree transduction and the tree languages generated by context-free graph grammars see Engelfriet and Maneth (1999).

Part IV

Conclusion and Outlook

Chapter 12

Conclusion

After presenting the "classical" technique of using MSO logic on multiple successor functions as a grammar formalism for P&P-based theories, we analyzed the strengths and weaknesses of this proposal. Since the approach stops short in two crucial respects, namely the generative capacity and the adequacy towards other (generative) grammar formalisms, we proposed in this monograph a two-step approach which retains the description language MSO logic on the denotational side and still has a provably equivalent operational interpretation via different types of automata.

All the constructions that have been cited as evidence for the need of context-sensitive grammatical devices for the description of natural languages seem to be amenable to an analysis within the framework of context-free tree grammars or multiple context-free grammars. Based on the Mezei and Wright (1967) result according to which structural accounts of the context-free tree level can be lifted to the regular tree level where composition and projection occur as explicit node labels, the third part of the book has focused on a fine-grained analysis of the process connecting the initial level of explicit trees with the intended level of context-free or macro trees. In accordance with the three types of classical approaches in formal language theory we have provided logical, grammatical and automata-theoretic characterizations of the homomorphism relating the initial tree algebra of (Lawvere) terms to the substitution algebra of macro terms. Along the way first steps were taken in the direction of "reverse" linguistics. For contemporary models such as Tree Adjoining Grammar and Minimalism it has been shown how to accommodate their main ideas within the algebraic framework outlined above.

Beyond these particular observations, it is interesting to see what the prominent existing approaches in linguistic theory look like when recast in this algebraic, two-step setting.

Building on the formulation of central proposals in tree adjoining grammar, categorial grammar, and even formulations of Chomskian minimalist grammars that have been formalized by the work of Stabler, Michaelis and others in an algebra of trees, the work presented in this work leads to precise ways of translating or "embedding" the proposals in one notation into proposals of other notations, allowing comparisons among theories that were not possible before. Already, the intertranslatability results have allowed parsing algorithms for one notation to be adapted to other notations (Stabler 1999a; Harkema 2000; Morawietz 2000a,b) and even influenced the development of formalisms in the minimalist tradition (Stabler and Keenan 2000). Further development of this perspective promises much deeper insight into the fundamental properties of human languages, properties that notational diversity is too often obscuring. In particular, ongoing work reveals that a very wide range of notations are intertranslatable, and with this development, the prospects for clear, precise and general statements of the universal properties of human languages look very good, including in particular, specifications of minimal sets of basic operations required to define human languages.

The influence of the formal work on minimalist grammars has led to a reformulation of Stabler's analysis of MGs. In Stabler and Keenan (2000) MGs are very close to MCFGs. This has an interesting effect on the generative capacity. While we have been careful in the course of this monograph to focus on the *weak* generative capacity, the new formalization is *strongly* equivalent, i.e., not only the sets of strings, but also the tree sets generated by MGs and the derived MCFGs are equivalent.

The question of strong and weak generative capacity with respect to TAGs and MCFTGs can also be answered. Analysis of the equivalence proof of TAGs and MCFTGs reveals that both generate "similar" tree sets. The fact that we are not dealing with equality but rather with similarity is due to the use of adjunction constraints in TAGs. These constraints have to be simulated in MCFTGs with different nonterminals. By constructing appropriate equivalence classes of these nonterminals, we can identify the tree generated by the TAG. So, in a certain limited sense, we have strong equivalence.

The price we have to pay for the extensions gained with the two-step approach is the loss of the naturalness of MSO logic as a description language for natural language syntax. It is no longer possible to write MSO formulas to directly encode principles as in Rogers's monograph. We now have to take a detour via the tree grammar formalisms.

Chapter 13

Outlook

Given the background of the general research agenda specified in this book, some areas of further research impose themselves that seem well suited to continue the work previously described.

Even though the existence of context-sensitive phenomena in natural languages is firmly established, an open debate continues about the exact level of complexity that has to be assumed for a descriptively adequate linguistic theory. As we presented in the introduction, the desiderata for a mildly context-sensitive grammar formalism include semi-linearity. But there might be one phenomenon, namely case-stacking in Old Georgian, which is not semi-linear (Michaelis and Kracht 1997). The empirical debate is still open, but if case-stacking is as productive as it is claimed to be, it cannot be formalized within multiple context-free grammars since those are semi-linear. The condition in the definition of multiple context-free grammars that is responsible for this weakness is the stipulation that each component of the value of an associated mapping is not allowed to appear in the value of the function more than once. Dropping this condition leads to a much larger class of languages where structures like unlimited case-stackings in Old Georgian can easily be described. The question which poses itself immediately is "Are natural languages semi-linear?". Further work has to be invested in this question on the empirical side. On the other hand, please note that Mönnich (1997b) has shown that CFTGs are powerful enough to account for the structures necessary to analyze Old Georgian case structures.

The question whether one can indeed characterize a class of languages with the proposed two-step approach is also open. It is a natural question which class of languages is captured by coupling an RTG with an MSO-definable transduction. But note that we are not addressing this general problem in our monograph. Rather, we are asking ourselves which class of languages can be characterized by RTGs in the special form of lifted Lawvere terms coupled with an MSO transduction implementing the unique homomorphism between the algebra of Lawvere terms to the underlying intended algebra. Again, this question is too ambitious to be answered here. But we have shown in this work that in the even more specific case that we are dealing with RTGs which result from lifting (linear) CFTGs or MCFGs, the transduction we proposed results in tree sets which are generated by (linear) CFTGs or MCFGs respectively. In this very special case, we indeed gave a characterization in the technical sense, and not only a description of the language classes involved.

In the conclusion we have stated that we are able to use our algebraic approach as a unifying framework for natural language formalisms. We have shown how to represent theories in the tradition of Government & Binding, Minimalism and Tree Adjoining Grammars both with an operational and an denotational semantics. A similar representation of the main missing contemporary formalism, namely HPSG, seems to be much more difficult. As is well known, the results by Büchi (1960), Thatcher and Wright (1968) and Doner (1970) and Rabin (1969) on the equivalence between logical and grammatical specifications of regular families of trees cannot be extended to graphs. However, recent results on the logical definability of graphs state that regular sets of trees over a fixed set of graph operations are second-order definable. The direction of further research now aims at a reformulation of feature logics such as the one proposed by King (1994a) into MSO logic. This attempt seems feasible since the regular set of trees which serves as the central ingredient of the MSO definable graph languages is again amenable to the techniques we presented in this book. The consequence of this reformulation would be not only an operational approach toward HPSG, but would also allow the analysis of the highly idiosyncratic feature logics with more standard mathematical means.

Further work must also be invested in the practical applications of the two-step approach. We already sketched the possible areas of web technology, i.e., the analysis, storage, retrieval and querying of structured documents via the developed logical tools. The development of MSO logic based systems seems a promising application of widespread use. The major obstacle here may be the non-elementary computational complexity of the logic-to-automaton compilation technique.

However, in recent research Neven and Schwentick (2002) have proposed a limited version of MSO logic, called *guarded* MSO, which has a far better complexity but is still as expressive as the original. The price one has to pay is that the guarded formulas may be exponentially longer than the original ones. It is an open question whether guarded MSO would be suitable for our purposes.

Furthermore, considering the need for finite-state calculi with a generative capacity higher than regular languages, it seems promising to develop and implement an MSO logic based toolkit for the specification of finite-state grammars. Since the generated tree automata are neutral with respect to the difference between generating and accepting devices there are no theoretical or practical obstacles concerning the level of regular tree sets which can be handled, although the additional control information has to be filtered by the intersection with a second finite-state device.

Building on such a toolkit, it would be extremely interesting to construct appropriate grammars and experiment with the resulting tree automata with respect to parsing and generation.

Maybe the most ambitious goal for further research is the isolation of linguistic universals. The algebraic approach allows us to treat a language as the closure of a set of basic items under defined operations. The algebraic approach towards language invariants developed by Ed Keenan and Ed Stabler has already been applied to several fragments of languages and has helped to put the comparison between different linguistic similarity types on a firm methodological basis Keenan and Stabler (1996, 1997); Stabler and Keenan (2000). So, the goal would be to reduce the needed operations to a small set of grammatical primitives. Naturally we have to differentiate between the artificial functions (e.g., composition, projection and tuple-formation) responsible for the recursive structure and the functions responsible for the linguistic structural similarity (e.g., case-marking or inflectional functions). The identification of such a (minimal) set for both classes of functions can then be tested against data from different languages. If these tests are successful one can claim the universality of the proposed linguistic functions.

Part V

Appendix

Appendix A

Acronyms

CCG	combinatory categorial grammar
CFTG	context-free tree grammar
FSA	finite-state automaton
FSLP	finite-state language processing
FST	finite-state transducer
FSTA	bottom-up finite-state tree automaton
FSTWA	finite-state tree-walking automaton
GB	government & binding
GPSG	generalized phrase structure grammar
HG	head grammar
HPSG	head-driven phrase structure grammar
IG	indexed grammar
LCFRS	linear context-free rewriting system
LIG	linear indexed grammar
LUSCG	linear unordered scattered context grammar
MCFG	multiple context-free grammar
MCFTG	monadic context-free tree grammar
MCTAG	set local multi-component tree adjoining grammar
MG	minimalist grammar
MSO	monadic second-order logic
MTT	macro tree transducer
PF	phonetic form
P&P	principles & parameters
RTG	regular tree grammar
TAG	tree adjoining grammar
TDTT	top-down tree transducer

Appendix B

MONA code

B.1 XBar Theory

```
# switch to tree mode
ws2s;

#################################################################
# VARIABLE DECLARATIONS
var1 x,y,z,a,b,c;
var2 Bar0,Bar1,Bar2,John,Sleeps,
     X,Y, Adj, N, V, I1,I2,I3,I4,I5,I6, Base, Trace, Parse;

#################################################################
#
# PREDICATE DECLARATIONS
#
#################################################################

#################################################################
# tree logic signature
# immediate dominance
pred id (var1 x, var1 y) = (x.0 = y) | (x.1 = y);
# transitive closure of immediate dominance
pred d (var1 x, var1 y) = (x < y);
# transitive reflexive closure of immediate dominance
pred rd (var1 x, var1 y) = (x <= y);
# precedence
pred p (var1 x, var1 y) = ex1 z,u,v: rd(u,x) & rd(v,y) &
                                      (z.0 = u) & (z.1 = v) &
                                      x ~= y;
```

```
#####################################################################
# auxiliary definitions

# all sets are a subset of the set in the first argument
pred Subs11( var2 X, var2 A, var2 B, var2 C, var2 D, var2 E,
             var2 F, var2 G, var2 H, var2 I, var2 J ) =
           A sub X & B sub X & C sub X & D sub X & E sub X &
           F sub X & G sub X & H sub X & I sub X & J sub X;

# disjointN: N the number of disjoint sets
pred disjoint2(var2 A, var2 B) =
        (~ (ex1 t: ( t in A & t in B )) );
pred disjoint3(var2 A, var2 B, var2 C) =
        (~ (ex1 t: ( t in A & t in B )) &
         ~ (ex1 t: ( t in A & t in C )) &
         ~ (ex1 t: ( t in B & t in C )) );
pred disjoint4(var2 A, var2 B, var2 C, var2 D) =
        (~ (ex1 t: ( t in A & t in B )) &
         ~ (ex1 t: ( t in A & t in C )) &
         ~ (ex1 t: ( t in A & t in D )) &
         ~ (ex1 t: ( t in B & t in C )) &
         ~ (ex1 t: ( t in B & t in D )) &
         ~ (ex1 t: ( t in C & t in D )) );
pred disjoint5(var2 A, var2 B, var2 C, var2 D, var2 E) =
        (~ (ex1 t: ( t in A & t in B )) &
         ~ (ex1 t: ( t in A & t in C )) &
         ~ (ex1 t: ( t in A & t in D )) &
         ~ (ex1 t: ( t in A & t in E )) &
         ~ (ex1 t: ( t in B & t in C )) &
         ~ (ex1 t: ( t in B & t in D )) &
         ~ (ex1 t: ( t in B & t in E )) &
         ~ (ex1 t: ( t in C & t in D )) &
         ~ (ex1 t: ( t in C & t in E )) &
         ~ (ex1 t: ( t in D & t in E )) );
pred disjoint6(var2 A, var2 B, var2 C, var2 D, var2 E, var2 F) =
        (~ (ex1 t: ( t in A & t in B )) &
         ~ (ex1 t: ( t in A & t in C )) &
         ~ (ex1 t: ( t in A & t in D )) &
         ~ (ex1 t: ( t in A & t in E )) &
         ~ (ex1 t: ( t in A & t in F )) &
         ~ (ex1 t: ( t in B & t in C )) &
         ~ (ex1 t: ( t in B & t in D )) &
```

```
        ~ (ex1 t: ( t in B & t in E )) &
        ~ (ex1 t: ( t in B & t in F )) &
        ~ (ex1 t: ( t in C & t in D )) &
        ~ (ex1 t: ( t in C & t in E )) &
        ~ (ex1 t: ( t in C & t in F )) &
        ~ (ex1 t: ( t in D & t in E )) &
        ~ (ex1 t: ( t in D & t in F )) &
        ~ (ex1 t: ( t in E & t in F )) );

# Rogers's thesis page 49/50
pred myroot( var1 x ) = (all1 y: rd(x,y));
pred InclRoot ( var2 X ) = ex1 x: (x in X & myroot(x));
pred Rooted ( var2 X ) =
     ex1 x: ( all1 y: (x in X & (y in X => rd(x,y))));
pred Connected ( var2 X ) =
    all1 x,y,z: ((x in X & y in X & rd(x,z) & rd(z,y)) =>
                 z in X);
pred Path( var2 X ) = Connected(X) &
    all1 x,y: ((x in X & y in X) => (rd(x,y) | rd(y,x)));
pred Subset( var2 X, var2 Y ) = X sub Y;

# trees are connected sets which contain the root
pred Tree (var2 Parse) =
    Connected( Parse ) & InclRoot( Parse );


###############################################################
#
# LINGUISTICALLY MOTIVATED DEFINITIONS
#
###############################################################

###############################################################
# LEXICON: a naive and small one
pred Lexicon ( var1 x, var2 N, var2 V, var2 John, var2 Sleeps ) =
    disjoint2(John,Sleeps) &
    ( x in John & x in N & x notin V ) |
    ( x in Sleeps & x in V & x notin N);

# c-command: a node x c-commands another one y in case all nodes
# which properly dominate it, also dominate the other and it does
# not dominate or equal y.
```

```
pred c_com (var1 x, var1 y) = all1 z: ( d(z,x) => d(z,y) ) &
     ~(rd(x,y));

# technical definitions to ensure equality of feature bundles
pred FEq (var1 x, var1 y, var2 N, var2 V ) =
    (x in N <=> y in N) &
    (x in V <=> y in V) ;
pred Projects (var1 x, var1 y, var2 N, var2 V ) =
    (x in N <=> y in N) &
    (x in V <=> y in V) ;

##############################################################
# Xbar - THEORY
#        on catories not on nodes

# auxiliary for category
pred Component ( var2 X, var2 Adj, var2 N, var2 V ) =
    Path(X) &
    all1 x,y: ((x in X & y in X) => FEq(x,y,N,V)) &
    all1 x,v: ex1 y: all1 z: ( (x in X & v in X & id(x,v)) =>
             (v notin Adj & id(x,y) & v ~= y & y in Adj &
                 (id(x,z) => (z = v | z = y))));
# a category is a maximal component
pred Category ( var2 X, var2 Adj, var2 N, var2 V ) =
    Component(X,Adj,N,V) &
    all2 Y: ((Subset(X,Y) & ~(Subset(Y,X))) =>
            ~(Component(Y,Adj,N,V)));
pred Category1 ( var2 X, var1 x, var2 Adj, var2 N, var2 V ) =
    Category(X,Adj,N,V) & x in X;
pred Cat ( var1 x, var1 y, var2 Adj, var2 N, var2 V ) =
    ex2 X: Category1(X,x,Adj,N,V) & Category1(X,y,Adj,N,V);
# highest and lowest element of a category
pred MaxSeg ( var1 x, var2 Adj, var2 N, var2 V ) =
    ex2 X: (Category1(X,x,Adj,N,V) & all1 y: (y in X =>
           rd(x,y)));
pred MinSeg ( var1 x, var2 Adj, var2 N, var2 V ) =
    ex2 X: (Category1(X,x,Adj,N,V) & all1 y: (y in X =>
           rd(y,x)));

# relations among categories
pred D( var1 x, var1 y, var2 Adj, var2 N, var2 V ) =
    all1 v: (Cat(x,v,Adj,N,V) => d(v,y));
```

```
pred Excludes( var1 x, var1 y, var2 Adj, var2 N, var2 V ) =
    all1 v: (Cat(x,v,Adj,N,V) => ~(rd(v,y)));
pred Includes( var1 x, var1 y, var2 Adj, var2 N, var2 V ) =
    ~(Excludes(x,y,Adj,N,V));
pred LeftOf( var1 x, var1 y, var2 Adj, var2 N, var2 V ) =
    Excludes(x,y,Adj,N,V) & Excludes(y,x,Adj,N,V) & p(x,y);
pred ID( var1 x, var1 y, var2 Adj, var2 N, var2 V ) =
    D(x,y,Adj,N,V) &
    ~( ex1 z: ((Excludes(z,x,Adj,N,V) & D(z,y,Adj,N,V)) |
               (z in Adj & Excludes(z,x,Adj,N,V) &
                     Includes(z,y,Adj,N,V))));

# command relations again
pred CCom( var1 x, var1 y, var2 Adj, var2 N, var2 V ) =
    ~(D(x,y,Adj,N,V)) & ~(D(y,x,Adj,N,V)) &
    all1 z: (D(z,x,Adj,N,V) => D(z,y,Adj,N,V));
pred MCom( var1 x, var1 y, var2 Adj, var2 N, var2 V,
           var2 Bar2 ) =
    ~(D(x,y,Adj,N,V)) & ~(D(y,x,Adj,N,V)) &
    all1 z: ((x in Bar2 & D(z,x,Adj,N,V)) => D(z,y,Adj,N,V));
pred ACCom( var1 x, var1 y, var2 Adj, var2 N, var2 V ) =
    CCom(x,y,Adj,N,V) & ~(CCom(y,x,Adj,N,V));

# identifying nodes with certain properties: Head, XP, Comp, Spec
pred HeadXP( var1 x, var1 y, var2 Adj, var2 N, var2 V ) =
    ID(y,x,Adj,N,V) &
    all1 z: ID(y,z,Adj,N,V) => ~(LeftOf(x,z,Adj,N,V));
pred HeadXBar( var1 x, var1 y, var2 Adj, var2 N, var2 V ) =
    ID(y,x,Adj,N,V) &
    all1 z: ID(y,z,Adj,N,V) => ~(LeftOf(z,x,Adj,N,V));

pred MaxProjection( var1 x, var1 y, var2 Bar2, var2 Adj, var2 N,
                    var2 V, var2 Base ) =
    ( y in Base | y in Bar2 ) &
    x in Bar2 & Includes(x,y,Adj,N,V) &
    all1 z: ((z in Bar2 & Includes(z,y,Adj,N,V)) =>
             Includes(z,x,Adj,N,V));
pred MaxProj( var1 x, var2 Bar2 ) =
    x in Bar2;

pred Head ( var1 x, var1 y, var2 Bar2, var2 Adj, var2 N,
            var2 V, var2 Base ) =
```

```
    ( y in Base | y in Bar2 ) &
    ex1 v,w: ( MaxProjection(w,y,Bar2,Adj,N,V,Base) &
               HeadXP(v,w,Adj,N,V) & HeadXBar(x,v,Adj,N,V));
pred Hea (var1 x, var2 Bar2, var2 Adj, var2 N, var2 V,
          var2 Base ) =
    ex1 y: Head(x,y,Bar2,Adj,N,V,Base);

pred Comp ( var1 x, var1 y, var2 Bar2, var2 Adj, var2 N,
            var2 V, var2 Base ) =
    ( y in Base | y in Bar2 ) &
    ex1 v,w: ( MaxProjection(w,y,Bar2,Adj,N,V,Base) &
               HeadXP(v,w,Adj,N,V) & ID(v,x,Adj,N,V) &
               ~(HeadXBar(x,v,Adj,N,V)));
pred Com(var1 x, var2 Bar2, var2 Adj, var2 N,
         var2 V, var2 Base ) =
    ex1 y: Comp(x,y,Bar2,Adj,N,V,Base);

pred Spec( var1 x, var1 y,
           var2 Bar2, var2 Adj, var2 N, var2 V, var2 Base ) =
    ( y in Base | y in Bar2 ) &
    ex1 w: ( MaxProjection(w,y,Bar2,Adj,N,V,Base) &
             ID(w,x,Adj,N,V) & ~(HeadXP(x,w,Adj,N,V)));
pred Spe(var1 x, var2 Bar2, var2 Adj, var2 N,
         var2 V, var2 Base ) =
    ex1 y: Spec(x,y,Bar2,Adj,N,V,Base);

################################################################
# PRINCIPLES

# distribution of the Adj feature
pred adj( var2 Parse, var2 Adj, var2 N, var2 V ) =
    all1 x where ( x in Parse ): ( x in Adj =>
          ( ex1 y,z where ( y in Parse & z in Parse):
               ( ex2 Y: id(y,x) & id(y,z) & Category(Y,Adj,N,V) &
                  y in Y & z in Y )));

# some more restrictions on Adjuncts
pred adjres( var2 Parse, var2 Bar0, var2 Bar2, var2 Adj, var2 N,
             var2 V, var2 Base, var2 Trace, var2 John,
             var2 Sleeps ) =
    all1 x,y where ( x in Parse & y in Parse): ( ( x in Adj &
                    id(x,y)) =>
```

```
                ( y notin Trace & ~ Lexicon(y,N,V,John,Sleeps) &
                ( (x in Bar0 & y in Bar0) |
                  (x in Bar2 & y notin Bar0)))) &
    ~(ex1 x,y where ( x in Parse & y in Parse):
                ( x in  Bar0 & id(x,y) & y in Adj &
                  y notin Base) );

# every node has to have a barlevel or be lexical
pred bar( var2 Parse, var2 Bar0, var2 Bar1, var2 Bar2, var2 N,
          var2 V, var2 John, var2 Sleeps  ) =
    all1 x where ( x in Parse ): ( x in Bar0 | x in Bar1 |
                   x in Bar2 | Lexicon(x,N,V,John,Sleeps) );

# conditions on xbar structure depending on barlevel
pred barZero( var2 Parse, var2 Bar0, var2 Adj, var2 N, var2 V,
              var2 Base, var2 John, var2 Sleeps  ) =
    all1 x where ( x in Parse ): (x in Bar0 =>
           (( ex1 y where ( y in Parse ):
               ( ID(x,y,Adj,N,V) &
                 all1 v where ( v in Parse ):
                        ( ID(x,v,Adj,N,V) =>
                          v = y ))) &
            ( all1 y where ( y in Parse ): ( ID(x,y,Adj,N,V) =>
                    (Lexicon(y,N,V,John,Sleeps) &
                     Projects(x,y,N,V) &
                     (x in Base <=> y in Base))))));
pred barOne( var2 Parse, var2 Bar0, var2 Bar1, var2 Bar2,
             var2 Adj, var2 N, var2 V ) =
    all1 x where ( x in Parse ): (x in Bar1 =>
           ( (ex1 y where ( y in Parse ): (
                    HeadXBar(y,x,Adj,N,V) &
                    y in Bar0 & Projects(x,y,N,V))) &
             (all1 y where ( y in Parse ): (
                      (ID(x,y,Adj,N,V) &
                       ~(HeadXBar(y,x,Adj,N,V))) =>
                      y in Bar2 ))));
pred barTwo( var2 Parse, var2 Bar1, var2 Bar2, var2 Adj, var2 N,
             var2 V, var2 Trace ) =
    all1 x where ( x in Parse ): (x in Bar2 =>
           (( x in Trace & (all1 y where ( y in Parse ):
                      (~(D(x,y,Adj,N,V))))) |
            ( ex1 y where ( y in Parse ): (
```

```
                    HeadXP(y,x,Adj,N,V) &
                    y in Bar1 & Projects(x,y,N,V)) &
              all1 y where ( y in Parse ): (
                      (ID(x,y,Adj,N,V) &
                       ~(HeadXP(y,x,Adj,N,V))) =>
                      y in Bar2 ))));

# the xbar principle
pred XBar ( var2 Parse, var2 Bar0, var2 Bar1, var2 Bar2,
            var2 Adj, var2 N, var2 V,
            var2 Base, var2 Trace, var2 John, var2 Sleeps  ) =
    adj(Parse,Adj,N,V) &
    adjres(Parse,Bar0,Bar2,Adj,N,V,Base,Trace,John,Sleeps) &
    bar(Parse,Bar0,Bar1,Bar2,N,V,John,Sleeps) &
    barZero(Parse,Bar0,Adj,N,V,Base,John,Sleeps) &
    barOne(Parse,Bar0,Bar1,Bar2,Adj,N,V) &
    barTwo(Parse,Bar1,Bar2,Adj,N,V,Trace);

##################################################################
# FEATURE PRINCIPLES
pred Features( var2 Parse, var2 Bar0, var2 Bar1, var2 Bar2,
               var2 Adj, var2 N, var2 V, var2 Base, var2 Trace,
               var2 John, var2 Sleeps ) =
    Subs11(Parse,Bar0,Bar1,Bar2,Adj,N,V,Base,Trace,John,Sleeps) &
    (~(ex1 x,y where ( x in Parse & y in Parse):
                  (x in John | x in Sleeps) & id(x,y)));

##################################################################
# GRAMMAR FORMULA
# we are interested only in a certain part of the result -> a
# labeled parse tree which has to be
#  -- finite
#  -- a tree
#  -- restrictions on the variables representing features
#      + all labels appear only in the tree (this makes the
#        automaton smaller)
#      + Bar levels are disjoint
#  -- linguistic modules
#      + X-Bar theory
#      + Government
#      + Lexicon (lexical entries are represented as disjoint
        sets)
```

```
#       + Binding & Control
#       + Chains
#      (+ Reconstruction )
pred Gram( var2 Parse, var2 Bar0, var2 Bar1, var2 Bar2,
           var2 Adj, var2 N, var2 V,
           var2 Base, var2 Trace, var2 John, var2 Sleeps  ) =
    Tree(Parse) &
    Features(Parse,Bar0,Bar1,Bar2,Adj,N,V,Base,Trace,John,
             Sleeps) &
    XBar(Parse,Bar0,Bar1,Bar2,Adj,N,V,Base,Trace,John,Sleeps);


##############################################################
# formula to compile

Gram(Parse,Bar0,Bar1,Bar2,Adj,N,V,Base,Trace,John,Sleeps);
```

B.2 Co-Indexation

We refrain from giving the full definition of the various disjointness predicates. They are further generalizations of the ones given in the previous section.

```
# switch to tree mode
ws2s;

##############################################################
# VARIABLE DECLARATIONS
var1 a,b,c;
var2 I1,I2,I3,I4,I5,I6,I7,I8, Trace, P;

##############################################################
#
# PREDICATE DECLARATIONS
#
##############################################################

##############################################################
# tree logic signature
# immediate dominance
pred id (var1 x, var1 y) = (x.0 = y) | (x.1 = y);

# transitive closure of immediate dominance
pred d (var1 x, var1 y) = (x < y);
```

```
# transitive reflexive closure of immediate dominance
pred rd (var1 x, var1 y) = (x <= y);
# precedence
pred p (var1 x, var1 y) = ex1 z,u,v: rd(u,x) & rd(v,y) &
                                     (z.0 = u) & (z.1 = v) &
                                     x ~= y;

##############################################################
# auxiliary definitions
# omitted:
# disjointN: N the number of disjoint sets

##############################################################
#
# LINGUISTICALLY MOTIVATED DEFINITIONS
#
##############################################################

##############################################################
# c-command: a node x c-commands another one y in case all nodes
# which properly dominate it, also dominate the other and it does
# not dominate or equal y.
pred c_com (var1 x, var1 y) = all1 z: ( d(z,x) => d(z,y) ) &
                                      ~(rd(x,y));

# additional conditions: directed, asymmetric c-command
pred da_ccom (var1 x, var1 y) = c_com(x,y) & ~( c_com(y,x)) &
                                p(x,y);

##############################################################
# INDEX THEORY: we need N different indices to mark the occurring
# chains; two nodes are co-indexed in case they are both in the
# same index and all other indices are either disjoint or equal.

# indexN: N the number of indices
pred index1 (var2 X, var2 I1) =
    (X = I1);
pred index2 (var2 X, var2 I1, var2 I2) =
    ((X = I1) | (X = I2)) & disjoint2(I1,I2);
pred index3 (var2 X, var2 I1, var2 I2, var2 I3) =
    ((X = I1) | (X = I2) | (X = I3)) & disjoint3(I1,I2,I3);
```

```
pred index4 (var2 X, var2 I1, var2 I2, var2 I3, var2 I4) =
    ((X = I1) | (X = I2) | (X = I3) | (X = I4)) &
     disjoint4(I1,I2,I3,I4);
pred index5 (var2 X, var2 I1, var2 I2, var2 I3, var2 I4,
                     var2 I5) =
    ((X = I1) | (X = I2) | (X = I3) | (X = I4) |
     (X = I5)) & disjoint5(I1,I2,I3,I4,I5);
pred index6 (var2 X, var2 I1, var2 I2, var2 I3, var2 I4,
                     var2 I5, var2 I6) =
    ((X = I1) | (X = I2) | (X = I3) | (X = I4) | (X = I5) |
     (X = I6)) & disjoint6(I1,I2,I3,I4,I5,I6);
pred index7 (var2 X, var2 I1, var2 I2, var2 I3, var2 I4,
                     var2 I5, var2 I6, var2 I7) =
    ((X = I1) | (X = I2) | (X = I3) | (X = I4) |
     (X = I5) | (X = I6) | (X = I7)) &
    disjoint7(I1,I2,I3,I4,I5,I6,I7);
pred index8 (var2 X, var2 I1, var2 I2, var2 I3, var2 I4,
                     var2 I5, var2 I6, var2 I7, var2 I8) =
    ((X = I1) | (X = I2) | (X = I3) | (X = I4) |
     (X = I5) | (X = I6) | (X = I7) | (X = I8) ) &
    disjoint8(I1,I2,I3,I4,I5,I6,I7,I8);

# co_idxN: N the number of indices
pred co_idx1 (var1 x, var1 y, var2 I1 ) =
    ex2 X: ( index1(X,I1) & x in X & y in X );
pred co_idx2 (var1 x, var1 y, var2 I1, var2 I2 ) =
    ex2 X: ( index2(X,I1,I2) & x in X & y in X);
pred co_idx3 (var1 x, var1 y, var2 I1, var2 I2, var2 I3 ) =
    ex2 X: ( index3(X,I1,I2,I3) & x in X & y in X );
pred co_idx4 (var1 x, var1 y, var2 I1, var2 I2, var2 I3,
                                var2 I4 ) =
    ex2 X: ( index4(X,I1,I2,I3,I4) & x in X & y in X );
pred co_idx5 (var1 x, var1 y, var2 I1, var2 I2, var2 I3,
              var2 I4, var2 I5 ) =
    ex2 X: ( index5(X,I1,I2,I3,I4,I5) & x in X & y in X );
pred co_idx6 (var1 x, var1 y, var2 I1, var2 I2, var2 I3,
              var2 I4, var2 I5, var2 I6 ) =
    ex2 X: ( index6(X,I1,I2,I3,I4,I5,I6) & x in X & y in X );
pred co_idx7 (var1 x, var1 y, var2 I1, var2 I2, var2 I3,
              var2 I4, var2 I5, var2 I6, var2 I7 ) =
    ex2 X: ( index7(X,I1,I2,I3,I4,I5,I6,I7) & x in X & y in X );
```

```
pred co_idx8 (var1 x, var1 y, var2 I1, var2 I2, var2 I3,
             var2 I4, var2 I5, var2 I6, var2 I7, var2 I8 ) =
    ex2 X: ( index8(X,I1,I2,I3,I4,I5,I6,I7,I8) & x in X &
            y in X );

############################################################
# ECP: if something is a Trace, then there has to exist a
#      c-commanding co-indexed antecedent.
# ecpN: N the number of indices
pred ecp1 (var2 P, var2 Trace, var2 I1) =
    all1 x: ((x in P & x in Trace) =>
            (ex1 y: ( y in P & c_com(y,x) & co_idx1(x,y,I1))));
pred ecp2 (var2 P, var2 Trace, var2 I1, var2 I2) =
    all1 x: ((x in P & x in Trace) =>
            (ex1 y: ( y in P & c_com(y,x) &
                     co_idx2(x,y,I1,I2))));
pred ecp3 (var2 P, var2 Trace, var2 I1, var2 I2, var2 I3) =
    all1 x: ((x in P & x in Trace) =>
            (ex1 y: ( y in P & c_com(y,x) &
                     co_idx3(x,y,I1,I2,I3))));
pred ecp4 (var2 P, var2 Trace, var2 I1, var2 I2, var2 I3,
          var2 I4) =
    all1 x: ((x in P & x in Trace) =>
            (ex1 y: ( y in P & c_com(y,x) &
                     co_idx4(x,y,I1,I2,I3,I4))));
pred ecp5 (var2 P, var2 Trace, var2 I1, var2 I2, var2 I3,
          var2 I4, var2 I5) =
    all1 x: ((x in P & x in Trace) =>
            (ex1 y: ( y in P & c_com(y,x) &
                     co_idx5(x,y,I1,I2,I3,I4,I5))));
pred ecp6 (var2 P, var2 Trace, var2 I1, var2 I2, var2 I3,
          var2 I4, var2 I5, var2 I6) =
    all1 x: ((x in P & x in Trace) =>
            (ex1 y: ( y in P & c_com(y,x) &
                     co_idx6(x,y,I1,I2,I3,I4,I5,I6))));
pred ecp7 (var2 P, var2 Trace, var2 I1, var2 I2, var2 I3,
          var2 I4, var2 I5, var2 I6, var2 I7) =
    all1 x: ((x in P & x in Trace) =>
            (ex1 y: ( y in P & c_com(y,x) &
                     co_idx7(x,y,I1,I2,I3,I4,I5,I6,I7))));
```

```
pred ecp8 (var2 P, var2 Trace, var2 I1, var2 I2, var2 I3,
           var2 I4, var2 I5, var2 I6, var2 I7, var2 I8) =
    all1 x: ((x in P & x in Trace) =>
             (ex1 y: ( y in P & c_com(y,x) &
                       co_idx8(x,y,I1,I2,I3,I4,I5,I6,I7,I8))));

####################################################################
# formula(s) to compile

# ecp1(P,Trace,I1);
# ecp2(P,Trace,I1,I2);
# ecp3(P,Trace,I1,I2,I3);
# ecp4(P,Trace,I1,I2,I3,I4);
# ecp5(P,Trace,I1,I2,I3,I4,I5);
# ecp6(P,Trace,I1,I2,I3,I4,I5,I6);
ecp7(P,Trace,I1,I2,I3,I4,I5,I6,I7);
# ecp8(P,Trace,I1,I2,I3,I4,I5,I6,I7,I8);
```

Appendix C

Additional MSO Definitions

C.1 The MSO Definition of Intended Dominance for Γ^L Structures

The translation via (5.3) on page 79 of the walking-language $W_\blacktriangleleft$ derived from the tree-walking automaton $\mathfrak{A}_\blacktriangleleft$ in Figure 11.2 on page 159 yields the following MSO-definition of $\blacktriangleleft_W$ for binary branching intended trees and underlying grammars with macros with at most four parameters. We allow ourselves a predicate $\mathsf{lexical}(x)$ which identifies all elements with a "lexical" label, i.e., in the example those are $\bullet'$, ε, a', b', c', and d'.

(C.1)
$$\begin{aligned} x \blacktriangleleft_W y \overset{def}{\iff}\ & \mathsf{trans}_{W_\blacktriangleleft}(x,y) \\ \overset{def}{\iff}\ & \mathsf{lexical}(x) \wedge (\exists z)[\mathsf{edg}_1(z,x) \wedge \\ & (\exists u)[(\mathsf{edg}_2(z,u) \vee \mathsf{edg}_3(z,u) \vee \mathsf{edg}_4(z,u) \vee \mathsf{edg}_5(z,u)) \wedge \\ & \quad (\forall X)(\forall v,w)[(v \in X \wedge (c\text{-}\mathsf{link}(v,w) \vee \\ & \qquad (\pi_1\text{-}\mathsf{link}(v,w) \vee \pi_2\text{-}\mathsf{link}(v,w) \vee \\ & \qquad \pi_3\text{-}\mathsf{link}(v,w) \vee \pi_4\text{-}\mathsf{link}(v,w))) \to \\ & \qquad w \in X) \wedge (u \in X \to y \in X)] \wedge \\ & \qquad \mathsf{lexical}(y)]]. \end{aligned}$$

(C.2)
$$c\text{-}\mathsf{link}(x,y) \overset{def}{\iff} C(x) \wedge \mathsf{edg}_1(x,y)$$

(C.3)
$$\begin{aligned} \pi_1\text{-}\mathsf{link}(x,y) \overset{def}{\iff}\ & \Pi_1(x) \wedge (\exists z)(\forall X)(\forall u,v)[(u \in X \wedge \\ & (\mathsf{edg}_2(v,u) \vee \mathsf{edg}_3(v,u) \vee \mathsf{edg}_4(v,u) \vee \mathsf{edg}_5(v,u)) \\ & \to v \in X) \wedge (x \in X \to z \in X) \wedge \\ & (\exists w)[\mathsf{edg}_1(w,z) \wedge \mathsf{edg}_2(w,y)]]. \end{aligned}$$

(C.4) $$\pi_2\text{-link}(x,y) \overset{def}{\Longleftrightarrow} \Pi_2(x) \wedge (\exists z)(\forall X)(\forall u,v)[(u \in X \wedge (\mathsf{edg}_2(v,u) \vee \mathsf{edg}_3(v,u) \vee \mathsf{edg}_4(v,u) \vee \mathsf{edg}_5(v,u)) \rightarrow v \in X) \wedge (x \in X \rightarrow z \in X) \wedge (\exists w)[\mathsf{edg}_1(w,z) \wedge \mathsf{edg}_3(w,y)]].$$

We omit the corresponding definitions for $\pi_3\text{-link}(x,y)$ and $\pi_4\text{-link}(x,y)$.

The edg-relations used above are instances of the following definition scheme suitable for the general, n-branching tree (note that it was already given in (5.4) on page 79):

(C.5) $$\mathsf{edg}_n(x,y) \overset{def}{\Longleftrightarrow} (\exists x_1,\ldots,x_{n-1})[x \lhd x_1 \wedge \cdots \wedge x \lhd x_{n-1} \wedge x \lhd y \wedge x_1 \prec x_2 \wedge \cdots \wedge x_{n-1} \prec y \wedge (\forall w)[x \lhd w \wedge w \not\approx x_1 \wedge \cdots \wedge w \not\approx x_{n-1} \wedge w \not\approx y \rightarrow y \prec w]]$$

In a similar vein, generalization of $\blacktriangleleft_W$ to the unrestricted case $\blacktriangleleft$ of the n-branching tree and macros of arity $i, n, i < \omega$ is trivial. The only changes required concern (C.1) and (C.3/C.4), again introducing a definition scheme in the case of (C.3'):

(C.1') $$x \blacktriangleleft y \overset{def}{\Longleftrightarrow} \mathsf{lexical}(x) \wedge (\exists z)[\mathsf{edg}_1(z,x) \wedge (\exists u)[(\bigvee_{1<n<\omega} \mathsf{edg}_n(z,u)) \wedge (\forall X)(\forall v,w)[(v \in X \wedge (c\text{-link}(v,w) \vee (\bigvee_{1<i<\omega} \pi_i\text{-link}(v,w))) \rightarrow w \in X) \wedge (u \in X \rightarrow y \in X)]] \wedge \mathsf{lexical}(y)].$$

(C.3') $$\pi_i\text{-link}(x,y) \overset{def}{\Longleftrightarrow} \Pi_i(x) \wedge (\exists z)(\forall X)(\forall u,v)[(u \in X \wedge (\bigvee_{1<n<\omega} \mathsf{edg}_n(v,u)) \rightarrow v \in X) \wedge (x \in X \rightarrow z \in X) \wedge (\exists w)[\mathsf{edg}_1(w,z) \wedge \mathsf{edg}_{i+1}(w,y)]].$$

Appendix D

Prolog Code

D.1 Apply a given MTT to a tree generated by an RTG

```
%% Apply an MTT to the trees generated by a regular tree grammar.
%% Output in Latex is possible.

:- ensure_loaded(library(lists)).

:- dynamic latexon/0.

%% Example grammars and MTTs
%:- ensure_loaded(iowa).
%:- ensure_loaded(tcs).
:- ensure_loaded(tag).

%% tree printing
:- ensure_loaded(tree_print).

%%%%%%%%%%%%%%%%%%%%%%%%%%%%%%%%%%%%%%%%%%%%%%%%%%%%%%%%%%%%%%%%%%%%%%
%% generate a tree with an RTG and transduce it using an MTT

%% process( +Tree, -Tree )
process( RTGTree, MTTTree ) :-
        internal_gen( Tree ),
        name_tree( Tree, RTGTree ),
        transduce( RTGTree, MTTTree ).

%%%%%%%%%%%%%%%%%%%%%%%%%%%%%%%%%%%%%%%%%%%%%%%%%%%%%%%%%%%%%%%%%%%%%%
%% tree generation via an RTG
%%
%% uses iterative deepening!
```

```
%% gen( -Tree )
%% gets the start symbol and starts walking and replacing from
%% there, prints the output. While it does so, it counts the
%% number of rule applications - iterative deepening!
gen(Tree) :-
        ssymbol(S),
        num(Steps),
        gen(S,Tree,0,Steps,Steps),
        print('Tree generated with '),
        print(Steps),
        print(' rule applications:'),
        treeprint(Tree).
%% the same as above but without output
internal_gen(Tree) :-
        ssymbol(S),
        num(Steps),
        gen(S,Tree,0,Steps,Steps).

%% gen( +Tree, -Tree, +Depth )
%% the predicate walks the tree, replacing each nonterminal it
%% finds with a tree from a corresponding rule and continues
%% walking. Three cases: we are looking at a terminal, a
%% nonterminal or at a branching node. Case one and three are
%% both handled by the second clause. The process allows exactly
%% Steps steps.
gen(X,Tree,In,Out,Max) :-
        In =< Max,
        atom(X),
        gr(X,LHS),
        NewIn is In+1,
        gen(LHS,Tree,NewIn,Out,Max).
gen(M/Ds,M/NewDs,In,Out,Max):-
        gen_aux(Ds,NewDs,In,Out,Max).

%% gen_aux( +ListOfTrees, -ListOfTrees )
%% simple double recursion needed to walk the daughters
gen_aux([],[],In,In,_Max).
gen_aux([H|T],[Tree|Trees],In,Out,Max):-
        gen(H,Tree,In,Out1,Max),
        gen_aux(T,Trees,Out1,Out,Max).
```

```
%%%%%%%%%%%%%%%%%%%%%%%%%%%%%%%%%%%%%%%%%%%%%%%%%%%%%%%%%%%%%%%%%%%
%% transduction predicates

%% transduce( +Tree, -Tree )
transduce(InTree,OutTree):-
        startstate(Q0),
        print('Input Tree:'),
        treeprint(InTree),
        transduce(Q0,InTree,[],OutTree),
        print('Output Tree:'),
        treeprint(OutTree).

%% transduce( +State, +InTree, +ListOfParameters, -OutTree )
%% InTree is given as (NodeName-Value)/ListOfDaughters
transduce(Q,(N-V)/Ds,Ps,OutTree):-
        rule(Q-[V/Ds,Ps],RHS),
        ( RHS = Sym/L ->                % if something is a
                                        % terminating rule
            ( alph(V) ->                % and belongs to the
                                        % original alphabet
                OutTree = (N-Sym)/L     % - record its node name as
                                        %   well
            ;
                OutTree = Sym/L         % - or else only pass it on
            )
        ;
            trans_star(RHS,OutTree)     % or else recurse on the RHS
        ).

%% trans_star( +RHS, -Tree )
%% is used to construct the parametres from R in Out, calls the
%% new resulting transduction .
trans_star(Q-[H|R],OutTree) :-
        trans_star_aux(R,Out),
        transduce(Q,H,Out,OutTree).

%% trans_star_aux( +ListOfSpecialTrees, -Tree )
%% recurses through the list and transduces the subtrees yielding
%% the parameters
trans_star_aux([],[]).
trans_star_aux([H|T],[R|Rs]) :-
        ( H = _Sym/_L ->               % if something is a tree
```

```
          R = H                    % pass it on
      ;
          H = Q-[Tree|Ps],         % if not transduce it
          transduce(Q,Tree,Ps,R)
      ),
      trans_star_aux(T,Rs).

%%%%%%%%%%%%%%%%%%%%%%%%%%%%%%%%%%%%%%%%%%%%%%%%%%%%%%%%%%%%%%%%%%%%%%%%%%%%%%%%%%%%%%%%%%%%
%% Auxiliaries

%% generates numbers via backtracking
num(1).
num(X) :-
        num(Y),
        X is Y+1.

%% walk a tree and name the nodes uniquely with 'nN', where N is
%% a number.
name_tree( In, Out ) :-
        nametree( In, 0, _, Out ).

%% nametree( +Tree, +NumbersSoFar, -MaxNum, -NewTree )
nametree( X/Ds, In, Out, (Name-X)/NewDs ) :-
        Out1 is In+1,
        make_name(In, Name),
        name_star( Ds, Out1, Out, NewDs ).

%% simple double recursion needed to transform the daughters
name_star([],In,In,[]).
name_star([H|T],In,Out,[Tree|Trees]):-
        nametree(H,In,Out1,Tree),
        name_star(T,Out1,Out,Trees).

%% make_name( +Number, -Atom )
make_name( N, Name ) :-
        number_chars(N,L),
        append([110],L,L1),
        name(Name,L1).
```

D.2 The Example Grammars

D.2.1 The CFTG Example: Γ^L and M_{Γ^L}

```
%%%%%%%%%%%%%%%%%%%%%%%%%% -*- Mode: Prolog -*- %%%%%%%%%%%%%%%%%
%% tcs.pl ---
%% Example grammar and MTT for the CFTG example: Gamma^L

%%%%%%%%%%%%%%%%%%%%%%%%%%%%%%%%%%%%%%%%%%%%%%%%%%%%%%%%%%%%%%%%%
%% Input examples: an alphabet, an RTG and an MTT
%% alphabet - the unlifted signature of the CFTG
alphabet([a,b,c,d,e,dot]).

%% transducer for the CFTG MTT
%% rule( LHS, RHS ).
%% LHS = State - [ AlphabetSymbol/ListOfDaughters,
%%                 ListOfParameters ]
%% RHS = State - ListOfSpecialTrees      or
%%       Tree
%% SpecialTrees can either be trees (daughters [Xs] or parameters
%%              [Ys] from LHS) or State - ListOfTree pairs
startstate(q0).

rule(q0-[c40/[X1,X2,X3,X4,X5],[]],q4-[X1,q0-[X2],q0-[X3],q0-[X4],
     q0-[X5]]).
rule(q0-[X/[],[]],X/[]).

rule(q2-[dot/[],[Y1,Y2]],dot/[Y1,Y2]).

rule(q4-[c44/[X1,X2,X3,X4,X5],[Y1,Y2,Y3,Y4]],
     q4-[X1,q4-[X2,Y1,Y2,Y3,Y4],q4-[X3,Y1,Y2,Y3,Y4],
     q4-[X4,Y1,Y2,Y3,Y4],q4-[X5,Y1,Y2,Y3,Y4]]).
rule(q4-[c24/[X1,X2,X3],[Y1,Y2,Y3,Y4]],
     q2-[X1,q4-[X2,Y1,Y2,Y3,Y4],q4-[X3,Y1,Y2,Y3,Y4]]).
rule(q4-[p41/[],[Y1,_Y2,_Y3,_Y4]],Y1).
rule(q4-[p42/[],[_Y1,Y2,_Y3,_Y4]],Y2).
rule(q4-[p43/[],[_Y1,_Y2,Y3,_Y4]],Y3).
rule(q4-[p44/[],[_Y1,_Y2,_Y3,Y4]],Y4).
rule(q4-[a/[],[_Y1,_Y2,_Y3,_Y4]],a/[]).
rule(q4-[b/[],[_Y1,_Y2,_Y3,_Y4]],b/[]).
rule(q4-[c/[],[_Y1,_Y2,_Y3,_Y4]],c/[]).
rule(q4-[d/[],[_Y1,_Y2,_Y3,_Y4]],d/[]).
rule(q4-[e/[],[_Y1,_Y2,_Y3,_Y4]],e/[]).
```

```
%% RTG (lifted CFTG for the language a^nb^mc^nd^m)
%% rules are: gr( LHS, RHS ) where LHS is a simple nonterminal
%%            and RHS is a lifted tree
%% Note that nonterminals do not have following daughters
ssymbol(s).

gr(s,e/[]).
gr(s,c40/[f,a/[],e/[],c/[],e/[]]).
gr(s,c40/[f,e/[],b/[],e/[],d/[]]).
gr(f,c44/[f,c24/[dot/[],a/[],p41/[]],p42/[],
          c24/[dot/[],c/[],p43/[]],p44/[]]).
gr(f,c44/[f,p41/[], c24/[dot/[],b/[],p42/[]],
          p43/[],c24/[dot/[],d/[],p44/[]]]).
gr(f,c24/[dot/[],c24/[dot/[],c24/[dot/[],p41/[],p42/[]],p43/[]],
     p44/[]]).
```

D.2.2 The TAG Example: Γ^L_{TAG} and $M_{\Gamma^L_{TAG}}$

```
%%%%%%%%%%%%%%%%%%%%%%%% -*- Mode: Prolog -*- %%%%%%%%%%%%%%%%
%% tag.pl ---
%% Example grammar and MTT for the TAG example: Gamma^L_TAG

%%%%%%%%%%%%%%%%%%%%%%%%%%%%%%%%%%%%%%%%%%%%%%%%%%%%%%%%%%%%%%%%%%%%%%%%%
%% Input examples: an alphabet, an RTG and an MTT
%% alphabet - the unlifted signature of the MCFTG
alphabet([a,b,c,d,e,st,st0]).

%% transducer for the MCFTG MTT
%% rule( LHS, RHS ).
%% LHS = State - [ AlphabetSymbol/ListOfDaughters,
%%                 ListOfParameters ]
%% RHS = State - ListOfSpecialTrees or
%%       Tree
%% SpecialTrees can either be trees (daughters [Xs] or parameters
%%              [Ys] from LHS) or State - ListOfTree pairs
startstate(q0).

rule(q0-[c10/[X1,X2],[]],q1-[X1,q0-[X2]]).
rule(q0-[X/[],[]],X/[]).
rule(q0-[X/[]],X/[]).

rule(q3-[st/[],[Y1,Y2,Y3]],st/[Y1,Y2,Y3]).
```

```
rule(q1-[st0/[],[Y1]],st0/[Y1]).
rule(q1-[c11/[X1,X2],[Y1]],
     q1-[X1,q1-[X2,Y1]]).
rule(q1-[c31/[X1,X2,X3,X4],[Y1]],
     q3-[X1,q1-[X2,Y1],q1-[X3,Y1],q1-[X4,Y1]]).
rule(q1-[p11/[],[Y1]],Y1).
rule(q1-[a/[],[_Y1]],a/[]).
rule(q1-[b/[],[_Y1]],b/[]).
rule(q1-[c/[],[_Y1]],c/[]).
rule(q1-[d/[],[_Y1]],d/[]).
rule(q1-[e/[],[_Y1]],e/[]).

%% RTG (lifted MCFTG for the langeuage a^nb^nc^nd^n)
%% rules are: gr( LHS, RHS ) where LHS is a simple nonterminal
%%            and RHS is a lifted tree
%% Note that nonterminals do not have following daughters
ssymbol(sp).

gr(sp,c10/[s,e/[]]).
gr(s,c11/[sb1,c11/[s,c11/[sb2,p11/[]]]]).
gr(s,c11/[st0/[],p11/[]]).
gr(sb1,c31/[st/[],a/[],p11/[],d/[]]).
gr(sb2,c31/[st/[],b/[],p11/[],c/[]]).
```

D.2.3 The MCFG Example: $\mathcal{G}'_{MCFG}$ and $M_{\mathcal{G}'_{MCFG}}$

```
%%%%%%%%%%%%%%%%%%%%%%%%% -*- Mode: Prolog -*- %%%%%%%%%%%%%%%%%
%% mcfg.pl ---
%% Example grammar and MTT for the MCFG example: G'_MCFG

%%%%%%%%%%%%%%%%%%%%%%%%%%%%%%%%%%%%%%%%%%%%%%%%%%%%%%%%%%%%%%%%
%% Input examples: an alphabet, an RTG and an MTT
%% alphabet - the unlifted signature of the MCFG
alphabet([a1,a2,a3,dot]).

%% transducer for the simple example MCFG
%% rule( LHS, RHS ).
%% LHS = State - [ AlphabetSymbol/ListOfDaughters,
                   ListOfParameters ]
%% RHS = State - ListOfSpecialTrees or
%%       Tree
%% SpecialTrees can either be trees (daughters [Xs] or parameters
%%               [Ys] from LHS) or State - ListOfTree pairs
```

```
startstate(q0).

rule(q0-[c031/[X1,X2],[]],q3-[X1,q01-[X2],q02-[X2],q03-[X2]]).
rule(q0-[X/[],[]],X/[]).

rule(q2-[dot/[],[Y1,Y2]],dot/[Y1,Y2]).

rule(q3-[p31/[],[Y1,_Y2,_Y3]],Y1).
rule(q3-[p32/[],[_Y1,Y2,_Y3]],Y2).
rule(q3-[p33/[],[_Y1,_Y2,Y3]],Y3).
rule(q3-[c301/[X1,_X2],[_Y1,_Y2,_Y3]],X1).
%% for the simplified case remove the rule above and uncomment
%% the following three rules
% rule(q3-[a1/[],[_Y1,_Y2,_Y3]],a1/[]).
% rule(q3-[a2/[],[_Y1,_Y2,_Y3]],a2/[]).
% rule(q3-[a3/[],[_Y1,_Y2,_Y3]],a3/[]).
rule(q3-[c321/[X1,X2],[Y1,Y2,Y3]],q2-[X1,q31-[X2,Y1,Y2,Y3],
                                          q32-[X2,Y1,Y2,Y3]]).

rule(q01-[c033/[X1,X2],[]],q31-[X1,q01-[X2],q02-[X2],q03-[X2]]).
rule(q01-[t03/[X1,_X2,_X3],[]],q0-[X1]).

rule(q02-[c033/[X1,X2],[]],q32-[X1,q01-[X2],q02-[X2],q03-[X2]]).
rule(q02-[t03/[_X1,X2,_X3],[]],q0-[X2]).

rule(q03-[c033/[X1,X2],[]],q33-[X1,q01-[X2],q02-[X2],q03-[X2]]).
rule(q03-[t03/[_X1,_X2,X3],[]],q0-[X3]).

rule(q31-[t33/[X1,_X2,_X3],[Y1,Y2,Y3]],q3-[X1,Y1,Y2,Y3]).
rule(q31-[t32/[X1,_X2],[Y1,Y2,Y3]],q3-[X1,Y1,Y2,Y3]).

rule(q32-[t33/[_X1,X2,_X3],[Y1,Y2,Y3]],q3-[X2,Y1,Y2,Y3]).
rule(q32-[t32/[_X1,X2],[Y1,Y2,Y3]],q3-[X2,Y1,Y2,Y3]).

rule(q33-[t33/[_X1,_X2,X3],[Y1,Y2,Y3]],q3-[X3,Y1,Y2,Y3]).

%% RTG (lifted MCFG for the language a1^n a2^n a3^n
%% rules are: gr( LHS, RHS ) where LHS is a simple nonterminal
%%            and RHS is a lifted tree
%% Note that nonterminals do not have following daughters
ssymbol(s).
```

```
gr(a,t03/[a1/[],a2/[],a3/[]]).
gr(s,c031/[c321/[dot/[],t32/[c321/[dot/[],t32/[p31/[],p32/[]]],
     p33/[]]],a]).

% for the simplified case, replace the subtree dominated by c301
% simply by the appropriate ai
gr(a,c033/[t33/[c321/[dot/[],t32/[p31/[],c301/[a1/[],t30/[]]]],
                c321/[dot/[],t32/[p32/[],c301/[a2/[],t30/[]]]],
                c321/[dot/[],t32/[p33/[],c301/[a3/[],t30/[]]]]],
           a]).
```

Notes

1 Formally one can show that the addition of a relation encoding free indexation to Rogers's formal system leads to undecidability via a reduction from the tiling problem.

2 Note that Rogers does not use this fact in his thesis. He used the full power of Rabin's result, namely that SωS, the strong theory of multiple successor functions, is decidable (Rabin 1969). The automata employed there – so called Rabin automata – work on infinite sets and therefore do not have efficient minimization algorithms. Thus, they cannot be used efficiently in applications.

3 If the MSO language $\mathcal{L}$ would contain constants, those would be terms too.

4 For an MSO language with constants c_i, we have to add the line $Free(c_i) = \emptyset$.

5 Note that the variable T denoting the set of nodes under consideration can be used to ensure the finiteness of the characterized trees since finiteness is definable in MSO logic via the lexicographic order ($\trianglelefteq$) inherent in trees: $Finite(X) \overset{def}{\Longleftrightarrow} (\forall Y)(\exists x)(\forall y)[\mathsf{Subset}(Y,X) \rightarrow (x \in Y \wedge (y \in Y \rightarrow y \trianglelefteq x))]$ with $\mathsf{Subset}(X,Y)$ defined as in (3.1) on page 37.

6 For nondeterministic FSAs we need the condition for membership in the language to read $\hat{\delta}(q_0, w) \cap F \neq \emptyset$ under the assumption that we have an appropriate extended transition function $\hat{\delta}$.

7 Note that *top-down* tree automata do not have this property: deterministic top-down tree automata recognize a strictly narrower family of tree sets. Whereas FSAs are reversible, this is not true for tree automata.

8 Sentential forms are built as follows: If $\sigma \in \Sigma^n$ and $t_1, \ldots, t_n$ are sentential forms, then $\sigma(t_1, \ldots, t_n)$ is also a sentential form. And, furthermore, if $q \in Q$ has rank $n+1$ for $n \geq 0$, $s \in T_\Sigma$ and $t_1, \ldots, t_n$ are sentential forms, then $q(s, t_1, \ldots, t_n)$ is a sentential form.

9 We will encounter the same phenomenon in Definition 10.1 on page 135 where we define derivations of context-free tree grammars.

10 There is yet another solution, which is often employed in practice. It is quite easy to assure as part of the construction of primitive automata that certain sets can contain only one member. In effect, this amounts to constructing the relevant cross product automaton, optimizing it and renaming the states.

11 We use this expression as a shorthand for a simple tree with a mother which is labeled with $\underline{0}^n$ and two daughters labeled with λ.

12 Recall from the discussion preceding Definition 4.6 on page 50, that we assume that the leaves of the trees are labeled with terminating λs. As an example, look at the tree displayed in Figure 3.1 on page 38. The node labeled with x is treated as being in state a_3 according to the topmost rule in the right column of the automaton.

13 The curious reader is referred to the proof of Lemma 11 in Thatcher and Wright (1968).

14 It may be more efficient to delay determinization until a negation is actually encountered, at which time we can also minimize the resulting automaton.

15 A detailed analysis of these notions in relation to $\mathcal{L}^2_{K,P}$ can be found in Rogers (1998).

16 The definite clauses in Figure 5.4 on page 77 are given such that the disjunction is reflected via multiple clauses. The constraints which decide whether a clause is applicable are enclosed in curly braces. Clearly, as given here, append constitutes a recursive definition. The auxiliary definitions serve as a (recursive) formalization of lists with appropriate heads and tails.

17 Using the append relation defined in Figure 5.4 on page 77, one can write a predicate successively generating all possible sequences of indices.

18 Note that using the string as a tree as discussed in Section 4.2 on page 49 does not help here since we are after the structure of the string. And, furthermore, we want the yield of a tree to represent the string, not the internal nodes.

19 Without reference to special properties of a particular software tool, in general if $P \Rightarrow Q$ is unsatisfiable then any MSO logic-to-automaton compiler will construct the empty automaton. In that case, $P \wedge \neg Q$ will be satisfiable and the resulting automaton can be used to generate counterexamples to the original query.

20 Note that the problem of estimating the number of indices a sentence will require is considerably simpler than the problem of estimating the number of traces it may contain. Roughly, every movable expression (overt or covert) is either headed by an overt lexical item or else licensed by an overt lexical item's selectional properties.

21 This happened even on the machines of the MONA crew (Nils Klarlund, p.c.).

22 Approaches to Minimalism in the tradition of categorial grammar (e.g., Cornell 1998, 1999a,b; Lecomte 1997, 1998) also address this issue. The advantage we offer with our approach is that we can treat not only Minimalism, but other formalisms such as TAGs and GB and maybe even HPSG (see Chapter 13 on page 187) within the same setup.

23 TAGs are not the focus of our work, but since they are so closely tied to a simplification of the techniques we need to deal with minimalist theories, we can easily incorporate them. For TAGs, the operational/denotational distinction has not been a major theme for research. There are approaches using logical formalisms (e.g. Rambow et al. 1995; Vijay-Shanker et al. 1995) as well as the standard operational one (e.g. Joshi et al. 1975; Joshi 1985, 1987) as well as hybrid ones (e.g., Kallmeyer 1999).

24 GB can still (trivially) be treated with the techniques introduced in the preceding part (going back to Jim Rogers's dissertation).

25 In the figure we also mention simple attribute transducer, which can also be used to implement the desired tree-transductions. But these ATTs are not within the scope of this monograph since they require many more prerequisites which would only distract from the main issues. A preliminary version of a transduction built upon them can be found in Michaelis et al. (2001). The paper by van Vugt (1996) contains more on the equivalence between some mildly context-sensitive grammar formalisms and restricted forms of attribute grammars.

26 The following paragraphs have been taken almost verbatim from Michaelis et al. (2001).

27 For all $\chi, \psi \in N_\tau$, $\chi \triangleleft_\tau \psi$ iff $\psi = \chi i$ for some $i \in \mathbb{N} \setminus \{0\}$, and $\chi \prec_\tau \psi$ iff $\chi = \omega i \chi'$ and $\psi = \omega j \psi'$ for some $\omega, \chi', \psi' \in (\mathbb{N} \setminus \{0\})^*$ and $i, j \in \mathbb{N} \setminus \{0\}$ with $i < j$. Recall that N_τ is a unique *prefix closed* and *left closed* subset of $(\mathbb{N} \setminus \{0\})^*$ (cf. Definition 2.8 on page 21).

28 $\mathsf{Base}_\varepsilon$ stands for $\mathsf{Base} \cup \{\varepsilon\}$.

29 For each (partial) mapping f from a set M_1 into a set M_2 we take $\mathrm{Dom}(f)$ to

denote the *domain of* f, the subset of M_1 for which f is defined.

30 Since all lexical entries are heads, we simply represent them by their respective (unique) labels.

31 MCFGs will be introduced formally in Section 10.1.2 on page 140. LCFRSs are weakly equivalent to MCFGs, but play no further role in this monograph.

32 Our definition uses a certain amount of handwaving and even ignores some aspects of TAGs such as for example adjunction constraints. Therefore it has to be taken with a grain of salt. However, nothing important has been left out such that the claims we make about this simplified version of TAGS are still valid for the full version.

33 We have to leave the question of how much generative capacity is needed open. While we presuppose in this book that mild context-sensitivity is enough, there exist discussions of phenomena which might go beyond, e.g., *Suffixaufnahme* in Old Georgian. We will come back to this point briefly in Chapter 13 on page 187.

34 Clearly, while this is true concerning the levels in the hierarchy, it is not true concerning the generative capacity.

35 Note that the string in the figure is turned by 90 degrees to emphasize the connection to the tree case.

36 Basic morphisms are concatenation, projection and tupling.

37 Here we have to recall the definitions concerning Lawvere algebras from Section 2.3 on page 22.

38 Note that we give the full formal definition although we are dealing with a single sorted set $\mathcal{S}$. The definition simplifies accordingly in the examples.

39 We do not need states for the composition symbols since each composition corresponds to a nonterminal due to the normal form.

40 Since Π-nodes are never leftmost daughters, the sublanguage $\mathrm{L}(x) \cdot \uparrow_1 \cdot (\downarrow_2 \cup \downarrow_3 \cup \downarrow_4 \cup \downarrow_5) \cdot (W_{\Pi_1} \cup W_{\Pi_2} \cup W_{\Pi_3} \cup W_{\Pi_4})^* \cdot W_C{}^* \cdot \mathrm{L}(x)$ would be even more accurate for our purposes. The trivial changes to $\mathfrak{A}_{\blacktriangleleft}$ required to compute exactly this language (adding an extra state and duplicating several transitions) only enlarge the automaton, decreasing its perspicuity without providing any new insights.

41 In this particular example, where we have only one projection node, the only potential fillers will either be a second daughter or the leftmost daughter of a

composition node which is a right daughter.

42 Note that using this solution requires a more general definition of an MSO transduction as well.

43 Note that we discussed the FSTWA defining the precedence relation only for lifted MCFTGs.

44 It is a simple task to translate this recursive definition into a Prolog program. But since we can simulate a Turing machine with Prolog, nothing much is gained on the formal side. In case one considers implementing the approach, it makes sense to use this simple homomorphism directly.

45 The CFTG Γ^L can be found in Example 10.11 on page 143.

46 Although it might seem overkill to present the rules both ways, as terms and as trees, we think that the reader can only profit from two different representations.

47 Recall that a leaf labeled with a term $a_{(3,1)}$ of type $(3,1)$ is a shorthand for the term $c_{(3,0,1)}(a_{(0,1)}, (\ )_{(3,0)})$.

48 Because of the limitation to the appearance of at most one nonterminal on each RHS, we indeed apply the rule to one tree only. Although the use of tuples ensures that more than one variable can be used in each function corresponding to a rule.

49 Note that this informal motivation for the needed states does not mean that the resulting transitions will refer to information about particular daughters.

50 Please recall that the transitions leading to constant symbols of type $(3,1)$ are artifacts of the simplification we alluded to in Example 10.14 on page 148. Note furthermore, that the use of more than one nonterminal on the RHS of an MCFG-rule entails, as outlined in Section 10.2.2 on page 145, extra tupling nodes which naturally have to be accommodated by the MTT. In particular, it has to make use of the additional superscripts to determine the appropriate daughter to find the correct value.

Bibliography

Aho, A. V.

1968 Indexed grammars – an extension to context free grammars. *J. ACM* 15: 647–671

Aho, A. V. and J. D. Ullman

1971 Translations on a context-free grammar. *Information and Control* 19: 439–475

Ayari, A., D. Basin, and A. Podelski

1998 LISA: A specification language based on WS2S. In: M. Nielsen and W. Thomas (eds.), *Computer Science Logic, 11th International Workshop, CSL'97, Annual Conference of the EACSL*, Aarhus, Denmark: Springer, LNCS

Barton, G. E., Jr. and R. C. Berwick

1985 Parsing with assertion sets and information monotonicity. In: *Proceedings of IJCAI-85*, pp. 769–771

Basin, D. and N. Klarlund

1995 Hardware verification using monadic second-order logic. In: *Computer-Aided Verification (CAV '95)*, Springer, vol. 939 of *LNCS*, pp. 31–41

1998 Automata based symbolic reasoning in hardware verification. *Formal Methods In System Design* 13: 255–288, Extended version of: "Hardware verification using monadic second-order logic," *CAV '95*, LNCS 939

Berwick, R. C. and A. Weinberg

1985 Deterministic parsing: A modern view. In: *Proceedings of NELS 15*, Brown University, Providence, RI, pp. 15–33

Blackburn, P. and C. Gardent

1995 A specification language for lexical-functional grammars. Tech. Rep. 51, Computational Linguistics at the University of the Saarland (CLAUS)

Blackburn, P., C. Gardent, and W. Meyer-Viol

1993 Talking about trees. In: *Proceedings of the 6th EACL*, pp. 21–29

1994 Linguistics, logic, and finite trees. Report CS-R9412, CWI, Amsterdam

Bloem, R. and J. Engelfriet

1997a Characterization of properties and relations defined in Monadic Second Order logic on the nodes of trees. Tech. Rep. 97-03, Dept. of Computer Science, Leiden University

1997b Monadic second order logic and node relations on graphs and trees. In: J. Mycielski, G. Rozenberg, and A. Salomaa (eds.), *Structures in Logic and Computer Science*, Springer-Verlag, vol. 1261 of *Lecture Notes in Computer Science*, pp. 144–161

Brody, M.

1995 *Lexico-Logical Form*. Cambridge, Ma.: MIT Press

Bryant, R. E.

1992 Symbolic boolean manipulation with ordered binary-decision diagrams. *ACM Computing Surveys* 24(3): 293–318

Büchi, J. R.

1960 Weak second-order arithmetic and finite automata. *Zeitschrift für mathematische Logik und Grundlagen der Mathematik* 6: 66–92

Carpenter, B.

1992 *The Logic of Typed Feature Structures*, vol. 32 of *Cambridge Tracts in Theoretical Computer Science*. Cambridge University Press

Chidlovskii, B.

2000 Using regular tree automata as XML schemas. In: *Proc. IEEE Advances in Digital Libraries Conference*

Chomsky, N.

1956 Three models for the description of language. *I.R.E. Transactions of Information Theory* 2: 113–124

1957 *Syntactic Structures*. The Hague: Mouton

1959 On certain formal properties of grammars. *Information and Control* 2(2): 137–167

1965 *Aspects of the Theory of Syntax*. Cambridge, Mass: MIT Press

1982 *Lectures on Government and Binding*. Dordrecht, Holland: Foris Publications

1985 *Barriers*. Cambridge, MA: MIT Press

1995 *The Minimalist Program*, vol. 28 of *Current Studies in Linguistics*. MIT Press

Cornell, T. L.
1992 *Description Theory, Licensing Theory, and Principle–Based Grammars and Parsers*. Ph.D. thesis, UCLA
1994 On determining the consistency of partial descriptions of trees. In: *32nd Annual Meeting of the ACL: Proceedings of the Conference*, Association for Computational Linguistics, Las Cruces, New Mexico, pp. 163–170
1996 Model-theoretic syntax. *Glot International* 2(1/2)
1998 Island effects in type logical approaches to the minimalist program. In: *Proceedings of FHCG-98 Joint Conference On Formal Grammar, Head-Driven Phrase Structure Grammar, and Categorial Grammar*, Saarbrücken, Germany
1999a Derivational and representational views of minimalist syntactic calculi. In: A. Lecomte, F. Lamarche, and G. Perrier (eds.), *Logical Aspects of Computational Linguistics (LACL '97)*, Berlin: Springer, no. 1582 in LNAI, pp. 92–111
1999b Representational minimalism. In: H.-P. Kolb and U. Mönnich (eds.), *The Mathematics of Syntactic Structure*, Mouton de Gruyter, no. 44 in Studies in Generative Grammar
2000 Parsing and grammar engineering with tree automata. In: *Algebraic Methods in Language Processing: Second AMAST Workshop on Language Processing*, Parlevink, University of Iowa, TWLT

Courcelle, B.
1990 Graph rewriting: An algebraic and logic approach. In: J. van Leeuwen (ed.), *Handbook of Theoretical Computer Science*, Elsevier, vol. B of *Handbook of Theoretical Computer Science*, pp. 193–242
1997 The expression of graph properties and graph transformations in monadic second-order logic. In: G. Rozenberg (ed.), *Handbook of Graph Grammars and Computing by Graph Transformation. Vol. I: Foundations*, World Scientific, chap. 5, pp. 313–400

Damgaard, N., N. Klarlund, and M. I. Schwartzbach
1999 YakYak: Parsing with logical side constraints. In: *Proceedings of DLT'99*

Devienne, P., P. Lebègue, A. Parrain, J. Routier, and J. Würtz
1994 Smallest horn clause programs. *Journal of Logic Programming* 19, 20: 1–41

Doner, J.
1970 Tree acceptors and some of their applications. *Journal of Computer and System Sciences* 4: 406–451

Duchier, D.
1999 Axiomatizing dependency parsing using set constraints. In: *Proceedings of MOL 6*, Orlando, Florida

Duchier, D. and S. Thater
1999 Parsing with tree descriptions: a constraint based approach. In: *Proceedings of* NLULP'99

Ebbinghaus, H.-D. and J. Flum
1995 *Finite Model Theory*. Berlin: Springer

Elgaard, J., A. Møller, and M. I. Schwartzbach
2000 Compile-time debugging of C programs working on trees. In: *Proceedings of European Symposium on Programming Languages and Systems*, Berlin: Springer, vol. 1782 of *LNCS*

Elgot, C. C.
1961 Decision problems of finite automata design and related arithmetics. *Trans. Amer. Math. Soc.* 98: 21–51

Engelfriet, J.
1997 Context-free graph grammars. In: G. Rozenberg and A. Salomaa (eds.), *Handbook of Formal Languages. Vol. III: Beyond Words*, Springer, chap. 3, pp. 125–213

Engelfriet, J. and S. Maneth
1999 Macro tree transducers, attribute grammars, and MSO definable tree translations. *Information and Computation* 154: 34–91
2000 Tree languages generated by context-free graph grammars. In: H.-J. K. H. Ehrig, G. Engels and G. Rozenberg (eds.), *Proceedings of Theory and Applications of Graph Transformations - TAGT'98*, no. 1764 in LNCS, pp. 15–29
2001 Macro tree translations of linear size increase are mso definable. Technical Report 01-08, Leiden Institute of Advanced Computer Science, Leiden University

Engelfriet, J. and V. van Oostrom
1996 Regular description of context-free graph languages. *Journal Comp. & Syst. Sci.* 53(3): 556–574

Engelfriet, J. and E. Schmidt
1977 IO and OI, part I. *J. Comput. System Sci.* 15: 328–353
1978 IO and OI, part II. *J. Comput. System Sci.* 16: 67–99

Engelfriet, J. and H. Vogler
1985 Macro tree transducers. *Journal of Computer and System Sciences* 31(1): 71–146

Fagin, R.
1974 Generalized first-order spectra and polynomial-time recognizable sets. In: R. Karp (ed.), *Complexity of Computation*, AMS, vol. 7 of *SIAM-AMS Proc.*, pp. 27–41

Fischer, M. J.
1968 Grammars with macro-like productions. In: *Proceedings of the 9th Annual Symposium on Switching and Automata Theory*, IEEE, pp. 131–142

Fong, S.
1992 *Computational Properties of Principle-Based Grammatical Theories*. Ph.D. thesis, MIT

Frank, R.
1990 *Computation and Linguistic Theory: A Government Binding Theory Parser using Tree Adjoining Grammar*. Master's thesis, University of Pennsylvania

Frank, R. and K. Vijay-Shanker
1995 C-command and grammatical primitives. Presentation at the 18th GLOW Colloquium, University of Tromsø
1998 Primitive c-command. Ms., Johns Hopkins University & Universtiy of Delaware

Fujiyoshi and Kasai
2000 Spinal-formed context-free tree grammars. *MST: Mathematical Systems Theory* 33

Gaifman, H.
1965 Dependency systems and phrase-structure systems. *Information and Control* 8(3): 304–337

Gazdar, G.
1988 Applicability of indexed grammars to natural languages. In: U. Reyle and C. Rohrer (eds.), *Natural Language Parsing and Linguistic Theories*, Dordrecht: D. Reidel, pp. 69–94

Gazdar, G., E. Klein, G. K. Pullum, and I. A. Sag
1985 *Generalized Phrase Structure Grammar*. Cambridge, Massachusetts: Harvard University Press

Gécseg, F. and M. Steinby
1984 *Tree Automata*. Budapest: Akadémiai Kiadó
1997 Tree languages. In: G. Rozenberg and A. Salomaa (eds.), *Handbook of Formal Languages: Beyond Words*, Berlin: Springer, vol. 3

Hanschke, P. and J. Würtz
1993 Satisfiability of the smallest binary program. *Information Processing Letters* 45(5): 237–241

Harkema, H.
2000 A recognizer for minimalist grammars. In: *Sixth International Workshop on Parsing Technologies, IWPT'2000*

Hays, D. G.
1964 Dependency theory: A formalism and some observations. *Language* 40(4): 511–525, prepared for US Air Force Project Rand

Höhfeld, M. and G. Smolka
1988 Definite relations over constraint languages. LILOG Report 53, IBM Deutschland, Stuttgart, Germany

Huybregts, M. A. C.
1976 Overlapping dependencies in Dutch. *Utrecht Working Papers in Linguistics* 1: 24–65
1984 The weak adequacy of context-free phrase structure grammar. In: G. J. de Haan, M. Trommelen, and W. Zonneveld (eds.), *Van periferie naar kern*, Dordrecht: Foris, pp. 81–99

Immerman, N.
1987 Languages that capture complexity classes. *SIAM J. of Computing* 16(4): 760–778

Janssen, T. M.
2000 An algebraic approach to grammatical theories for natural language. In: A. Nijholt, G. Scollo, T. Rus, and D. Heylen (eds.), *Algebraic Methods in Language Processing, AMiLP 2000*, University of Iowa

Jensen, J. L., M. E. Joergensen, N. Klarlund, and M. I. Schwartzbach
1997 Automatic verification of pointer programs using monadic second-order logic. In: *PLDI '97*

Johnson, D. and P. Postal
1980 *Arc Pair Grammar*. Princeton, NJ: Princeton University Press

Johnson, M.
1988 *A Logic of Attribute-Value Structures and the Theory of Grammar*. Stanford/Chicago: CSLI/Chicago University Press

Johnson, M.
1990 Expressing disjunctive and negative feature constraints with classical first-order logic. In: *Proceedings of the 28th Meeting of the Association for Computational Linguistics*, Association for Computational Linguistics, Association for Computational Linguistics

1991 Features and formulae. *Computational Linguistics* 17(2): 131–151

Johnson, M. and E. P. Stabler
1993 Topics in principle based parsing. Notes for a course taught at the LSA Summer Institute, Columbus, OH, 1993

Joshi, A. K.
1985 Tree adjoining grammars: How much context-sensitivity is required to provide reasonable structural description. In: D. Dowty, L. Karttunen, and A. Zwicky (eds.), *Natural Language Parsing*, Cambridge, UK: Cambridge University Press, pp. 206–250
1987 An introduction to tree adjoining grammars. In: Manaster-Ramer (ed.), *Mathematics of Language*, Amsterdam: John Benjamins

Joshi, A. K., L. S. Levy, and M. Takahashi
1975 Tree adjunct grammars. *Journal of Computer and System Sciences* 10: 136–63

Joshi, A. K. and Y. Schabes
1997 Tree adjoining grammars. In: G. Rozenberg and A. Salomaa (eds.), *Handbook of Formal Languages*, Berlin: Springer, vol. 3: Beyond Words of *Handbook of Formal Languages*, pp. 69–123

Kallmeyer, L.
1999 Underspecification in tree description grammar. In: H.-P. Kolb and U. Mönnich (eds.), *The Mathematics of Syntactic Structure: Trees and their Logics*, Mouton de Gruyter, no. 44 in Studies in Generative Grammar

Kaplan, R. M. and J. Bresnan
1983 Lexical-functional grammar: A formal system for grammatical representation. In: J. Bresnan (ed.), *The Mental Representation of Grammatical Relations*, Cambridge, Mass: MIT Press, pp. 173–381

Kasper, R. T.
1987a *Feature Structures: A Logical Theory with Application to Language Analysis*. Ph.D. thesis, University of Michigan
1987b A unification method for disjunctive feature descriptions. In: *ACL Proceedings, 25th Annual Meeting*, Stanford, CA, pp. 235–242

Kasper, R. T. and W. C. Rounds
1986 A logical semantics for feature structures. In: *ACL Proceedings, 24th Annual Meeting*, Columbia University, New York, NY, pp. 257–271

Kay, M.
1983 Unification grammar. Tech. rep., Xerox Palo Alto Research Center, Palo Alto, CA

1984 Functional unification grammar: a formalism for machine translation. *COLING-84* pp. 75–78

Kayne, R. S.
1994 *The Antisymmetry of Syntax*, vol. 25 of *Linguistic Inquiry Monographs*. Cambridge, Mass. and London, England: MIT Press

Keenan, E. L. and E. P. Stabler
1996 Abstract syntax. In: A.-M. DiSciullo (ed.), *Configurations: Essays on Structure and Interpretation*, Somerville, Massachusetts: Cascadilla Press, pp. 329–344
1997 Syntactic invariants. In: *6th Annual Conference on Language, Logic and Computation*, Stanford

Kelb, P., T. Margaria, M. Mendler, and C. Gsottberger
1997 MOSEL: A flexible toolset for monadic second-order logic. In: E. Brinksma (ed.), *Tools and Algorithms for The Construction and Analysis of Systems: International Workshop*, TACAS '97, Lecture Notes in Computer Science 1019, Springer, pp. 183–202

King, P. J.
1989 *A Logical Formalism for Head-Driven Phrase Structure Grammar*. Ph.D. thesis, Manchester University, Manchester, England
1994a An expanded logical formalism for head–driven phrase stucture grammar. Arbeitspapiere des SFB 340 59, SFB 340, Universität Tübingen
1994b Typed feature structures as descriptions. In COLING-94

Klarlund, N.
1998 MONA & Fido: The logic-automaton connection in practice. In: M. Nielsen and W. Thomas (eds.), *Computer Science Logic, 11th International Workshop, CSL'97, Annual Conference of the EACSL*, Aarhus, Denmark: Springer, LNCS

Klarlund, N. and A. Møller
1998 *MONA Version 1.2 User Manual*. BRICS Notes Series NS-98-3, Department of Computer Science, University of Aarhus

Klarlund, N., A. Møller, and M. I. Schwartzbach
2000 MONA implementation secrets Proceedings of CIAA 2000

Klarlund, N. and M. I. Schwartzbach
1993 Graph types. In: *Conference Record of the Twentieth ACM SIGPLAN-SIGACT Symposium on Principles of Programming Languages*, Charleston, South Carolina: ACM Press, pp. 196–205

1997 A domain-specific language for regular sets of strings and trees. In: *Proceedings of the Conference on Domain-Specific Languages*, USENIX, Santa Barbara, Ca.

Kleene, S. C.
1956 Representation of events in nerve nets and finite automata. In: C. Shannon and J. McCarthy (eds.), *Automata Studies*, Princeton University Press

Kolb, H.-P., J. Michaelis, U. Mönnich, and F. Morawietz
2003 An operational and denotational approach to non-context-freeness. *Theoretical Computer Science* 293: 261–289

Kolb, H.-P., U. Mönnich, and F. Morawietz
1999a Logical description of cross-serial dependencies. In: *Proceedings of the Workshop Finite Model Theory and its Applications at FloC '99*, Trento, Italy
1999b Regular description of cross-serial dependencies. In: *Proceedings of MOL 6*, Orlando, Florida
2000 Descriptions of cross-serial dependencies. *Grammars* 3(2/3): 189–216

Kolb, H.-P. and C. L. Thiersch
1991 Levels and empty categories in a principles and parameter approach to parsing. In: H. Haider and K. Netter (eds.), *Reptresentation and Derivation in the Theory of Grammar*, Dordrecht: Kluwer

Kracht, M.
1993 Mathematical aspects of command relations. In: *Sixth Conference of the European Chapter of the Association for Computational Linguistics*, EACL, pp. 240–249
1995 Syntactic codes and grammar refinement. *Journal of Logic, Language and Information* 4: 41–60
1999 Adjunction structures and syntactic domains. In: H.-P. Kolb and U. Mönnich (eds.), *The Mathematics of Syntactic Structure: Trees and their Logics*, Mouton de Gruyter, no. 44 in Studies in Generative Grammar

Kunze, J.
1977 Dependency grammar as syntactic model in several procedures of automatic sentence analysis. *Linguistics* 195: 46–62

Lambek, J.
1958 The mathematics of sentence structure. *American Mathematical Monthly* 65: 154–169

Lang, B.
1992 Recognition can be harder than parsing. In: *Proc. of the 2nd Int. Workshop on Tree Adjoining Grammars. Philadelphia, PA, June 1992*

Lautemann, C., T. Schwentick, and D. Thérien
1995 Logics for context-free languages. In: L. Pacholski and J. Tiuryn (eds.), *Computer Science Logic '94*, Springer, pp. 205–216, LNCS 933

Lawvere, F. W.
1963 *Functorial Semantics of Algebraic Theories*. Ph.D. thesis, Columbia University, Braunschweig

Lecomte, A.
1997 POM-nets and minimalism. In: C. Casadio (ed.), *Proceedings of the IV Roma Workshop: Dynamic Perspectives in Logic and Linguistics*, Università di Roma Tre
1998 Categorial minimalism. In: *Proceedings of LACL'98*, Grenoble, France

Levy, J.
1996 Linear second-order unification. In: H. Ganzinger (ed.), *Proceedings of the 7th International Conference on Rewriting Techniques and Applications (RTA-96)*, Berlin: Springer-Verlag, vol. 1103 of *LNCS*, pp. 332–346

Lewis, H. R. and C. H. Papadimitriou
1998 *Elements of the Theory of Computation*. Upper Saddle River, New Jersey: Prentice-Hall, Inc.

Lloyd, J.
1984 *Foundations of Logic Programming*. Berlin: Springer

Macías, B.
1990 *An Incremental Parser for Government-Binding Theory*. Ph.D. thesis, University of Cambridge

Maibaum, T. S. E.
1974 A generalized approach to formal languages. *J. Comput. System Sci.* 88: 409–439

Marcus, M. P., D. Hindle, and M. M. Fleck
1983 D-theory: Talking about talking about trees. In: *21st Annual Meeting of the ACL: Proceedings of the Conference*, pp. 129–136

McCawley, J. D.
1986 *Encyclopedic Dictionary of Semiotics*, Mouton de Gruyter, chap. Syntax, pp. 1061–71

Mezei, J. and J. B. Wright
1967 Algebraic automata and contextfree sets. *Information and Control* 11: 3–29

Michaelis, J.
1999 Derivational minimalism is mildly context-sensitive. *Linguistics in Potsdam (LiP)* 5, Institut für Linguistik, Universität Potsdam, Available under http://www.ling.uni-potsdam.de/~michael/
2001a Derivational minimalism is mildly context-sensitive. In: M. Moortgat (ed.), *LACL '98*, Berlin: Springer, vol. 2014 of *LNAI*
2001b *On Formal Properties of Minimalist Grammars*. Ph.D. thesis, University of Potsdam

Michaelis, J. and M. Kracht
1997 Semilinearity as a syntactic invariant. In: C. Retoré (ed.), *Proceedings of the 1st International Conference on Logical Aspects of Computational Linguistics (LACL-96)*, Berlin: Springer, vol. 1328 of *LNAI*, pp. 329–345

Michaelis, J., U. Mönnich, and F. Morawietz
2000a Algebraic descriptions of derivational minimalism. In: *Algebraic Methods in Language Processing: Second AMAST Workshop on Language Processing*, Parlevink, University of Iowa, TWLT
2000b Derivational minimalism in two regular and logical steps. In: *Proceedings of the Tag+5 Conference*, Paris
2001 On minimalist attribute grammars and macro tree transducers. In: C. Rohrer, A. Rossdeutscher, and H. Kamp (eds.), *Linguistic Form and its Computation*, CSLI Publications, pp. 287–326

Møller, A. and M. Schwartzbach
2001 The pointer assertion logic engine. In: C. Norris and J. J. B. Fenwick (eds.), *Proceedings of the ACM SIGPLAN '01 Conference on Programming Language Design and Implementation (PLDI-01)*, N.Y.: ACMPress, vol. 36.5 of *ACM SIGPLAN Notices*, pp. 221–231

Mönnich, U.
1993 Algebraic refinement of the Chomsky hierarchy. Course notes, 5th European Summer School in Logic, Language and Information, Lisbon
1997a Adjunction as substitution. In: G.-J. M. Kruijff, G. Morill, and R. Oehrle (eds.), *Formal Grammar '97*, Aix-en-Provence, pp. 169–178
1997b Lexikalisch kontrollierte Kreuzabhängigkeiten und Kongruenzmorphologien. Talk at Meeting of the SFBs 471, 340 and 282, Available under http://tcl.sfs.uni-tuebingen.de/~tcl/uwe/uwe_moennich.html
1998 TAGs M-constructed. In: *TAG+ 4th Workshop, Philadelphia*

1999 On cloning contextfreeness. In: H.-P. Kolb and U. Mönnich (eds.), *The Mathematics of Syntactic Structure*, Mouton de Gruyter, no. 44 in Studies in Generative Grammar, pp. 195–229

Morawietz, F.

1999 Monadic second order logic, tree automata and constraint logic programming. In: H.-P. Kolb and U. Mönnich (eds.), *The Mathematics of Syntactic Structure*, Mouton de Gruyter, no. 44 in Studies in Generative Grammar

2000a Chart parsing and constraint programming. In: *Proceedings of COLING-2000*

2000b Chart parsing as constraint propagation. In: F. Morawietz (ed.), *Some Aspects of Natural Language Processing and Constraint Programming*, Universität Tübingen, no. 150 in Arbeitspapiere des SFB 340, pp. 29–50

Morawietz, F. and T. L. Cornell

1997a Approximating Principles and Parameters Grammars with MSO Tree Logics. In: *Proceedings of LACL '97*, Nancy, France

1997b On the recognizability of relations over a tree definable in a monadic second order tree description language. Arbeitspapiere des SFB 340 85, SFB 340, Universität Tübingen

1997c Representing constraints with automata. In: *Proceedings of the 35th Annual Meeting of the ACL and the 8th Conference of the EACL*, Madrid, Spain: Association for Computational Linguistics, pp. 468–475

1999 The Logic-Automaton Connection in Linguistics. In: *Proceedings of LACL 1997*, Springer, no. 1582 in LNAI

2001 A model-theoretic description of tree adjoining grammars. *Electronic Notes in Theoretical Computer Science 53* (53), Formal Grammar/MOL Conference 2001. Elsevier Science

Moschovakis, Y. N.

1974 *Elementary Induction on Abstract Structures*. Amsterdam: North-Holland

Moshier, M. A.

1988 *Extensions to Unification Grammar for the Description of Programming Languages*. Ph.D. thesis, University of Michigan

1993 On completeness theorems for feature logics. CLAUS Report 31, Universität des Saarlandes, Saarbrücken, Germany

Moshier, M. A. and W. C. Rounds
1987 A logic for partially specified data structures. In: ACM (ed.), *POPL '87. Fourteenth Annual ACM SIGACT-SIGPLAN Symposium on Principles of programming languages, January 21–23, 1987, Munich, W. Germany*, New York, NY, USA: ACM Press, pp. 156–167

Neven, F.
1999 *Design and Analysis of Query Languages for Structured Documents – A Formal and Logical Approach*. Ph.D. thesis, Limburgs Universitair Centrum

Neven, F. and T. Schwentick
1999 Query automata. In: ACM (ed.), *Proceedings of the Eighteenth ACM SIGMOD-SIGACT-SIGART Symposium on Principles of Database Systems: PODS 1999: Philadelphia, Pennsylvania, May 31–June 2, 1999*, New York, NY 10036, USA: ACM Press, pp. 205–214
2000 Expressive and efficient pattern languages for tree-structured data. In: *Proceedings of the Nineteenth ACM SIGMOD-SIGACT-SIGART Symposium on Principles of Database Systems*, ACM, pp. 145–156
2002 Automata- and logic-based pattern languages for tree-structured data. Manuscript, URL: http://alpha.luc.ac.be/~lucg5503/publs.html

Niehren, J. and A. Podelski
1992 Feature automata and recognizable sets of feature trees. In: M.-C. Gaudel and J.-P. Jouannaud (eds.), *Proccedings of the 4th International Joint Conference on Theory and Practice of Software Development*, Orsay, France: Springer, no. 668 in LNCS, pp. 356–375

Parikh, R.
1966 On context-free languages. *Journal of the ACM* 13: 570–581

Peacock, G.
1830 *A Treatise on Algebra*. Cambridge

Pereira, F. C. N. and M. D. Riley
1997 Speech recognition by composition of weighted finite automata. In: Roche and Schabes (1997)

Peters, P. S. and R. W. Ritchie
1971 On restricting the base component of transformational grammars. *Information and Control* 18(5): 483–501
1973 On the generative power of transformational grammars. *Information Sciences* 6: 49–83

Pollard, C. J.
1984 *Generalized Context-Free Grammars, Head Grammars and Natural Language*. Ph.D. thesis, Stanford University

Pollard, C. J. and I. A. Sag

1987 *Information-Based Syntax and Semantics*, vol. 13 of *CSLI Lecture Notes*. CSLI Publications

1994 *Head-Driven Phrase Structure Grammar*. University of Chicago Press and CSLI Publications

Post, E.

1946 A variant of a recursively unsolvable problem. *Bulletin of the American Mathematical Society* 52: 264–268

Pullum, G. and G. Gazdar

1982 Natural languages and context-free languages. *Linguistics and Philosophy* 4(4): 471–504

Rabin, M. O.

1969 Decidability of second-order theories and automata on infinite trees. *Transactions of the American Mathematical Society* 141: 1–35

Rabin, M. O. and D. Scott

1959 Finite automata and their decision problems. *IBM Journal of Research and Development* 3: 114–125

Rambow, O. and G. Satta

1999 Independent parallelism in finite copying parallel rewriting systems. *Theoretical Computer Science* 223(1–2): 87–120

Rambow, O., K. Vijay-Shanker, and D. Weir

1995 D-Tree Grammars. In: *Proceedings of ACL*

Rizzi, L.

1990 *Relativized Minimality*. MIT Press

Roche, E. and Y. Schabes (eds.)

1997 *Finite-State Language Processing*. Language, Speech, and Communication Series, MIT Press

Rogers, J.

1994 *Studies in the Logic of Trees with Applications to Grammar Formalisms*. Ph.D. thesis, University of Delaware, Dep. of Computer & Information Sciences, Newark, DE 19716, Published as Technical Report No. 95-04

1996 A model-theoretic framework for theories of syntax. In: *Proc. of the 34th Annual Meeting of the ACL*, Santa Cruz, USA

1997 On descriptive complexity, language complexity, and GB. In: P. Blackburn and M. de Rijke (eds.), *Specifying Syntactic Structures*, CSLI Publications

1998 *A Descriptive Approach to Language-Theoretic Complexity*. Studies in Logic, Language, and Information, CSLI Publications and FoLLI

Rounds, W. C.
1970a Mappings and grammars on trees. *Mathematical Systems Theory* 4: 257–287
1970b Tree-oriented proofs of some theorems on context-free and indexed languages. In: *Proceedings of the 2nd Annual ACM Symposium on Theory of Computing*, pp. 109–116

Sandholm, A. and M. I. Schwartzbach
1998 Distributed safety controllers for web services. In: E. Astesiano (ed.), *Fundamental Approaches to Software Engineering, FASE'98, LNCS 1382*, Springer-Verlag, no. 1382 in Lecture Notes in Computer Science, pp. 270–284, Also available as BRICS Technical Report RS-97-47

Seki, H., T. Matsumura, M. Fujii, and T. Kasami
1991 On multiple context-free grammars. *Theoretical Computer Science* 88(2): 191–229

Shieber, S. M.
1985 Evidence against the context-freeness of natural language. *Linguistics and Philosophy* 8: 333–343

Stabler, E. P.
1992 *The Logical Approach to Syntax: Foundations, Specifications and Implementations of Theories of Government and Binding*. Cambridge, Ma.: MIT Press
1994 The finite connectivity of linguistic structure. In: C. C. Jr., L. Frazier, and K. Rayner (eds.), *Perspectives on Sentence Processing*, Hillsdale, New Jersey: Lawrence Erlbaum, pp. 303–336
1997 Derivational minimalism. In: C. Retoré (ed.), *Logical Aspects of Computational Linguistics*, Berlin: Springer, pp. 68–95, LNAI 1328
1999a Performance models for a derivational minimalism. Presented at the Workshop *Linguistic Form and its Computation* of the SFB 340 in Bad Teinach, Draft
1999b Remnant movement and complexity. In: G. Bouma, G.-J. M. Kruijff, E. Hinrichs, and R. T. Oehrle (eds.), *Constraints and Resources in Natural Language Syntax and Semantics*, CSLI, vol. II of *Studies in Constrained Based Lexicalism*, pp. 299–326

Stabler, E. P. and E. L. Keenan
2000 Structural similarity. In: A. Nijholt, G. Scollo, T. Rus, and D. Heylen (eds.), *Algebraic Methods in Language Processing, AMiLP 2000*, University of Iowa

Steedman, M.
1988 Combinators and grammar. In: R. Oehrle, E. Bach, and D. Wheeler (eds.), *Categorial Grammar and Natural Language Structures*, Dordrecht: Reidel, pp. 417–442

Thatcher, J. W.
1970 Generalized sequential machines. *J. Comput. System Sci.* 4: 339–367

Thatcher, J. W. and J. B. Wright
1968 Generalized finite automata theory with an application to a decision problem of second-order logic. *Mathematical Systems Theory* 2(1): 57–81

Thomas, W.
1990 Automata on infinite objects. In: J. van Leeuwen (ed.), *Handbook of Theoretical Computer Science*, Elsevier Science Publishers B. V., chap. 4, pp. 133–191
1997 Languages, automata, and logic. In: G. Rozenberg and A. Salomaa (eds.), *Handbook of Formal Languages*, Berlin: Springer, vol. 3: Beyond Words, pp. 389–455

Veenstra, M.
1998 *Formalizing the Minimalist Program*. Ph.D. thesis, University of Groningen

Vijay-Shanker, K., D. Weir, and O. Rambow
1995 Parsing d-tree grammars. In: *Proceedings of the International Workshop on Parsing Technologies*, ACL/SIGPARSE, Prag, pp. 252–259

Vijay-Shanker, K. and D. J. Weir
1994 The equivalence of four extensions of context-free grammars. *Mathematical Systems Theory* 27(6): 511–546

van Vugt, N.
1996 *Generalized Context-Free Grammars*. Ph.D. thesis, Leiden University, Leiden, The Netherlands

Wagner, E. G.
1994 Algebraic semantics. In: S. Abramsky, D. M. Gabbay, and T. S. E. Maibaum (eds.), *Semantic Structures*, Oxford University Press, vol. 3 of *Handbook of Logic in Computer Science*, pp. 323–393

Weinberg, A.
1988 *Locality Principles in Syntax and in Parsing*. Ph.D. thesis, MIT

Weir, D. J.
1992 Linear context-free rewriting systems and deterministic tree-walk transducers. In: *30th Meeting of the Association for Computational Linguistics (ACL'92)*

Whitehead, A. N.
1911 *An Introduction to Mathematics*. London: Williams and Northgate, Reprinted by Oxford University Press

Yu, S.
1997 Regular languages. In: G. Rozenberg and A. Salomaa (eds.), *Handbook of Formal Languages: Word, Language, Grammar*, Berlin: Springer, vol. 1

Mathematical Symbols

$\mathcal{A}$	a Σ-algebra	22
A	a finite set of symbols	18
A^*	the set of all words over A	18
$\mathfrak{aut}$	an automaton constructor	68
$\mathfrak{A}$	an automaton	44
$c_{n,k}$	a composition symbol	142
$c_{(u,v,w)}$	a composition symbol	23
δ	the transition function of a finite state machine	44
$\hat{\delta}$	the extended transition function of a finite state machine	45
$\downarrow_i$	a directive of an FSTWA: go down	53
$\uparrow_i$	a directive of an FSTWA: go up	53
$\triangleleft$	the relation of immediate dominance	39
$\blacktriangleleft$	the immediate dominance relation on lifted structures	155
$\triangleleft^*$	the relation of reflexive dominance	39
$\blacktriangleleft^*$	the dominance relation on lifted structures	155
ε	the empty word	18
F	the set of final states of a finite state machine	44
G	a minimalist grammar	117

Index

Bei Fragen zur Produktsicherheit wenden Sie sich bitte an:
If you have any questions regarding product safety,
please contact:

Walter de Gruyter GmbH
Genthiner Straße 13
10785 Berlin
productsafety@degruyterbrill.com